James Canton teaches at th[   ]d
Theatre Studies at the Univer[   ]i
Essex universities, gaining a Pl   ....g..t widely in
the UK and Egypt, and has himself travelled extensively across the
Middle East.

'*From Cairo to Baghdad: British Travellers in Arabia* is a major
contribution to our understanding of British interest in, and
understanding of, the Middle East between the occupation of
Egypt in 1882 and the invasion of Iraq in 2003. James Canton
deftly probes into ways that travel writing produced during this
period was unavoidably caught up and complicit in the twin
developments of mass tourism and imperialism. Organised
chronologically and thematically, this study reveals a much richer
and more complex range of cultural interactions and mutual
engagements than the still powerful notion of a clash between
civilisations. Canton examines justly celebrated works by a variety
of well-known travel writers – from Marmaduke Pickthall and St
John Philby, to T. E. Lawrence, Mark Sykes, Gertrude Bell,
Rosita Forbes and Freya Stark – alongside fascinating accounts by
lesser-known figures, such as "Captain Shakespear" and S. C.
Rolls. Interviews with celebrated writers William Dalrymple, Tim
Mackintosh-Smith, Jonathan Raban, and Colin Thubron, offer
fascinating insights into the artistry and politics of travel. This is
essential reading for all who are interested in travel writing and
the history of cultural interactions between the Christian West
and the Islamic East.'
Gerald MacLean, Professor of English, University of Exeter

'In *From Cairo to Baghdad*, James Canton offers an important
account of the British travels in Arabia since Britain's occupation
of Egypt in 1882. Canton provides historical depth to British
involvement in the Middle East with a nuanced discussion of
how travel writing is implicated in colonial relations of power.
The book will be required reading for scholars of travel writing
and postcolonial studies.'
**Ali Behdad, John Charles Hillis Professor of Literature,
UCLA, and author of *Belated Travellers: Orientalism in the
Age of Colonial Dissolution***

FROM CAIRO
— *to* —
BAGHDAD

British Travellers in Arabia

JAMES CANTON

I.B. TAURIS
LONDON · NEW YORK

New paperback edition first published in 2014 by
I.B.Tauris & Co. Ltd
6 Salem Road, London W2 4BU
175 Fifth Avenue, New York NY 10010
www.ibtauris.com

Distributed in the United States and Canada exclusively by Palgrave
Macmillan, 175 Fifth Avenue, New York NY 10010

First published in hardback in 2011 by I.B.Tauris & Co. Ltd

ISBN: 978 1 78076 987 5
eISBN: 978 0 85773 571 3

A full CIP record for this book is available from the British Library
A full CIP record is available from the Library of Congress

Library of Congress catalog card: available

To the memory of my father

CONTENTS

Acknowledgements   *ix*
List of Maps and Illustrations   *xi*
Maps   *xiii*

Introduction   1

1   Missionaries and Pilgrims   13

2   The Empty Quarter   37

3   Imperial Wars   57

4   Modernising Arabia   83

5   Women in Arabia   105

6   Baghdad and Beyond   129

7   Southern Arabia   155

8   After Empire   191

Notes   *217*
Appendix   *233*
Bibliography   *271*
Index   *289*

ACKNOWLEDGEMENTS

The book before you grew from my PhD dissertation at the University of Essex. I am very grateful to Kate Rhodes for her suggestion that I have a chat with her former doctoral tutor at Essex. Her tutor was to become mine. To Peter Hulme I offer my sincerest thanks, not only for his guidance through the years, nudging my development on, but for his patience, dedication and cups of tea. His academic standing and gentle humanity have been an inspiration.

There are many other friends and colleagues who have played valuable roles in providing supervision, advice, feedback and support. In particular, I would like to thank Fiona Venn, Jeff Geiger, Claire Finburgh, Tim Youngs, Jonathan Masterson and Nadia Atia. My editor, Minna Cowper-Coles, has always shown unstinting support and enthusiasm for the book, while Susan Forsyth has been outstanding in editing, proofing and indexing the work. My thanks to them both.

I should like to express my gratitude for the time and thoughts of William Dalrymple, Jonathan Raban and Colin Thubron who willingly provided interviews, and to Tim Mackintosh-Smith who conducted a vibrant email exchange from San'a and read Chapter 7, assuring me he couldn't think of anyone he'd prefer to be compared to than Joyce Grenfell.

To the staff at the British Library, SOAS library and the National Archives at Kew, I also offer my thanks. I appreciate the assistance of G. M. C. Bott, formerly at Jonathan Cape archives, and wish to recognise that print run figures for *Seven Pillars of Wisdom* are reproduced with the kind permission of Seven Pillars of Wisdom Trust and held in Random House archives. The Imperial War Museum kindly granted permission to use the photograph of T. E. Lawrence entering Damascus in a motor car in October 1918.

I should also like to thank my sister, Helen Canton, for her time and dedication in proofreading each chapter and my mother for the finds passed my way from her rummaging in Oxfam Bookshop. My love and thanks to Hannah who has given me the time and space to work and to Eva who arrived somewhere in the middle of this project and towards the end would potter into my study to play. She has ensured valuable breaks from the workplace.

LIST OF MAPS AND ILLUSTRATIONS

Maps

1   The Middle East in 1926   xiii

2   The Arabian Peninsula   xv

Illustrations

1   Reverend Haskett Smith. From *Patrollers of Palestine*
     (London: Edward Arnold, 1906)   26

2   Arthur Wavell. From *A Modern Pilgrim in Mecca: And a
     Siege in Sanaa* (London: Constable, 1912)   30

3   T. E. Lawrence arrives at Damascus in a Tin Lizzie
     (October 1918). Detail from Stephen E. Tabachnick
     and Christopher Matheson *Images of Lawrence* (London:
     Cape, 1988). Copyright Imperial War Museum,
     London.   89

4   Rosita Forbes as a 'Beduin Sheikh'. From *The Secret of
     the Sahara: Kufara* (London: Cassell, 1921)   113

5   Wyman Bury as 'Abdullah Mansûr'. From *The Land of
     Uz* (London: Macmillan, 1911)   171

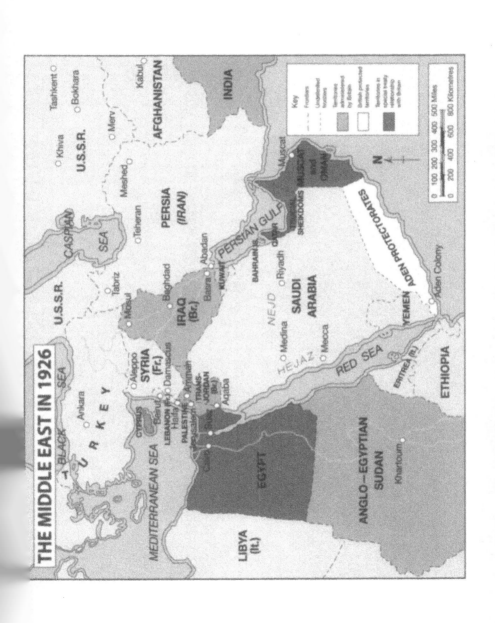

THE MIDDLE EAST IN 1926

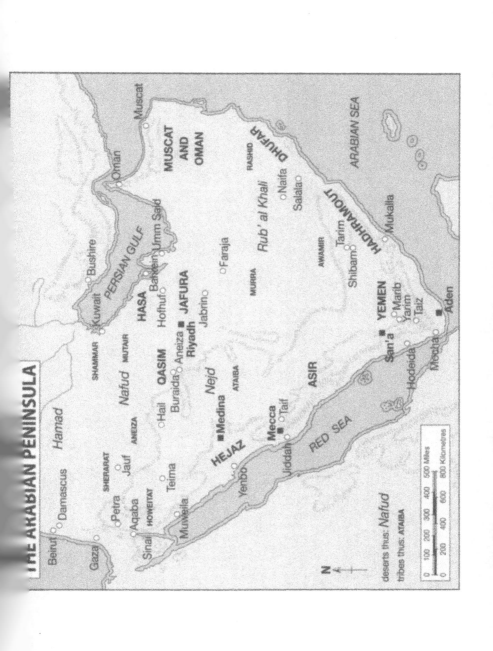

THE ARABIAN PENINSULA

deserts thus: *Nafud*
tribes thus: ATAIBA

N

| 0 | 100 | 200 | 300 | 400 | 500 Miles |
| 0 | 200 | 400 | 600 | 800 Kilometres |

INTRODUCTION

On 20 March 2006, the *Independent* newspaper led with a special edition to remember 'Three Years of War in Iraq'. The article was written by Robert Fisk, who noted:

> For the truth, we should turn to a well-known analyst who warned us that in Iraq, the British have been 'led into a trap from which it shall be hard to escape with dignity and honour. They have been tricked into it by a steady withholding of information. The Baghdad communiqués are belated, insincere, incomplete. Things have been far worse than we have been told. Our administration more bloody and inefficient than the public knows ... We are today not far from a disaster.' This is the most concise and accurate account I have yet read of our present folly.[1]

Fisk reveals that the words are those of 'Lawrence of Arabia' written about the British occupation of Iraq in 1920. The disclosure serves to remind the reader that British military activity in Iraq is nothing new. However, it also emphasises that while T. E. Lawrence will be ever mythologised as a British explorer sweeping through Arabian deserts alongside tribes of Bedouin, he was first and foremost a British military and intelligence officer. In 1920, Lawrence was known to the British public only thanks to the publicity of Lowell Thomas, whose entertaining music-hall lectures dramatised Lawrence's First World War escapades in the Arabian desert. His first draft of *Seven Pillars of Wisdom* had been lost or stolen at Reading train station in 1919. The general edition would not appear until after his death in 1935. Yet, before Lawrence's best-selling travel text had even materialised, his thoughts were refining British military policy in Arabia. In 1921, when Winston Churchill, as Colonial Secretary, drew up a Middle East department, Lawrence was employed as 'an advisor on Arab affairs'.[2] A year after publicly criticising government policy on Iraq, Lawrence was instrumental in the British-inspired coronation of Hashemite leader Feisal as the constitutional monarch of Iraq in July 1921. In T. E. Lawrence, there is personified the complex and intimate relationship between Britain's imperial project in Arabia, the travellers who explored those lands and the travel writing they produced.

*

The aim of this book is to explore, uncover, analyse and comment on written accounts of British travels in Arabia published after Britain's occupation of Egypt in 1882. In one sense the work is a gentle untying of the entanglement of travel writing and British imperial history, for the two are intricately linked. When British forces invaded Egypt in 1882, they cleared the ground for a colonial administration and the structures of imperial rule. Of course, many Britons had visited Egypt previously, particularly from the 1860s when Thomas Cook started his tours, but with the planting of an imperial base in Egypt, a new era of exploration began. In the twentieth century, other Arab countries would come under varying degrees of British political influence. Once parts of Arabia came under British control, so travellers' accounts of the region started to appear in greater numbers. Furthermore, as the British Empire in Arabia expanded so travellers' tales proliferated, and, later, when British rule receded so the travelogues dried up. Many who wrote travelogues were colonial administrators or their wives, missionaries, military officers, intelligence officials and spies. The very nature of travel in Arabia for British travellers was tempered by Britain's imperial presence. Even apparently independent travellers often used the existing structures of imperialism to frame their journeys. Colonial outposts could provide home comforts and occasionally life-saving medical support. In the 1950s, Wilfred Thesiger took time out from exploring the marshes of southern Iraq, using the British Consulate in Basra as a refuge to enjoy long baths and collect his post. When struck down with a mystery fever in 1935, Freya Stark employed the services of the RAF to airlift her from the isolation of Shibam in the Hadhramaut and deliver her to the English hospital in Aden.[3]

There is a plurality of terms which could potentially be applied to define the geographical region under consideration. 'Arabia' is the most specific and appropriate. The term Arabia describes an area comprising the Arabian Peninsula and neighbouring Arab lands. While expressions such as 'the Middle East' or even 'the Near East' are commonly used to refer to an area that also encompasses Iran, Israel and Turkey, and 'the Levant' and 'the Orient' have almost no specificity, Arabia is a culturally coherent region with a shared, common language whose very title derives from the Arabic tongue to delineate the lands of the Arab peoples – unlike the other terms which carry Western perspectives of positioning.[4] When I interviewed Jonathan Raban he expressed a similar stance over terminology, declaring it had been his deliberate policy to use the term 'Arabia' rather than 'the Middle East' when writing *Arabia: Through the Looking Glass* (1979).[5]

This study illustrates the breadth of British travel writing on Arabia from the end of the nineteenth century through the twentieth century, drawing to a close as another era of imperial conflict commenced. The temporal parameters have been chosen to emphasise the associations between British imperial enterprises in Arabia and British travel writing on the region. On 11 July 1882, a British naval fleet bombarded Alexandria in northern Egypt. The action was the start of a military campaign that would conclude with the wiping out of the Egyptian army at Tel el Kebir and Britain assuming control over Egyptian affairs for the next seventy-four years until the Suez Crisis in 1956. The British occupation of Egypt is the chronological starting point for this work, while 2003 dates its conclusion as British forces returned once more to Arabia, this time to invade Iraq.

Operating within these parameters yields a great deal of research material. British travellers, colonial administrators, and military personnel wrote accounts and memoirs of time spent in Arabia. Some writers, like Harry St John Philby, were prolific in their output. Others, such as Gerard Leachman or Captain William Shakespear, travelled extensively in Arabia but wrote little. However, a vast body of personal reflections on the region was written by British hands, often individuals brought into Arabian lands to serve the British imperial mission and now long forgotten. Some of the leading figures of this imperial enterprise left accounts of their experiences: Gertrude Bell, for example, wrote two travel texts on the region and then, once employed in imperial governance, produced many more narrative pieces on the lands and peoples of Arabia, aimed specifically to inform and educate members of the British colonial service. While her intended readership may have altered, Bell was still writing travel literature. A broad array of writers and travel narratives are cited and referenced here in order to provide thorough coverage and to emphasise the extent of British travel writing on Arabia from 1882 to 2003. This approach ensures space is given to those whose tales of travel in Arabia were once well-received yet now are rarely retold. Lesser-known texts are presented alongside works that have achieved critical acclaim and/or wide readership throughout this period and beyond. The Arabian travel writings of Charles Doughty, Gertrude Bell, T. E. Lawrence, Bertram Thomas, Freya Stark, Wilfred Thesiger, James (later Jan) Morris, Colin Thubron, Jonathan Raban, William Dalrymple and Tim Mackintosh-Smith are all closely considered.

*

The relationship between British imperial activity in Arabia and travel writing about the region is intimate. In the period prior to 1882, travels were undertaken by singular individuals (or married explorers), without exception from the upper reaches of British society, who possessed independent incomes and the freedom to plan, execute and write up their adventures. These Victorian explorers included the formidable figures of Sir Richard Burton, Wilfred Scawan Blunt and Charles Doughty. Burton journeyed to Mecca disguised as a Muslim in 1853, recounting his travel in the three-volumed *Personal Narrative of a Pilgrimage to El-Medinah and Meccah* (1855). Blunt, with his wife Anne, headed to Arabia in the 1870s to buy horses for their stud in Sussex, and later became an ardent opponent of the emergent British imperial project in Egypt, producing his *Secret History of the English Occupation of Egypt* (1907). Charles Doughty's voyage into central Arabia in 1876 lasted close to two years. Neither disguising his nationality nor his religion, Doughty's tale of a remarkable meander took ten years to reach publication, finally appearing in 1888 as *Travels in Arabia Deserta.*

Three distinct phases within the historical period under consideration can be delineated. With the occupation of Egypt in 1882, ostensibly to protect the Suez Canal passage to India, came a collective British curiosity about Arabia. Increasing financial interest accompanied the new wave of missionaries, archaeologists, military and administrative personnel, not only in Egypt, but in the Christian

Holy Lands and Greater Syria. In the first phase, which runs from 1882 through to 1917, a growing number of travellers was concerned not merely with seeking novel landscapes and peoples, but with appropriating knowledge of the region by plotting and mapping the land. Scientific methodology became an essential component of many expeditions. The pocket theodolite, thermometer and barometer became invaluable travelling companions. The varied experiences of these neophyte travellers ensured an ever-burgeoning travel literature. However, Britain's presence in Arabia was limited to specific external, coastal sites from which a few explorers could venture into the 'interior'. In 1798, as Napoleon began his campaign in Egypt, Britain had agreed a treaty with the Sultan of Muscat in an attempt to safeguard British political and commercial activities in the Indian Ocean from piracy. Aden, on the southern coast of the peninsula, was seized by the British navy in 1839 to protect the sea passage to India. With the opening of the Suez Canal in 1869, that colonial traffic swelled significantly and the stopping-off point en route to India which Aden provided became a vital safe harbour for British interests. Yet the vision from Aden was not inwards to the shimmering deserts of southern Arabia, but rather out to merchant shipping on the Arabian Sea.

As the First World War rolled into Arabia, so increasing numbers of British soldiers came to make their own voyages into the foreign landscape. The establishment of the Arab Bureau in Cairo, under the directorship of D. G. Hogarth, brought together figures such as T. E. Lawrence and Gertrude Bell, already well-travelled in the region, in a concerted effort to spark an Arab revolution against the Ottoman Empire. In Mesopotamia, British troops secured Basra as early as October 1914. By 1917, both Baghdad and Jerusalem were under British control. With Cairo already occupied, three key cities of Arabia lay in British military hands.

The second period, from 1917 to 1956, has been dubbed 'Britain's moment in the Middle East' by Elizabeth Monroe, based on the calculation that 'forty years is only a moment in the life of a region with a recorded history of four millennia'.[6] This was the period of greatest British colonial activity in Arabia. It was a time when British dominance brought ever greater numbers of British citizens to Arabia for financial, military, religious, travel or tourist reasons. That migration was accompanied by increasing numbers of travelogues and memoirs published for a British readership both in England and across

Arabia. The processes of modernisation and mechanisation gathered pace. New means of transport were becoming available. Cars, rarely glimpsed before 1914, had been imported during the First World War and the 'Tin Lizzies', as the early Fords were named, ventured further into Arabia's interior. Aircraft had shrunk the vast distances of Arabia. In the 1920s and 1930s, when the emergence of the oil industry brought in prospectors seeking 'black gold', British and US diplomacy battled for contracts with Arabian states, with the Americans securing Ibn Saud's valuable signature.

British intrigue now extended to those parts of Arabia that had previously eluded the vision of 'imperial eyes'.[7] During this period of escalating British involvement in Arabia, most travelogues came from colonial and military sources. Though the First World War had fashioned Lawrence's *Seven Pillars of Wisdom* it was not until his death in 1935 that the book was published for the general public. Many other tales emerged from the pens of British military travellers and colonial administrators in far-flung quarters, though none caught the public imagination like Lawrence's epic crusade. The Second World War then brought thousands more British soldiers to Egypt and ensured a steady stream of books about their experiences. However, Indian independence in 1947 signalled the beginning of the end for British imperialism. In 1956, the Suez Crisis forced Britain to reluctantly rethink its entire colonial policy. The days of Britain's imperial presence in Arabia were numbered.

The third phase, from 1956 to 2003, witnessed British withdrawal from Arabia. The high tide of British imperialism in Arabia had seen a surge in travel writing in the first half of the twentieth century. The subsequent British departure in the second half of the century ensured a distinct decline in the production of travel texts. After Suez, it was the lamenting voice of Wilfred Thesiger, that most belated imperial traveller, which rang out in *Arabian Sands* (1959) and *The Marsh Arabs* (1964). Oil wealth and modernisation had forever altered Arabia both for its inhabitants and for travellers. Nostalgia for a vanishing land and people now reigned. The scarcity of travelogues was most noticeable in the thirty years that followed Britain's withdrawal from Aden in 1967. In embryonic form, in the early works of Colin Thubron, the post-imperial travelogue retained a hint of that Thesiger-esque nostalgia. But in Jonathan Raban's *Arabia: Through the Looking Glass* (1979) it found its feet. The desert obsession of previous travellers was gone, replaced by an excited exploration of the modern Arab world produced by petrodollars. Individual Arabs were now given greater voice; their words, thoughts, and dreams were presented in a contemporary, urban Arabia. Yet Raban's work stood alone. No British travelogue of note was produced in the 1980s. It was not until 1997 that other post-imperial works followed, with the appearance of William Dalrymple's *From the Holy Mountain* and Tim Mackintosh-Smith's *Yemen*. The link between British travel writing and imperial interest in Arabia was as clearly illustrated by the relative silence following withdrawal from Aden, as it was by the legion of books that had appeared during the heyday of the 1920s and 1930s.

The genre of travel writing houses a loosely defined collection of narratives. While the boundaries of the form escape definitive delineation, travel writing as a field of study has found itself increasingly under scrutiny by an expanding band of academics including literary scholars, geographers, historians, social scientists, anthropologists and cultural commentators. All have nuanced approaches to the subject. Theoretical and critical considerations from ethnography, discourse theory and cultural studies have impacted on literary models employed to unpack and analyse travel texts. The mounting academic interest in travel writing can arguably be traced to one work: Edward Said's *Orientalism* (1978). The wide-ranging debate that followed its publication not only forced academics to question the nature of imperialism and East-West representations but recognised travel writing now as an important and distinct form of literature. Though *Orientalism* may have kick-started a scholarly approach to travel writing, it might also have acted as a powerful deterrent to prospective travellers in the 1980s thinking of writing on Arabia. The label of 'Orientalist' now held a distinctly unwelcome stigma. However, the process of accumulated knowledge and power over the East, which 'Orientalism' represented, was never as monolithic or organised as Said originally envisaged. Rather, the accreted information should perhaps be seen as the result of a more organic process; a heterogeneous collation of thought and data, uneven and fractured, as the writing of Lisa Lowe, Ali Behdad, and others have illustrated.

The relationship between colonial rule and travel literature is continually emphasised in this study. Writing on lands and peoples either militarily occupied or under the scrutiny of British colonial travellers was a central part of the process by which parts of the wider world could be tamed and brought home to the readers back in Britain. Many of those who wrote of their travels in Arabia employed a colonial discourse which belittles and infantilises the locals and their concerns. Many also sought an appropriate narrative to describe, map and plot the landscape they crossed, often with a concern for Western scientific precision.

Many travellers supported Britain's presence in Arabia. Some did not. Here we see Gertrude Bell's eulogy to Lord Cromer's policy in Egypt in the form of a preface to her travelogue *Amurath to Amurath* (1911). We hear of Freya Stark's endeavours on behalf of the British government in 1940 to counter Yemen's isolationist stance by showing Pathé newsreels to the ladies of the royal court in San'a. Yet the tale of Harry St John Philby's spilt with British officialdom and his subsequent expeditions under the aegis of Ibn Saud is also told. Many travellers were deeply affected by their time in Arabia, and held complex personal and political views. Marmaduke Pickthall is seen in Chapter 1 despairing at the attitude and actions of a late-nineteenth-century British Christian missionary. However, when Pickthall converted to Islam in 1917, after spending some twenty years as an active Christian, he remained a public supporter of Britain's occupation of Egypt. I have uncovered archive material which demonstrates how aspects of British imperial history in Arabia closely tie to individual travel tales. In Chapter 3, T. E. Lawrence's reader's report on an unpublished biography of Colonel Leachman written by Harry St John Philby, graphically illustrates, in Lawrence's own words, just how divergent Lawrence and Leachman were as British military travellers. Secret political documents reveal the divisions that formed between individual travellers and British officials. In Chapter 7, Foreign Office archives are used to show how travellers into Turkish Yemen could be harshly treated by the British government when caught in disguise by a rival imperial power. The relationship between travellers and the British government was not always a rosy one.

The chapters that follow are organised thematically, combining both temporal and spatial considerations. In a style adapted from Erich Auerbach's *Mimesis* (1946), each chapter opens with an extended passage of primary source material chosen to introduce the chapter's central topic. Three chapters examine sites of Arabia while five concentrate on particular themes. When plotted together, these eight chapters provide a rich map of British travel writing across the defined region of Arabia from 1882 to 2003.

The three sites explored are the Empty Quarter, Iraq (comprising Baghdad and the marshes of southern Iraq), and southern Arabia, the lands neighbouring Aden. Though the dimensions of the sites may vary, each was a place of specific interest to British travellers and the wider imperial project in Arabia. At the peak of British imperial activity in Arabia in 1931, the Empty Quarter was the arena for a memorable race of exploration as two Englishmen vied to be the first man (Westerner) across its apparently waterless wastes. London newspapers reported Bertram Thomas's successful crossing of one of the world's most inhospitable places. Arabia was firmly fixed in Britain's thoughts.

Baghdad, romantically entwined in *Arabian Nights* mythology, was significant for British military plans in Arabia during the First World War, emerging as a base for British imperial administration and home to many travellers, Gertrude Bell being the best remembered of them. The marshes of southern Iraq were often viewed disparagingly by British travellers of the 1920s but became a wild, rural haven for Wilfred Thesiger to explore in the 1950s. The area of southern Arabia, centred on Aden, was fundamental to British imperialism in Arabia. Not only was Aden Britain's first Arabian acquisition, it was essential as a coaling station for British shipping to India. Using archive material, I investigate those British travellers who ventured into both Yemen and the Aden Protectorate to provide valuable intelligence information on the unknown lands neighbouring Aden.

Five central themes are identified: religion; the changing nature of Arabia across the twentieth century; imperial wars; British women travellers; and the nature of travel writing after Britain's imperial withdrawal. I demonstrate how each is vital to understanding the particular nuances and concerns of British travel writing on Arabia from 1882 to 2003. Each of these themes reflects imperial matters. For example, numerous women travellers came to the region as the wives of colonial administrators, and single women such as Freya Stark or Gertrude Bell lived in Baghdad supporting the British imperial presence there. Similarly, once Cairo became British-controlled, missionary activity in Arabia dramatically increased, illustrating how religious-based travel was closely tied to an imperial presence. Western desire for oil was a significant factor in changing the nature of Arabia across the twentieth century. While petrodollars radically transformed some societies, the arrival of car and air transport brought British travellers more swiftly into the furthest reaches of Arabia.

The chapters are presented in an order which is broadly chronological. For instance, Chapter 1 considers religious-based travel texts. Many of these travelogues were published in the late nineteenth and early twentieth centuries and so this topic makes a logical opening chapter. I distinguish two distinct forms of religious-based travel texts: those emphasising the perspective of a Christian traveller in Arabia, largely in the Christian Holy Lands; and those detailing journeys undertaken (largely in disguise as Muslims) to explore the Holy Cities of Islam.

Subsequent chapters cover a largely sequential focus, even though some are concerned with much of the 120-year-period while others explore a far shorter time span. Chapter 2 is chiefly concerned with the years 1930-31 when Bertram Thomas and Harry St John Philby competed to become the first non-Arab to cross that vast area of Arabia called the Empty Quarter. Chapter 3 examines the writing of British military travellers across three twentieth-century conflicts, covering the period from 1914 to 1956. While the First World War produced the widely romanticised exploits of T. E. Lawrence, the Second World War in Arabia was a far more mechanised conflict. I consider Keith Douglas's *Alamein to Zem Zem* (1946) as the finest travelogue to emerge from this imperial war. The chapter ends with a view of the Suez War of 1956, a crucial moment in British imperial history. Chapter 4 then explores depictions of the changing face of Arabia from 1902 to the 1970s. As railways, motor cars and airplanes came to Arabia, so new patterns of travel emerged and new destinations became feasible for both travellers and tourists. The discovery of oil and its resultant impact provides the backdrop to the second half of the chapter.

Gertrude Bell holds a remarkable place in the history of British involvement in Arabia, remembered for her travels, her travel writing and her role as a leading figure in the imperial construction and administration of Iraq. In Chapter 5, she is discussed alongside an impressive array of women travellers venturing into a land and society traditionally seen as male dominated. The chapter opens with Louisa Jebb and Victoria Buxton heading down the Euphrates in 1904 aboard a raft of goatskins. Their experiences, like those of Margaret Fountaine, Rosita Forbes and Freya Stark, serve to illustrate the rich variety of women's travel writing on Arabia from the 1880s to the 1970s. How these women travellers fitted within the British military and colonial administration network forms a thread running through the chapter.

Chapters 6 and 7 then refocus on specific sites of interest. Chapter 6 is concerned with British travellers' impressions of Baghdad from

1908. The contrasting rural world of the Marsh Arabs forms the subject of the second half of the chapter. Chapter 7 turns to exploration in southern Arabia, following those figures who stepped beyond the confines of Aden. Archive material is used to investigate a number of journeys made into Yemen and the Aden Protectorates by British travellers from the 1890s to the 1940s and the value of certain travellers to Britain's imperial project in Arabia. Tim Mackintosh-Smith's account of Yemen in the 1990s then provides a more contemporary commentary.

In the concluding Chapter 8, the spotlight is on the nature of the travel literature that emerged between Britain's declining imperial presence in Arabia in the 1960s and 2003 when British troops returned to invade Iraq. I investigate how the shift from imperial to post-imperial Arabia is reflected in British travel writing, drawing on material from interviews with four contemporary travel writers to analyse the evolution of the post-imperial travel text.

From Cairo to Baghdad commences as Britain seizes control in Egypt in 1882 under William Gladstone's political rule and ends with the invasion of Iraq in 2003 led by Prime Minister Tony Blair. Throughout that period, individual voices offered evocative accounts of their travels in Arabia. This study is a commentary on the voyages undertaken by those travellers who ventured into Arab lands, either independently or as part of that vast military and colonial machine. While the British assault on Iraq in March 2003 may designate the end point to this study, the moment is more significantly marked as the return of British imperial and military might to Arabia. Commentators such as Robert Fisk are keen to recognise the complex correspondence between this latest incursion into Iraq and the last, back in 1914. *From Cairo to Baghdad* illustrates how similarly close connections exist between Britain's imperial activity in Arabia and British travel writing on the region.

1

MISSIONARIES AND PILGRIMS

'A marvel!' [Suleymân] exclaimed after a moment spent in
gazing. 'Never, I suppose, since first this village was created,
have two Franks approached it in a single day before. Thou art
as one of us in outward seeming,' he remarked to me; 'but
yonder comes a perfect Frank with two attendants.'

We looked in the direction which his finger pointed, and
beheld a man on horseback clad in white from head to foot,
with a pith helmet and a puggaree [turban used as sun-shade],
followed by two native servants leading sumpter-mules
[packhorses].

'Our horses are in need of water,' growled Rashîd,
uninterested in the sight. 'It is a sin for those low people to
refuse it to us.'

'Let us first wait and see how this newcomer fares, what
method he adopts,' replied Suleymân, reclining once more at
his ease.

The Frank and his attendants reached the outskirts of the
village, and headed naturally for the spring. The fellâhîn,
already put upon their guard by Rashîd's venture, opposed
them in a solid mass. The Frank expostulated. We could hear
his voice of high command.

'Aha, he knows some Arabic. He is a missionary, not a
traveller,' said Suleymân, who now sat up and showed keen
interest. 'I might have known it, for the touring season is long
past.'

He rose with dignified deliberation and remounted. We
followed him as he rode slowly down towards the scene of
strife. When we arrived, the Frank, after laying about him

vainly with his riding-whip, had drawn out a revolver. He was
being stoned. His muleteers had fled to a safe distance. In
another minute, as it seemed, he would have shot some
person, when nothing under Allah could have saved his life.

Suleymân cried out in English: 'Don't you be a fool, sir!
Don't you fire!'

The Frank looked round in our direction, with an angry
face; but Suleymân bestowed no further thought on him. He
rode up to the nearest group of fellahin, crying aloud:

'O true believers! O asserters of the Unity! Bless the
Prophet, and inform me straightaway what has happened!'

Having captured their attention by this solemn adjuration,
he inquired:

'Who is the chief among you? Let him speak, him only!'

Although the crowd had seemed till then to be without a
leader, an old white-bearded man was thrust before him, with
the cry:

'Behold our Sheykh, O lord of judgment. Question him!'

Rashîd and I heard nothing of the conversation which
ensued, except the tone of the two voices, which appeared
quite friendly, and some mighty bursts of laughter from the
crowd. No more stones were thrown, although some persons
still kept guard over the spring.

At length Suleymân returned to us, exclaiming:

'All is well. They grant us leave to take what water we
require. The spring has been a trouble to these people through
the ages because the wandering tribes with all their herds
come here in time of drought and drink it dry. But now they
are our friends, and make us welcome.'

He called out to the Frank, who all this while had sat his
horse with an indignant air, more angry, as it seemed, to be
forgotten than to be assailed:

'It is all right. You take the water and you pay them five
piastres.'

'It is extortion!' cried the Frank. 'What right have they to
charge me money for the water of this natural spring, which is
the gift of God? I will not pay.'

'No matter. I pay for you,' shrugged Suleymân.

I tried to make the missionary – for such he proved to be
upon acquaintance – understand that the conditions in that

desert country made the spring a valued property, and gave a price to every pitcherful of water.

'What! Are you English?' was his only answer, as he scanned my semi-native garb with pity and disgust. 'And who, pray, is that person with you who was rude to me?'

'His name is Suleymân. He is a friend of mine.'

'A friend, I hardly think,' replied the Frank fastidiously.'[1]

The passage is taken from *Oriental Encounters* (1918) by Marmaduke Pickthall which is a reconstruction of Pickthall's youthful travels in Palestine and Syria from 1894 to 1896. Pickthall is journeying through northern Arabia with an entourage consisting of Suleyman, his rather disreputable dragoman, Rashid, a Syrian soldier bought from Turkish servitude for five pounds, and an unnamed cook. On the outskirts of a desert village one travel party espies another. The incongruity between the two Englishmen is painted in the initial vision of the missionary dressed all in white, with pith helmet on his head, astride a horse, his servants traipsing behind. He does not even recognise Pickthall as a fellow countryman due to his 'semi-native garb' and certainly cannot comprehend his friendship with one of the locals. The missionary is the evangelical Victorian traveller of the nineteenth century heading out into distant lands for the sake of God and country, with the Bible in one hand and a gun in the other. He is an archetype who receives recognition merely as 'the Frank'. Pickthall accounts him no more personal respect than that. When the Englishmen meet, the outrage expressed by the missionary is due to the disparity between the two. While the missionary maintains a rigid stance as an Englishman and a Christian in Arabia, Pickthall has undergone a process of assimilation, his clothing and his mannerisms reflecting his immersion into the ways of the Arab. He has made friends with his dragoman and shows sympathy for his companions' thoughts and feelings. Yet both men are distinct from the simple tourist; both have learnt some Arabic in order to ease their separate paths.

In the following chapter, 'The Parting of the Ways', the difference in the two Englishmen's philosophies becomes more apparent. Pickthall has gone to the missionary's tent and, 'thinking to make him laugh', tells an anecdote on local methods of pest control:

Rashîd had spoken of the virtues of a certain shrub; but Suleymân declared the best specific was a new-born baby.

This, if laid within a room for a short while, attracted every
insect. The babe should then be carried out and dusted. The
missionary did not even smile.

The basis of the joke is the inhumanity of the Arab who could employ
a young baby to remove insects from a tent. In drawing this picture of
Suleyman's primitive nature, Pickthall appeals to the missionary's
willingness to define their Arab attendants as racially inferior. He tries
to unite the two Englishmen by a light-hearted prod at the locals. It
does not work:

> 'The brutes!' he murmured. 'How can you, an Englishman,
> and apparently a man of education, bear their intimacy?'
>   They have their good points, I asserted – though, I fear, but
> lamely; for the robustness of his attitude impressed me, he
> being a man, presumably, of wide experience, and, what is
> more, a clergyman – the kind of man I had been taught to
> treat with some respect. (97)

Pickthall's tone may seem ironic, yet powerful Christian voices had
indeed been influential in his life. He is moved to a momentous
epiphany as he wonders whether he should accede to the missionary's
approach to the Arabs. A new dawn begins to break on the horizon:

> And suddenly my mind grew clear. I cared no longer for the
> missionary's warning. I was content to face the dangers which
> those warnings threatened; to be contaminated, even ruined as
> an Englishman. The mischief, as I thought it, was already
> done. I knew that I could never truly think as did that
> missionary, nor hold myself superior to eastern folk again. If
> that was to be reprobate, then I was finished. (104)

Pickthall's father and grandfather had both been clergymen. It was
with Christian missionary friends that he first went to stay in Palestine
in 1894.[2] When back in Damascus in 1907, Pickthall stayed with the
chaplain, J. E. Hanauer, editing his *Folk-lore of the Holy Land*, and
providing the introduction and a number of the tales told in the book
which recognised the shared nature of many traditions within
Christianity and Islam.[3] However, in 1917, whilst writing *Oriental
Encounters* in a cottage in the heart of the English countryside in

Suffolk, he renounced the Christianity he practised and openly embraced Islam. The dawn revelation quoted above can therefore be viewed as an expression of apostasy. Just as in 'The Parting of the Ways', Pickthall makes a decisive shift in his religious identity, striking away from Christianity and a stance of assumed eminence over the Arab world. In *Oriental Encounters*, Pickthall decides he can no longer maintain a position as dictated by the missionary and so opts for friendship with the 'eastern folk' even though such an attitude threatens his ruination as an Englishman. In person, Marmaduke Pickthall went much further in his conversion. For the final twenty years of his life, he was a leading light of the British Muslim community. Yet his religious convictions were only part of his identity. His political position was far more intricate than merely extolling blanket approval of Arab independence. Pickthall remained a Tory and an opponent of Pan-Arab nationalism even after his conversion to Islam. He has been aptly described as 'an upholder of the British empire who unrelentingly banged on the tub of Disraelian Toryism'.[4] Indeed Pickthall backed the British rule of Egypt under Lord Cromer, publicly declaring his advocacy despite being an adherent of Islam, seeing 'small harm in the British occupation, so long as it left the inhabitants in peace'.[5] While Pickthall may have ignored the cries of Egyptian nationalists, he wrote fervently in support of the Young Turk revolution. Though the two positions were viewed by many as incongruous, Pickthall saw no inconsistency.

*

For Charles Montagu Doughty the idea of being turned to Islam through time spent travelling in Arabia was anathema. His oft-quoted quip that 'the sun made me an Arab, but never warped me to Orientalism' contrasts vividly with Marmaduke Pickthall's experiences in Arabia. Following Cambridge, where he studied geology, and a four-year period of travel around Europe, Doughty headed for the Holy Lands in 1874, settling in Damascus where he learnt Arabic and lived the life of a Christian Arab. Doughty openly introduced himself to all as a Christian or 'Nasrâny'. By 1876, he was prepared to journey further into the Arabian Peninsula on an extraordinary expedition that lasted close to two years. *Travels in Arabia Deserta* (1888) was the record of Doughty's wanderings into the Arabian desert until his exit from Jeddah in August 1878. The work was not ready to be published for ten years, only then accepted by Cambridge University Press with some reluctance after being rejected by four other publishing houses.[6] The problem for the publisher was Doughty's adherence to a distinctly abstruse Chaucerian style. Richard Burton, who had travelled to Mecca in disguise some twenty years earlier detailing his adventures in *A Pilgrimage to Mecca* (1853), was less than enamoured with Doughty's anti-Muslim sentiments. According to Doughty's biographer, D. G. Hogarth, 'the obstinacy of "Khalil Nasrâny's" contempt for Islam was in itself a challenge to one who had thought it necessary to adopt that faith and still professed it'.[7] Burton, like Marmaduke Pickthall, had become a Muslim; Doughty always remained devoutly Christian.

The arch-Christian Charles Doughty chose to travel with the vast collection of Muslims heading south from Damascus to the Holy Cities of Islam. He joined the convoy of 6,000 hajji and their accompanying 10,000 camels, mules and asses but travelled always as an outsider, as one with, but not of, the hajj. Just as the hajj was a declaration of his Muslim companions' faith, Doughty's voyage would be an assertion of his own religious belief. Rather than Mecca, the Nabataean monuments of Medain Saleh were the object of his travels, and in order to safely reach them, he travelled with a *mukowwem* [hajj camel master] who agreed to escort Doughty for the price of 1,000 piastres, or ten English pounds. While he travelled with the Persian Shia pilgrims, he was noticeably a stranger. On the *Derb el-Haj* [Pilgrim road] near Maan a gang of Bedouin demanded, 'And who is he?' to which the reply came; 'A Nasrâny'.[8] Thoroughly aware of the incitement of being a Christian on the hajj, Doughty apparently did nothing to hide the fact. 'All the Damascene servants in our Persian company knew me to be a Nasrâny' (63). Consequently, Doughty's insistence on declaring his religion, or at least not disguising it, became a continual cause of conflict throughout his time in Arabia. It was his open declaration of Christian faith that provoked ridicule, curses and violence.

The only possible sign of religious compromise was in Doughty's acceptance of an adopted Muslim form of his first name: 'He became known under the name of Khalil, which he caused to be engraved upon a seal, for use in Arabia.'[9] Whilst writing *Arabia Deserta*, Doughty distanced himself from his old travelling persona by the use of a third-person referent. Replacing the 'I' of the self, the narrator becomes at times, 'Khalil' and at others, 'the Nasrâny' or another epithet. The effect is two-fold in creating both an antiquated sense to the narrative and a dissociation from the narrator. It is a process by which Doughty conveys remoteness from his former self. Here rests the distinction between Doughty the travel writer and Doughty the traveller. One biography has noted: 'His constant use of the terms, "the Nasrâny," "the kafir," and "the God's adversary," in reference to himself is the clearest indication of his detachment.'[10] Doughty travelled openly as the Christian Khalil throughout his time in Arabia, the moniker becoming a pet name back in England. After he married Caroline Amelia McMurdo in October 1886, it was the name by which she would call him for the rest of his life.[11]

Thus it is Khalil who reaches his declared destination of Medain Saleh where he comes under the temporary protection of Mohammed Aly who is the guardian of the kella, a stronghold or tower designed to protect the chief watering-holes on the hajj route.

> Mohammed Aly had said to them that I was a Sîr Amîn, some secretary sent down upon a government errand. This was a short illusion, for as the Moslems pray openly and Khalîl was not seen to pray, it was soon said that I could not be of the religion. Mohammed Aly was a hater of every other than his own belief and very jealous of the growing despotism in the world of the perilous Nasâra [Christian peoples]; - thus they muse with a ferocious gloom over the decay of the militant Islam. Yet he could regard me pleasantly, as a philosopher, in whom was an indulgent natural opinion in all matter of religion. - These were the inhabitants of the kella, a tower seventy feet upon a side, square built. (93)

The detachment signified by the indirect referent Khalil has been replaced by Doughty's direct reference to himself as 'I'. It is as though there are two characters, two 'Nasâra', not praying. While Mohammed Aly is prepared to lie to his fellow Muslims in order to protect the true identity of the itinerant traveller, Khalil is unwilling to play along with the game. On this occasion, he manages to escape assault by the other inhabitants of the kella thanks to the protection of Mohammed Aly. In the future, he will be less fortunate.

Doughty remained for the next three months in Medain Saleh, exploring and recording the various monuments that lie there. The Nabataean and Himyaric inscriptions he found were a source of great excitement. No Westerner had seen them before. For the local inhabitants, including Mohammed Aly, the novelty of Doughty's presence soon wore off. He continued to rest as a guest in the kella, travelling to the surrounding ancient sites under the paid guidance of Zeyd, a sheikh of the local Fejir Bedouin. Eventually, the long-suffering Mohammed Aly's patience wore out and he attacked Doughty, beating him round the head and 'snatching my beard with canine rage' (164). Yet Doughty continued to explore the desert lands as a Christian 'almost at the door of the holy places' (103), perceiving his own presence in the eyes of the Arab population as an exciting intrigue that had gradually dissipated:

> When tumblers come to a town the people are full of novelty, but having seen their fill they are as soon weary of them; so these few peaceable days ended, I saw the people's countenances less friendly; the fanatical hearts of some swelled to see one walking among them that rejected the saving religion of the apostle of Ullah. If children cried after the heathen man, their elders were now less ready to correct them. A few ill-blooded persons could not spare to crake where I passed from their street benches: 'Say Mohammed rasûl Ullah!' but others blamed them. In an evening I had wandered to the oasis side; there a flock of the village children soon assembling with swords and bats followed my heels, hooting, 'O Nasrâny! O Nasrâny!' and braving about the kàfir and cutting crosses in the sand before me, they spitefully defiled them, shouting in such a villainous carol, 'We have eaten rice with *halîb* (milk) and have made water upon the *salîb* (cross).' The knavish boys followed ever with hue and cry, as it were in driving some uncouth beast before them, until I came again to the town's end, where they began to stone me. (155-6)

Doughty, comparing his presence to that of a circus performer with whom the crowd has become bored and then irritated, now makes reference not to Khalil or 'the Nasrâny' or any other of his Christian based epithets but to the 'kàfir' or unbeliever. It is to him, wholly isolated and abandoned, that the taunts and stones of the children are directed. Again, the Christian pilgrim is saved by the intervention of a local protectorate, this time one of the boys who bravely declares 'the stranger is a guest of Ullah' (156). Once more, Doughty emerges from the pages of *Arabia Deserta* as an ersatz Christ-like figure, wandering the heart of Arabia with a distinctly masochistic urge as though the stonings and beating inflicted on him served to reinforce his Christian righteousness.

When he has copied the inscriptions from the monuments of Medain Saleh and sent back his drawings to Damascus with the returning hajj caravan, there is a sense in which Doughty has completed his intended task. With this archaeological endeavour achieved his winding path over Arabia could now truly meander: Doughty headed off with Zeyd and the Fejir Bedouin into the open sand plains of the desert. Rekindling his passion for geology, he turned west into the 'Titanic desolation' (381) of the volcanic Harrat al 'Uwayrid, passing the summer of 1877 in the protective embrace of the Moahib tribesmen. Doughty wound his way through a series of potentially disastrous situations, often initiated by the avowal of his Christian identity, until he finally found himself at Ayn el Zeyma, deep into sacred Arabia. It was here that 'the final act in the drama of Doughty's Arabian wanderings ... took place as near Mecca as it is lawful for a Christian to approach'.[12]

At the green oasis of Ayn el Zeyma, the news that a Nasrany was on his way preceded Doughty. As he approached, he watched an injured camel being butchered by a frenzy of knives that worked to 'hack the not fully dead carcase' (484 vol II) and thought 'in a few minutes, my body might be likewise made a bloody spectacle' (485).[13] Soon he heard 'a voice of ill augury behind us, "Dismount, dismount! – Let me alone I say, and I will kill the kafir"' (486). It was the cry of a Bedouin sharif named Salem. He was old and infirm but wielded his *khánjar* [curved knife] with blatant intent. Doughty's companion whispered the advice, 'Only say, Khalil, thou art a Moslem, it is but a word, to appease them.' Doughty's response was typically grandiose: 'If it please God I will pass, whether they will or no' (486). As Salem attacked, Doughty stood still. His saviour on this occasion was Maabub whose reasoning was based on how the imperial might of England might respond:

What is this, he said, sheríf Sâlem? You promised me to do nothing by violence! Remember Jidda bombarded! – and that was for the blood of some of this stranger's people; take heed what thou doest. They are the Engleys, who for one that is slain of them send great battleships; and beat down a city. (487)

He recalls 1858 when the British frigate *Cyclops* shelled Jeddah following the murder of 'the British and French vice-consuls and fourteen Christian subjects'.[14] Salem yields to the memory of British naval firepower only after a final threat to kill the Christian. Doughty is reprieved but transported away to Ta'if to answer the grievances of his would-be assassin.

In Ta'if there is to be one final twist as Doughty reveals the loaded pistol he has carried unused around his neck all across Arabia for close to two years. He is faced by the still incensed Salem and a dozen cameleers whose hands are on their knives. The scene is 'an image straight from the Victorian pantheon of *Boy's Own* heroes: Gordon at Khartoum, perhaps, in Joy's famous painting'.[15] It is the moment where the hordes of murderous savages confront the lone, white Englishman. Yet unlike so many of his imperial counterparts, Doughty does not begin a bloodbath and once more manages to escape. He turns the pistol, offering the butt to one of his enemies. This last act of supplication leaves Doughty's life utterly dependent on the grace of those around him. He will sacrifice anything but his religion. The action saves him – just. Five of the bullets are fired into the air 'with a wonderful resonance' while Salem cries, 'Leave one of them!' (497). But the bullet reserved for Doughty is not shot. Salem is playing a macho game. He declares he would rather watch him hang. Instead, Doughty is rescued by Maabub and passed into the hands of Sharif Hussein of Ta'if who not only treats him with dignity and respect but arranges for him to be handed over into 'the open hospitality of the British Consulate' (539) in Jeddah. Once more, Doughty is saved. The near two-year wander of 'Khalil Nasrâny' across Arabia is finally brought to a safe conclusion.

*

While Pickthall sought friendships on his travels with both British missionaries and locals, Doughty remained aloof and alone. His reluctance to find common ground with those Arabs he met, combined with his refusal to cloak his Christianity, ensured a rough ride through firmly Muslim regions. Yet both Pickthall and Doughty travelled with religion as a central guiding light. The call of the Holy Lands had brought these travellers from the confines of England to forge their own distinct pilgrimages in Arabia. For Doughty the journey through Arabia became a deliberate expression of his faith; the more hostile the environment, the stronger his religious belief was forged. For Marmaduke Pickthall, Arabia became an area where he would question and doubt his Christianity, even though he had arrived there thanks to the support by the missionary movement.

Christian missionary work in the Arabian Peninsula only truly commenced in the second half of the nineteenth century. Prior to this time, 'Muslim lands had tended to be neglected by Christian missions in comparison with more productive fields'.[16] Following the British military seizure of Egypt in 1882, the Church Missionary Society launched its own offensive in March 1885, sanctioning Aden 'a jumping-off point for the interior'.[17] However, the early missionaries did not thrive. Thomas Valpy French came from the Church Missionary Society in India, where he had been Bishop of Lahore since 1877. In 1891, at the age of sixty-five, he declared he would lead the evangelical movement in Arabia and headed to the distant town of Muscat. French died within three months, though his 'Church in Arabia' was duly established. The mission was not a success: in the following fifty years it recorded merely five converts. In Egypt, the imposition of British imperial control in 1882 promoted a renewal of missionary zeal ensuring: 'from that time on Anglican work in the country was resumed. The C.M.S. [Church Missionary Society] hospital in Old Cairo was the centre of evangelical as well as of medical work.'[18] In Palestine, the English Christianity of Anglicanism had been in place rather longer; the position of Anglican Bishop of Jerusalem had been maintained since 1841.[19]

By the early twentieth century there was a growing collection of missionary travel texts concerned either with guiding the Christian pilgrim through the Holy Lands of Palestine or providing a broadly exegetic outline of the religion of Islam. The view of Islam was not always entirely sympathetic. In *The Reproach of Islam* (1909), the Reverend Gairdner openly recognises this aspect of his text, stating that 'Chapter IV is, the writer confesses, a frank criticism of Islam'. The author was better known as Temple Gairdner of Cairo, celebrated as a missionary travel writer, his work being 'the fruit of ten years spent in the east in one of the great centres of Islam'.[20] British-controlled Cairo provided Gairdner and other Christians with many more home comforts in their evangelical missions than French's earlier venture into Arabia. In her biography of Gairdner, Constance Padwick relates that *The Reproach of Islam* 'was written to give "study circles" some grasp of the main outlines of Islam'. Though only published by the Society for Promoting Christian Knowledge rather than a mainstream publisher, by 1920 it was in its fifth edition.[21] Other texts were equally damning in their reviews of Islam. *The Religion of the Crescent* (1895) by the Reverend William St Clair-Tisdall offered English readers a similarly biased vision. Some writers presented a more appreciative approach to Islam. S. H. Leeder tells of his journeying about Cairo, exploring the Mosques when able and discussing questions of Islam with various sheikhs. He is a sympathetic traveller who is keen to stress the links between the religions of Islam and Christianity rather than the divisions. Leeder hopes that his *Veiled Mysteries of Egypt and the Religion of Islam* (1912) will promote 'greater fairness and better understanding and appreciation of the motives and ideals of the followers of Mohammed'.[22]

The sites of the Christian Holy Lands meant Palestine offered rich material for the missionary travel writer. The Reverend James Neil's *Palestine Explored* (1881) was in its twelfth edition by 1907. British readers back in Edwardian London might instead choose W*alks About Jerusalem* (1910) published by the London Society for Promoting Christianity Amongst the Jews. Its author was the same Damascus-based chaplain, James Hanauer, who had befriended Marmaduke Pickthall during his time in Arabia. Alternatively, there was *Six Months in Jerusalem* (1898) by the Reverend Charles Biggs, with its patriotic subtitle 'Impressions of The Work of England in and for the Holy City'.[23] In *Patrollers of Palestine* (1906) the Reverend Haskett Smith offered a lighter version of the Christian travelogue. His book is the tale of a group of eleven English travellers journeying around Palestine who are all given amusing sobriquets based on a caricature of their physical or personal nature. For instance, the group includes a large middle-aged woman constantly getting the wrong end of the stick who is known as 'The Malaprop'. A humorous, well-travelled member of the party is 'Monte Carlo'. A first-time traveller, excited by all he comes across, receives the title of 'The Enthusiast'. It is the leader of the group who is most intriguing. His pseudonym is 'The Sheikh':

He had resided for many years in the Holy Land, wearing for the most part the costume of the natives, speaking their language, adapting himself to their daily manners and customs, partaking of their hospitality, conducting business relations with them, indulging in every opportunity of social intercourse and conversation with them, and closely studying the various idiosyncrasies of their dispositions and ideas.

By these means he had succeeded in penetrating beneath the surface of the Oriental character, and had become thoroughly imbued with Oriental modes and thoughts of expression.

Moreover, he had travelled frequently and in all directions through Eastern, Western, and Northern Palestine, so that there was scarcely a town or village which he had not visited from Baalbek to Gaza, from Damascus to Kerak, or from the Mediterranean to the Great Syrian Desert.

Nevertheless, he was a true-born Englishman, and English to the core – a typical John Bull in appearance and character. A journalistic interviewer had once described him as 'a pleasing, practical, portly parson, this patroller of Palestine, of robust form and full round voice, with the cool confidence of a clear-headed cosmopolitan who has seen places and people innumerable in variety, and who has a way of taking his companions along with him, not so much as a personal conductor, but as a genial friend, philosopher, and guide.'

One phrase of this description so fascinated the Sheikh's companions that they appropriated it to themselves, and they became known to their friends as 'The Sheikh and his Tribe; or The Patrollers of Palestine.'[24]

A 'true-born Englishman' dressed as an Arab leads his 'tribe' of English tourists from their steamer around the Holy Lands. It is a peculiar version of the romantic desire of the British traveller to adopt Arab clothes and ways exemplified earlier by Marmaduke Pickthall. Having compiled his tableaux of characters, largely stereotypes of English travellers, Smith then uses the arrangement as a narrative tool by which to describe the sites and scenes of Palestine to the reader. Conversations between the tourists and 'The Sheikh' offer historical, social and geographical information on the lands that they are visiting. In the Preface there is a thinly veiled declaration of ownership by the author concerning the opinions of 'The Sheikh': 'I only hold myself responsible for the statements of the Sheikh.' The clear inference is that an Anglican missionary chaplain has appropriated the persona of an Arabian tribal leader. If he does not, like Pickthall, actually convert to Islam, then temporarily, at least, he is mimicking the mannerisms of a Muslim chief. On the frontispiece to *Patrollers of Palestine* is a

Reverend Haskett Smith.

photograph of 'The Sheikh' in full Arab garb (see opposite). It is, of course, of the author, the Reverend Haskett Smith.

For H. V. Morton the rewards for writing on Palestine and the Christian Holy Lands were financial rather than spiritual. In the 1930s, Morton wrote three best-selling religious travelogues commencing with *In the Steps of the Master* (1934) in which he traced the path of Jesus:

> The story I tell in this book is a simple one. It describes the adventures of a man who went to the Holy Land to see the places associated with the life of Christ and to find out what new light the historian and the archaeologist have cast upon the world of the Gospels.[25]

Morton presents an image of himself as a humble pilgrim. Yet there is no deeply held religious drive to Morton's pilgrimage. His biographer Michael Bartholomew has stated that 'nothing, either in his early diaries or in his mature Memoir, suggests that he was driven by a Christian impulse to go on a pilgrimage to the holy places'.[26] The aspect of Morton's religious identity is carefully shrouded throughout his role as narrator of *In the Steps of the Master* and its follow up *In the Steps of St Paul* (1936). He is an ambiguous Christian traveller who never states his faith nor denies it. Morton concocts the sense of a lone Christian pilgrim traversing the lands of Palestine and beyond in the footsteps of Jesus and St Paul in order to provide a suitable narrative vehicle for his English audience to view the Holy Lands. In reality, Morton was either 'ferried around by local drivers' or travelled with his second wife Mary.[27] The nature of his apparent travel was deliberately modified to assume the characteristics of the religious figures whose footsteps he was purportedly following. It seems that Morton was equally content to fictionalise incidents: 'Whether every one of the encounters recorded in the Middle Eastern books actually took place is another question. It is likely, given Morton's general practice, that at least some were imaginatively elaborated, or invented from scratch.'[28] What is certain is his sales success. 200,000 copies of *In the Steps of St Paul* were printed in October 1936 and the book sold out, securing over £20,000 in royalties. In November 1936, Morton was able to note in his diaries that his two Middle Eastern travel texts had sold nearly half a million copies.[29]

*

The early twentieth century saw a growth of British travel texts and religious commentaries concerned with the religion of Arabia. It was in this vein that in 1902 the *Morning Post* sent its 'Special Correspondent' Hadji Khan, a Persian Sufi, on the hajj to Mecca. His experiences were then written up as *With the Pilgrims to Mecca* (1905) under the guidance of Wilfrid Sparroy. The result was a travelogue that detailed the various components of the hajj and Meccan life for a British readership:

> To the North of Mussah-street is situated the Soueygha Bazaar, where goods (especially the belongings of dead pilgrims) are sold by auction twice a day, in the morning and in the evening, and there also slaves are exhibited and knocked down to the highest bidder.[30]

The narrative is precise and exact as though for an audience that may wish to use the information to find their way amongst the markets of Mecca the next time they visit. Of course, few, if any, of the readership will ever visit Mecca. Yet the narrative is still written *as if* a guide to potential tourists. This is spurious. The meticulous nature of the analysis is voyeuristic, a vision of an impossible world for its British readership. It is an inspection of Arabia which defines that other world by carefully recording the minutiae of Mecca and the hajj, the text providing the British reader with a spyglass scrutiny of Arab religious life and customs. The result is a curious concoction of the personal experiences of a Muslim on the hajj (though not an Arab) which are distilled by an English co-author. When the pilgrim's text ends there is a commentary from Wilfrid Sparroy in an appendix entitled 'Some Reflections on the Existence of a Slave Market in Mecca'. He outlines the 'Musselman's attitude to slavery'. It is contrasted with that of the British:

> Now, the British are the champions of freedom: under their flag every man is born free. Nothing is more hateful, to their way of thinking, than one human being should be the slave of another.[31]

So the final words of *With the Pilgrims to Mecca* are those, not of the Muslim pilgrim, but of his English co-writer. While the text has guided

the British reader along the route of the hajj, has exhaustively
illustrated life in Mecca and given an educated insight into the religion
of Mohammed, the last hurrah of the book is to the glory of British
imperial endeavour.

There were two further British travelogues written before 1930 with
a specific focus on the Holy Cities of Islam. Like Charles Doughty,
their authors traced well-defined hajj trails towards Mecca and Medina,
but unlike their Victorian forefather they journeyed in religious and
cultural disguise in order to reach them. They travelled as faux
Muslims in order to experience and explain the customs and actions of
the hajji even though they were both Christian. In his survey *Christians
in Mecca* (1908), Augustus Ralli comments:

> It is possible to glean from the centuries a few examples of
> fearless Europeans, who, taking their lives in their hands,
> disguised in Mohammedan dress and outwardly conforming to
> Mohammedan customs, surmounting the difficulties of
> language and ritual, herding with strange companions,
> undergoing hardships by sea or on land journeys in torrid
> climates, have come scatheless with their hard-won knowledge
> out of the 'lions' den of Islam'.[32]

Ralli's metaphor of a lions' den hints at the notion that Mecca is just
another barbarian corner of the world to be tamed by brave Christian
explorers. The statement appears to be a gauntlet thrown down into
the sand for the next 'fearless' traveller to take up. It fell to Arthur
Wavell, who set off from Marseilles on his journey to Mecca in
September 1908 with Masaudi, 'a Mombasa Swahili', and Abdul
Wahid, 'an Arab from Aleppo'.[33] Half a century had passed since the
eminent Victorian traveller Sir Richard Burton had travelled as Sheikh
Hajj Abdullah. It was a short and distinguished list that Wavell was to
join.

In order to avoid detection, Wavell 'wore a turban and black jubba
[long coat], and was hence generally credited with coming from the
Hedjaz' (50). The matter of disguise is far more than mere dress:

> The main thing is to keep one's eyes open and one's mouth
> shut. It is wonderful how easy it is to acquire foreign habits
> when one is really living in their atmosphere. The secret, I
> believe, is in playing a part as little as possible consciously, and

Arthur Wavell.

in trying to identify one's self as closely as may be with the assumed character, in private as well as in public. (41)

A sense of the danger of discovery is an essential element to the travel Wavell has undertaken. It forms the central appeal to the travelogue which he was to write of his journey into sacred Islam. He travels not directly as an employee of British secret services though he is spying upon the rarely seen world of Mecca. As he seeks the visual requisition of the sacred Muslim sites for readers back home, the narrative delights in minute description and draws parallels to the world of England in order to ground the exotic.

When Wavell safely reaches the sacred city, he performs the required prayers, struggling in the throng of devotees to reach the Kaaba:

> We had considerable difficulty in kissing the black stone. The Kaaba was now dressed in its new covering, and the hole left for the purpose had not yet been widened sufficiently to admit more than one head at a time. A crowd of Bedou Arabs surrounded it, amongst whom we pushed our way, Masaudi and I, for Abdul Wahid was not for risking broken ribs in the crush. The whole thing resembled what we used to call a 'loose hot' at Winchester football. At last I got my head through, getting it violently bumped in the process, kissed the stone, and emerged from the throng minus the shoulder-cloth of my Ihram and a good deal of skin belonging to different parts of my anatomy. (163)

Wavell's analogy to the games of his English public school at Winchester is in keeping with his journeying as an English gentleman traveller. Amidst the multitudes of Muslims, though outwardly as one of them, beneath the layers of disguise there lies the body of a Christian. For Wavell, this reference to days at Winchester exemplifies the 'schoolboyish spirit of adventure' that drives him into the most sacred places of Islamic Arabia.[34]

It was less than seventeen years after Arthur Wavell had ventured to Arabia that Eldon Rutter also headed for Mecca. Rutter sets out alone from Cairo in May 1925. The Wahhabis of Ibn Saud had invaded the Hejaz in 1924, seizing Mecca from the more Western-friendly Hashemites and so making the region even more dangerous for a

British Christian traveller.[35] But Eldon Rutter travels covertly. He mirrors the approach of Wavell rather than Doughty. Voyaging from Port Tewfik, near Suez, by steamer, he arranges to travel with two Meccan *mutawwifs* [pilgrim guides], Abdullah and Jamil, who are to 'carry' him from Massawa, in Eritrea, to Mecca. Neither of the Arabs is aware of either Rutter's religion or where he is actually from: "'What is your nationality, O Hajji Ahmad?'" asked Abdullah kindly. "My origin is from Damascus," I replied, "but I have lived long in Egypt.'"[36] When they arrive in Massawa, all three travellers change clothes: 'Our two youths sold their European suits and their tarbûshes in the market-place, and resumed the turban and thawb, or gown, of Mekka. I donned somewhat similar dress' (15). Here is a complicated and layered undressing as the two Meccan guides remove their adopted European/Turkish cloaks and return to their own clothes. The British interloper's dress change is a yet more subtle reversal. He has already stepped from the colonial uniform of Cairo into the assumed disguise of a Syrian. Now he joins his fellow travellers in pulling on Meccan clothing.

Soon attention turns more directly to Rutter. Abdullah asks for more money as guide. At Rutter's refusal, Abdullah's response is to call him a dog, a Jew and finally a 'Nasrâni!' (40). Rutter explains for the reader the danger of being called, and discovered as, a Christian: 'There is only one person in a better position to arouse the fanatical hate of Muhammadans than a Christian on the way to Mekka, and that is a Christian who has already arrived in that forbidden city' (41). There are the endless examples of Doughty's trials as an Englishman who refuses to hide his Christianity to illustrate the point. But for Rutter, in disguise, the matter is eventually settled with a single guinea handed over to Abdullah. He leaves the care of his two Meccans only to meet them a few days later as they prepare to start the trek to the Holy Cities. Rutter's cover is secure. He has both the linguistic ability in Arabic and the religious knowledge and practice to fool his companions. At sunset they 'formed in a row to repeat the sunset prayer' (60).

In Mecca he pretends to perform the rites of the hajj alongside his fellow devotees. When they reach the Kaaba, 'rubbing the stone with my hands, I made a feint of kissing it, and passed on' (109). Yet for most of the text he only occasionally conveys a sense of the fear of discovery as a Christian infidel. Rutter is certainly in no hurry to leave. For eight months he rents rooms in Mecca which offer some respite from his disguise: 'Excepting at meal times, I could nearly always count upon being left alone if I shut the outer door of this apartment, and thus in Mekka I experienced no difficulty in writing my notes without fear of being observed' (149).

From these notes, he creates a detailed guide to all aspects of these sacred places. The Meccan's daily life is examined and delineated with microscopic precision from procedures for prayers and domestic arrangements to ablutions and sewerage. Interspersed with this carefully considered vision of Arabia are recollections of conversations, passages that convey personalised, individual portraits of Arabian contemporaries and friends. The majority of the narrative is a dry descriptive of places and customs. Having guided the Western reader through the journey to the Holy City and then through the rituals of the hajj, Rutter spends the next two chapters outlining 'Geographical and Historical Notes on Mekka' and 'Topographical Description of Mekka' (Chapters 10 and 11). The approach and content mirror the concerns of texts such as the Reverend Gairdner of Cairo's *The Reproach of Islam* in precisely defining Muslim practice for a confirmedly Christian audience. In Chapter 4 of volume II, Rutter turns to 'Manners and Customs of the Mekkans' echoing the encyclopaedic work of Edward Lane's *An Account of the Manners and Customs of the Modern Egyptians* (1836).

In Chapter 16, 'Encounters', Rutter's disguise is broken. He is recognised by Husni, an old acquaintance, 'who had known me as an Englishman in Egypt' (229). Rutter surreptitiously attempts to tell Husni he has adopted Syrian as his nationality but fails. Instead, Husni turns to his Bedouin escort:

'This one,' said he, effusively, 'is one of the greatest of the English, and a Muslim.'

As he heard the word 'Inkilîzi,' Husni's companion looked serious and careful.

'But are you of a truth an Inkilîzi?' he asked, regarding me earnestly.

'Inkilîzi!' said Husni in a tone of finality.

'Ay, yes!' I replied. 'I am an Inkilîzi.'

'But a Muslim – of course,' he persisted.

Again Husni anticipated me with his effusive exaggeration.

'Muslim! This is one of the learned!' he cried with conviction.

'Naturally – a Muslim,' I assured the Bedouin.

At that his gaze grew less intent. 'El hamdu Lillah!' exclaimed he, as we turned to walk up the street.

'But say not thus to others than ourselves, O Sallâh ed-Dîn!' said Husni. 'The ignorant ones do not understand. You have told them?'

'No,' I replied. 'They understand that I am of the people of Syria.'

'Wallah, it is better so!' said he. 'Neither will we tell it.' (231-2)

The fact that Rutter has been discovered in Mecca as an Englishman is accepted by both Arabs on the unfounded belief that he is a Muslim, and a learned one at that. In the eyes of both, his true nationality as an Englishman is not worthy of whistle-blowing to the authorities. Rutter has already explained that the consequence of being discovered a Christian in Mecca is death. Being discovered as an Englishman in fact enhances his travel experience. The recognition of his nationality gets Rutter an audience with Ibn Saud, the powerful Arab leader of the Wahhabis and ruler of Mecca.

In 'Final Departure from Mekka', Rutter prepares to leave but is struck down with a 'violent fever' (129 vol II).[37] In the delirium that the fever brings on, Rutter becomes conscious of betraying himself: 'I was obsessed, however, by the idea or delusion that in speech lay imminent danger. Therefore I restricted my replies to mono-syllables' (130). Rutter tells how, in the grip of his sickness, he 'feared to say things which might incriminate me with these watching fanatics – incriminate me falsely, perhaps, but none the less disastrously'. He dreams of Europe: 'I thought, if only I could climb to some mountain-top, and lie there among the winds which came out of Europe and Africa' (131). His visions reflect the complicated dual identity he has adopted:

It seemed to me that I had become two persons who were closely in league one with the other. We two were engaged throughout the night in fighting some intangible enemy. We constantly spoke words of encouragement to one another during the conflict; but what it was we fought, and whether we fought with swords or schemes, I do not know. All was dim and unreal; but among the broken threads of thought, and speech, and imagined action, which crossed and re-crossed one another in the woven experiences of that night, there was one shining strand which I constantly encountered with the utmost satisfaction. That was the fact that the door of the fortress which we defended was securely locked. (135)

The whole incident is a particularly violent clash of personal identities. Rutter has spent months under the exhausting yoke of disguise with the constant threat of being discovered as an unbeliever in Mecca, now in the power of the religious extremism of the Wahhabis. Revealing his true self would have meant certain death. Now, as he prepares to leave Mecca, the fever that descends appears to be symptomatic of the psychological stress he has put himself under in the last eight months. Yet Rutter offers no such analysis of his thoughts.

Having sufficiently recovered from this strange contagion, Rutter leaves Mecca for the final time. After a few months visiting the sites of Medina and the surrounding environs, Rutter heads for 'Yanbua', the coastal town from which he will leave Arabia. He is becoming deranged by his Arabian experiences: 'In the heat of the day I was now in a sort of dazed lethargy. I had lived as a hâjji in Arabia for more than a year, and the hardships of that life had blunted my sensibilities' (271). He takes a berth on an Egyptian steamer:

I would travel on her to Port Sudan, and thence by Khartum to Cairo.

Having spoken to the captain, I retired to a cabin which was allotted to me. Here I shaved my chin, and put on a suit of drill and other articles of European dress. Some of these I purchased in the marketplace of Yanbua, and others from the steward of the steamer.

For the first time for more than a year I now ate with a knife and a fork. I was still seated at table with my fellow-passengers when the anchor was heaved up and the propeller began to revolve. Presently I left the saloon and leant on the rail to obtain a last view of Arabia. Beyond the blue waters lay the silent yellow plain, and far away to the eastward the high peak of Rodhwa was fading slowly. The steamer had swung round the sandy islet which protects the harbour, and was heading for the open sea. (280)

Rutter takes little time to return to his old identity. With a shave and a change of clothes he discards his articles of disguise and slips gently back into his true self as an English Christian traveller heading back up the Red Sea, returning to the safety and comfort of British-run Egypt.

2

THE EMPTY QUARTER

The virgin Rub' al Khali, the Great Southern Desert! To have laboured in Arabia is to have tasted inevitably of her seduction, and six years ago when I left the Administration of Transjordan for the Court of Muscat and Oman I already cherished secret dreams. The remote recesses of the earth, Arctic and Antarctic, the sources of the Amazon, and the vast inner spaces of Asia and Africa, have one by one yielded their secrets to man's curiosity, until by a strange chance the Rub' al Khali remained almost the last considerable *terra incognita*, which is surprising considering the great antiquity of settled Arabia, the borderlands of which touched the early civilisations of Egypt and Babylonia.

Yet Arabia has remained the forbidden land. Throughout the centuries scarce twenty European explorers have been able usefully to penetrate to her inhospitable heart. For this there are two main reasons. First, lack of rain and the merciless heat of the Arabian desert permit of but scattered and semi-barbarous nomad societies, which are at such perpetual war that, even for themselves, life is insecure. Secondly, the religion of these desert men, at least in practice, is fanatical and exclusive. From time to time, they hold it virtuous to enforce Islam with the sword. In Arabia proper all European visitors have been individual men, and only once in all her history, and that in Roman times, has she – the then supposed Eldorado – excited the cupidity of European invaders, so that among her inhabitants, left so severely to themselves, insularity, bigotry, and intolerance are indigenous growths with a long pedigree. Hence an area equal to half the superficies of Europe had remained a blank on our maps.[1]

The passage is from the Introduction to *Arabia Felix* (1932), in which Bertram Thomas outlines the build-up to his 1930-31 crossing of the Empty Quarter. He draws a portrait of the land he has traversed. The desert is feminine: an untouched 'virgin' and yet a seductress to all Europeans who have lived in Arabia. Such erotic framing can be traced back to Elizabethan travelogues.[2] The romanticisation is all the more affected by the use of the name 'Rub' al Khali'. The term 'The Empty Quarter' is a direct translation from the Arabic which expresses the wilderness nature of the area. The Arabic Rub' al Khali exoticises the region by adding Eastern mystique for a British readership, engendering its fascination and feminisation. But the vision of an Oriental beauty soon vanishes from the text. Her allure hides an 'inhospitable heart'. This foreign land does not welcome guests. Both the environment and its peoples are dangerously hot and hostile. The lack of European visitors to Arabia has starved these desert inhabitants of healthy society. Without the calming touch of Western culture they have stewed in unwholesome ways. It is as though the Rub' al Khali was a fabled Queen of Sheba but her peoples had remained a barbaric, primitive horde without the civilising influence of the West.

Thomas heightens the sense of romance by printing a copy of Walter de la Mare's poem *Arabia* on the page before his own travel narrative commences. De la Mare also personifies Arabia as a feminine beauty, mirroring Thomas's metaphor for the Rub' al Khali. In the poem, a traveller to Arabia is bewitched by her charms:

> No beauty on earth I see
> But shadowed with the dream recalls
> Her loveliness to me:
> Still eyes look coldly upon me,
> Cold voices whisper and say –
> 'He is crazed with the spell of far Arabia,
> They have stolen his wits away.'

Thomas sees himself in an advantageous position to face her. He has spent thirteen years since the First World War acclimatising to Arabia. He has learnt the dialects and ways of many Arab tribes. Most importantly, as chief minister to the Sultan of Oman, Thomas has developed relations with some of the most powerful Arabs in south-eastern Arabia, nurturing 'a general attitude of tolerance towards me, an Englishman and a Christian, without which I could never have dreamt of moving off the beaten track' (xiii-xiv). Yet it was without the express permission of either the Sultan of Oman or British authorities that Thomas began exploring the Rub' al Khali.

The Rub' al Khali, or Empty Quarter, is an expanse of desert in the south of the Arabian Peninsula. It is a land of dunes and gravel plains, punctuated occasionally by water holes offering sparse and bitter refreshment. To the local Bedouin it is known simply as 'the Sands'. The scale of the region is simply vast. It measures some three million square kilometres; a space the size of India or the combined area of Germany, France and Spain.³ In the early twentieth century it remained one of the few regions of the world virtually unobserved by Western travellers. Geographical inhospitability does not entirely account for this fact: it was bordered by a population considered religiously fanatical. The Empty Quarter was an area which no Briton had yet crossed, let alone tamed. The occupation of Aden in 1839 had signalled Britain's imperial entrance into southern Arabia, yet the desire to protect shipping lanes to India ensured the focus remained seaward from Aden. Hundreds of miles inland, the Rub' al Khali remained unknown. In this chapter, I chart the legendary contest between two British travellers to claim the title of first to cross this forbidding desert, and Wilfred Thesiger's later journeys to more fully explore these lands.

In 1930 two Englishmen, Bertram Thomas and Harry St John Philby, were in positions from which they could attempt to traverse the Empty Quarter. They were both serving as consultants to Arab rulers, posts that had evolved from their involvement in British imperial administration: Thomas was political adviser, or wazir, to the Sultan of Oman; Philby held a more informal advisory role to Ibn Saud, ruler of Saudi Arabia. The competition that emerged between them to be the first to cross these sands was resonant of earlier imperial exploration enterprises in distant undiscovered lands. Unlike Robert Scott's heroic failure to beat Norwegian Roald Amundsen to the South Pole in 1911, this race was an all British affair. London newspapers ran regular reports on the two travellers' exploits in unknown Arabia. In accounts of their respective crossings both wrote of imperial expeditions to extract knowledge from an unfamiliar land. Both travelled as though on missions of discovery in British colonial lands. In reality, the Rub' al Khali was a large blank space on the world map.

The colonial race to be the first to conquer the Rub' al Khali was won by Bertram Thomas early in 1931. *The Times* reported the news, stating: 'At last an explorer has traversed the Great Desert of Southern Arabia and by its conquest has achieved one of the greatest geographical exploits of modern times.' Thomas could now be considered in the 'first rank of British explorers'.[4] A week later, Thomas was sent a telegram of congratulations from King George V. He had spent years preparing for the expedition and made three preliminary investigations into the southern areas of the Empty Quarter.[5] Now he had triumphed. Three months later, Thomas would be back in London receiving praise and medals from the Royal Geographical Society and the Royal Asiatic Society. He had already published a report of his exploration over five days in *The Times*, which would form the preliminary basis of *Arabia Felix* to be published in 1932 with a foreword by T. E. Lawrence. Such were the rewards for being first across the Empty Quarter.

*

Thomas commences his narrative of the journey in a spirit of espionage redolent of the imperial spy novel: 'It was midnight of the 4th-5th October 1930. The little Arab port of Muscat lay asleep.' Under the cover of night he slips from his political responsibilities to the Sultan of Oman into a rowing boat, 'secretly embarking on my long-cherished ambition to unveil the unknown southern Arabian desert' (1). There is a full moon to witness his drawing alongside the HMS *Cyclamen* where he collects his mascot for the expedition – a copy of De la Mare's *Arabia*. He heads for the open sea. He has procured a lift with a British oil tanker, laden and returning to England. It is a carefully arranged operation. Thomas will be safely transported half-way down the southern coast of Arabia to the region of Dhufar where, via a dinghy and an Arab dhow, he will reach the shore. As a sense of stealth is woven into these opening paragraphs of his text, Thomas is presented as an imperial agent undertaking a dangerous expedition into unknown and hostile lands. Rather than a travelogue, the narrative begins as an adventure novel; a reinvented *Riddle of the Sands* set in far Arabia.

Thomas has made a 'secret arrangement' with a Bedouin of the Rashid tribe to provide a camel party and guide him across the sands. The previous year 'Sahail the Rashidi' had been 'secretly' given a down payment of 200 dollars and a dagger. He had sworn only death would prevent him returning as a guide. Now, as Thomas lands in Salala he hears of tribal war and blood-feuds between the Rashid and Sa'ar Bedouin. Sahail has not showed up. 'My ambitious plans so carefully laid and secretly cherished for the year past seemed to be utterly at an end' (5-6). All he can do is wait and hope.

The hiatus in the expedition is reflected in the text of *Arabia Felix*. The break allows time for Thomas's ethnological concerns. Chapter III is titled 'Skull-Measuring and Devil Dancing'. Thomas has come 'prepared with head callipers to make and record skull measurements, for such measurements are vital to anthropologists'. He notes how the mind of the foreigner conditioned to Arabia, 'becomes unconsciously stamped with the physical characteristics of the natives, and is therefore acutely aware of aberrations from racial types when he meets them' (22). His vision sits squarely with the argument that during the 'latter phase of European imperialism, the active ideology of geographical discovery – a genuine passion for filling blank spaces in an ever more detailed map of the world ... coexisted with the formation of increasingly contemptuous and rigid racial stereotypes'.[6] Thomas's zeal to explore the question of Arab ethnicity appears to know few bounds: 'I had early entertained hopes of unearthing and sending home ancient skulls, but the dangers of offending religious susceptibilities in Arabia were great' (24). He confesses that on an earlier expedition, he had stolen a skull from a cave, hiding it in his bedding. It is at this point that *Arabia Felix* starts to emerge as straddling that 'unsettled frontier' between 'the discourses of adventurous travel and scientific exploration'.[7] His reconstruction of the journey has now shifted generic boundaries from the romanticised spy format of the opening scene to one that employs the language of scientific investigation. Thomas's adventure involves a peculiar form of imperial surveillance – scientific espionage. In the role of the ethnologist, Thomas is far less stealthy. His fieldwork is no mere observational study. He is after head measurements and hopefully a few stolen skulls.

While Thomas awaits his camel party for the great adventure across the sands, he collects data. He acts with the inquisitive tastes of earlier Orientalists, obsessively hoarding up information on the area that he is crossing. By seeing himself in this role of amateur scientist and anthropologist Thomas mimics those Victorian scientific travellers plotting and charting the creatures, peoples and lands of an expanding British Empire.[8] While the Rub' al Khali is not part of the Empire, Thomas still acts and writes with the same imperial zeal. He extracts as much detail as possible on the geography, geology, flora and fauna of the region. He shoots to gain specimens, collecting samples of the local wildlife: hyena, wolf, snake, fox and even badger form part of his skinned assortment of 'trophies' (105). Accompanying naturalistic concerns are anthropological investigations. He offers an explanation of food customs and circumcision rites, detailing tribal practices before turning to darker matters: 'Illness, such as failure of milk in their animals, is readily ascribed to the Evil Eye – *'Ain Balis* ... Exorcism is by a frankincense rite, performed usually at sunrise or sunset, of which I was on more than one occasion an interested witness' (80).

After some six weeks waiting, Thomas received news that the desert party had arrived. So too had the 'Muscat State gunboat *Al Sa'idi*' with a letter from his employer the Sultan of Oman to ferry him back to Oman. But Thomas makes a bold rebuttal:

> I would send the gunboat back without me to Muscat. I would attempt the return by another way. I would join fortune with those attractive ruffians below, strangers all, and take the plunge with them into the uncharted wilderness. (107)

The language of the imperial adventure novel has returned. The local Bedouin are now 'attractive ruffians'. Thomas will dive recklessly into the unknown. But he has his chronometers, thermometers and barometers to operate and there is the ongoing endeavour of collecting objects 'of great interest to the Natural History Museum' (135). The narrative of *Arabia Felix* provides the reader with the delicate outlines of the region, its wadis and water-holes, though anthropological concerns remain as Thomas explains tribal structure and marriage arrangements. The text switches from being a tale of derring-do in the distant wastes of the world to detailing a scientific/ethnological study of the southern Arabian desert, the narrative swinging between these two generic poles. The journey progresses and the scientific information amasses. Thomas breaks from the expedition to provide 'A Geographical Note on the Rub' Al Khali'. Then it is back to the adventure. The tale of the journey unfurls. The party is reduced to twenty. They head west towards Shanna. There, at a watering hole, the party is cut again; down to twelve with five pack camels. The objective is Doha, on the Persian Gulf, some 330 crow-miles north. By day there is the toil of endless footsteps through the sands. Steadily they edge closer to the sea. They step 'furtively' into Wahhabi territory, knowing the 'Puritans of Islam', will not take kindly to a British Christian on their lands. But the end is nigh.

In early February, at dawn, Thomas and two Murra guides, Hamad and Talib, clambered up the 'towering hill of Nakhala' and caught a view of the Persian Gulf: 'The vast, almost uninhabited wastes of Rub' al Khali stretched for weeks behind us, before us lay but a march of four days to the dwellings of man' (293). The weather offered little in the way of encouragement. It was English weather; a steady drizzling rain that accompanied them on their last night. But in the morning all were cheerful:

> The Badawin moved forward at a sharp pace, chanting their water chants. Our thirsty camels pricked up their ears with eager knowingness. The last sandhill was left behind. After the next undulation we saw in the dip of the stony plain before us Na'aija, where we had planned a final watering, and beyond it the towers of Doha silhouetted against the waters of the Persian Gulf. Half an hour later we entered the walls of the fort. The Rub' al Khali had been crossed. (298-9)

It was 3 February 1931. Bertram Thomas had triumphed in the imperial race to traverse the Empty Quarter.

*

Harry St John Philby took the news of Thomas's success rather badly. He 'shut himself indoors for a whole week'. While he publicly offered his congratulations, it was a bitter personal blow. Philby had put even more of his life into the project than Thomas. He talked of the 'single obsession' that had taken fifteen years to find fruition. Even his religious conversion to Islam in 1930 appeared linked, as 'becoming a Muslim seemed to him the only way of accomplishing the exploit of his dreams - the crossing of the Rub al Khali'.[9] His Introduction to *The Empty Quarter* (1933) explained the build-up in the race to cross the desert. Since 1917, he had nurtured a close friendship with Ibn Saud,

King of Arabia. In December 1930, Philby accompanied Ibn Saud to Riyadh, where they talked of an expedition into the Rub' al Khali. His travels into southern Arabia would involve a political aspect. A journey into the Empty Quarter would not only gain Philby personal kudos but be valuable 'to extend the bounds of Ibn Saud's kingdom – or at least to prepare the ground for an attempt to extend them'.[10] Philby's hopes were raised. Then, in January 1931, the King told Philby that the journey was cancelled. He knew Thomas had already left Muscat. For Philby 'it was not till March 6th that I knew the full bitterness of my own disappointment. He had won the race, and it only remained for me to finish the course'.[11] The competitive element to the expedition is clear. Yet Philby would certainly not turn back just because Thomas had triumphed. If Thomas had won the race, then Philby would take his time and show it was he who really knew the desert, he who had truly explored the Empty Quarter for the first time.

The following winter Philby got the go ahead. On Christmas Day 1931, Philby arrived in Hufuf, the north-western oasis that was to be the starting point of his journey. Ibn Jiluwi, who had blocked the previous project, now made all the arrangements for Philby. There were delays but in early January 1932 with a party of thirteen men and thirty-two camels they got going. The Bedu were warned: 'See that you avoid danger, but take him whither he would go. For his life you answer with yours. Forget not that' (7). The morning was bitter and foggy, hardly an auspicious start to the expedition, though Philby was elated to be finally under way.

In *The Empty Quarter* (1933), Philby reconstructed his journey, writing the travelogue almost immediately the travel was completed. He presents the reader with all the daily happenings of his party, creating a narrative of each day in the saddle and each night at camp. It is a thorough and precise detailing of the journey but it does nothing to aid easy consumption. The following describes a section of a day on the approach to Jabrin:

> We marched at first over a rough and dirty patch of salt-flat and then in an easy, gently undulating tract of sand and gravel, towards which the steppe desert ran down in a series of low, degenerate, echeloned tongues. Passing by the end of the chalky sandstone ridge of Al Usba', with a hillock called Al Thaniya far to our right and the headland of Khashm Na'aiyim to our right front, we rode on over more undulating

sand and gravel to a plain strewn with broken fragments of
flint and chert, among which I could detect no sign of ancient
artefacts. (93)

Philby's text is dense and difficult. Wilfred Thesiger apparently
found it 'stodgy'.[12] The writing style is wordy and often long-winded.
For that reason, as McLoughlin has noted, his diaries are often more
readable than his published travel accounts. 'Philby ... would pile fact
on fact, labour for effect and produce in many a reader that
exasperation summed up in one memorable criticism of Philby's many
works: "All those damned wadis ...!"'.[13] Over description is rife in *The
Empty Quarter*.

Unlike Thomas, Philby lingers less on matters anthropological or
ethnological. Though he shares the collective urge of Thomas, Philby
soon finds himself without the time to preserve specimens but still
manages to recover 'some seventy or eighty birds and mammals from
the Rub'al Khali' (54). Philby is focussed on providing a scientific
perspective on the geological nature of the desert. In this respect, he
echoes one of the narrative preoccupations of Charles Doughty in
Arabia Deserta:

> Fossiliferous deposits of Miocene age are exposed in the lower
> strata of the Anbak and Judairat cliffs ... Nothing surely can
> be of greater interest than an attempt to throw back the veil
> which hundreds or tens of thousands of years have drawn
> over the earth as it was when our earliest ancestors knew it or
> as it was even before the crowning glory of Creation. It is
> perhaps a bold task for a layman to embark on, but it is well
> enough if he bring with him to lay at the feet of the professors
> the material needful for the testing of his fancy's flights. (61)

Philby sees his role as that of the gentleman scientist. Like Thomas,
he is an amateur but unperturbed by the fact. He will explore the
unexplored and make known the geological truths of the physical
landscape he finds. He is the first Westerner to step onto those sands
and he is keen to record their nature. In offering a first survey of this
environment, Philby can be seen as staking a claim over that land. As a
scientific traveller, he gains knowledge of the desert; as an exploratory
emissary, his detailing of the desert enhances the territorial claims of
King Ibn Saud. Ownership of the Empty Quarter, and in particular its

geology, would prove pivotal not only to the emerging Saudi nation but the wider world community; within a few years, American prospectors would discover huge deposits of oil in the Rub' al Khali. Philby's preoccupation with geomorphology in *The Empty Quarter* may have turned much of the text into a physical geography handbook but it pre-empted Western interest in that aspect of the 'Great South Desert'.

At Jabrin, Philby and his party have their last meeting with humanity for 53 days. A local Bedu, Jabir ibn Fasl, comes across their tracks and assumes them to be government tax collectors. On finding they are not, he presents them with a young saluki bitch named al Aqfa and the hare she has recently caught. It is a poignant meeting. Jabir sacrifices a camel colt for a farewell feast. Philby's response is to press twenty silver dollars in the palm of Jabir's son. The scene is of a stereotyped dichotomy: the poor, simple Bedouin offers his livestock; the British traveller responds with the riches of money. Philby clearly appreciates the moment as symbolic and significant to his expedition. He hands Jabir his collected geological samples to be returned to Ibn Jiluwi at Hufuf:

> So we went our ways – we with the bitch that had hunted for him to hunt for us, and he with my box of stones and fossils. And we shall see in due course how God kept us all in the days yet to come as we turned our backs on the castle of ashes and fared forth into the great wilderness of the south. (106)

The religious imagery is of a stark and sterile place. For Philby, the barren nature of the desert emphasised the spiritual aspect of his journey. It may well also be true that he 'saw himself as the prophetic outsider ... for whom the desert was the ultimate sanctuary'.[14] Religious metaphors were regularly used by Philby to describe the desert. In the Introduction, he complains that for seven years he 'had laboured in vain as Jacob of old for Rachel'. The Rub' al Khali was 'the bride of my constant desire' (xv). The biblical form of Rachel has replaced the virgin temptress of *Arabia Felix* as a suitable object of conquest. Yet the metaphorical yearning for a Christian female figure occurs in the same paragraph in which Philby explains his conversion to Islam and the 'austere mantle of Wahhabi philosophy'. It is an incongruous religious match. When Bertram Thomas reviewed Philby's *The Empty Quarter*, he returned to this Old Testament symbol.

As Philby's epic journey reached its goal at Sulaiyil, Thomas wrote that 'Rachel had been won'.[15]

The text of *The Empty Quarter* teases out each event of the journey such that by its conclusion the reader feels they too have been through a trial. The route was not a straight dash across the desert as Thomas made. Philby had the backing of Ibn Saud so could travel at will, comparatively free from fear of Bedouin attack. His party reach Shanna after some 600 miles travel. Philby intends to end his exploration in the Hadhramaut, a further 300 miles south-west yet is forced to compromise when his journeymen refuse. They agree to head for Sulaiyil but turn back after six of the camels break down. Writing of the subsequent retreat to Naifa, Philby lingers on each aspect of the exhausting return march, dragging the painful trek out to excruciating effect. It is typical Philby; each moment of the journey seemingly relived for the reader. Even the sorry state of his tea rations is intricately explained:

> Unfortunately Sa'dan had without any previous warning announced during the day that my supply of tea was exhausted. I had told him to keep the leaves of my last pot for a second brew and it was weak stuff which I had to put up with that evening after dinner. The same leaves were used for a third brew before I retired to sleep, leaving something in the pot to drink cold – and it was deliciously cold – before starting on our march in the early hours of the morrow. (278)

At Naifa, a camel is killed and swiftly butchered. The party and al Aqfa, their adopted saluki bitch, engorge on the meat for the next two days, the remainder being 'dry-cured in sun and wind without salt'. A desert storm reduces the camp to shreds but preparations commence for the final push across the 'waterless waste' (291). The 375 miles to the oasis of Sulaiyil take just nine days. They will go on to reach Mecca in time for the pilgrimage, on the ninetieth day since the journey begun back at Hufuf. If Bertram Thomas had the honour of being first across the Rub' al Khali, Philby could certainly say that he knew the Empty Quarter better.

*

Wilfred Thesiger arrived in Arabia some thirteen years after Philby reached Sulaiyil, but when he left in 1950 he could rightly claim to have travelled even more of the Empty Quarter. Though Thesiger travels into the desert under the guise of tracking locust movements his true *raison d'être* is to explore the remaining uncharted territories. He heads to areas where Thomas and Philby have not been. As such, he maintains continuity with the sense of an imperial mission of knowledge requisition, of filling the blanks on Western maps. The break comes in the nature of the writing up of his travels.

Both Thomas and Philby operated ostensibly from an explorative perspective. They surveyed the travelled landscape with scientific precision and presented it to the reader with the same concerns for empirical validity. Both *Arabia Felix* and *The Empty Quarter* offer discrete objective travelogues detailing the minutiae of the Rub' al Khali as seen on their prospective journeys. While there are passages of personal expression, the overriding concern is with mapping the uncharted desert, capturing the Empty Quarter. Just as explorers, scientists and missionaries wrote in such a vein in Victorian times, so Thomas and Philby often adopted a similar style as they wrote the first Western explorations of the Rub' al Khali.

Thesiger's *Arabian Sands* may detail crossings of desert unknown to Western eyes, but it is written in a very different narrative style. There is far more memoir and inventiveness at play. Helen Carr has recognised this shift in twentieth-century travel writing 'to a more impressionistic style with the interest focused as much on the travellers' responses or consciousness as their travels'.[16] In the Empty Quarter, time is distorted. The fact that the area was only 'discovered' in 1931 meant Thomas and Philby mimicked the defined style of earlier nineteenth-century exploratory forefathers in order to map the land with appropriate exactness for the imperial information-gathering process. The emergence of modernist styles of travel writing could only concern lands already known and explored. For the first explorers of the unknown, a scientific description is what is demanded by the imperial community. Then can follow other forms of travelogue. Subsequent writers gain a greater liberty over their narrative style. This is the literary freedom Thesiger explores. As a later imperial traveller to the Empty Quarter he does not need to specify the scientific aspects of the desert. Instead, he is free to draw portraits of the Bedouin he has befriended and detail his own experiences in that desert.

Thomas and Philby eagerly wrote their accounts on completing their travels, both keen to profit from the immediate fame their exploration had brought. In contrast, Thesiger was persuaded to write his book by a literary agent and the publisher Mark Longman.[17] He reconstructed his journeys and recorded them to paper ten years after they were completed and the sense of consideration is apparent. That time period has been called a 'natural editorial process' which vanquished the 'blow-by-blow, inch-by-inch reportage of Philby's works'.[18] There is a concern with style and literariness in the narrative unseen in the earlier texts.

In the prologue of his text, Thesiger starts to allow his writing to flourish:

> A cloud gathers, the rain falls, men live; the cloud disperses without rain, and men and animals die. In the deserts of southern Arabia there is no rhythm of the seasons, no rise and fall of sap, but empty wastes where only the changing temperature marks the passage of the year. It is a bitter, desiccated land which knows nothing of gentleness or ease. Yet men have lived there since earliest times. Passing generations have left fire-blackened stones at camping sites, a few faint tracks polished on the gravel plains. Elsewhere the winds wipe out their footprints. Men live there because it is the world into which they were born; the life they lead is the life their forefathers led before them; they accept hardships and privations; they know no other way. Lawrence wrote in *Seven Pillars of Wisdom*, 'Bedouin ways were hard, even for those brought up in them and for strangers terrible: a death in life.' No man can live this life and emerge unchanged. He will carry, however faint, the imprint of the desert, the brand which marks the nomad; and he will have within him the yearning to return, weak or insistent according to his nature. For this cruel land can cast a spell which no temperate clime can match. [19]

In the opening line the delicate divide between life and death in the Empty Quarter is dramatically drawn. Desert living is austere and brutal, a form of masochism promising oblique pleasure with the pain of daily existence, as Lawrence knew so well. Thesiger, like Thomas, personifies the land as a sorcerer. It bewitches. Travellers will be

forever enchanted. In the final line he echoes the romanticism of
Walter de la Mare's *Arabia*, quoted earlier, providing a resonance to the
mascot which Bertram Thomas carried across the Rub' al Khali in
1930.

In Chapter 1, Thesiger focuses not on the start of his journey but
on details of his own start. He tells of his birth in a mud hut in Addis
Ababa, 1910; then of his explorations through Ethiopia into the
Danakil region in 1935 aged twenty-four. In England, Eton and
Oxford provided one education. He heads on to Sudan, Darfur and
later the Nuer district for another. The detailing of these adventures is
akin to a portfolio being unfolded presenting the explorer's credentials
to the reader. In Sudan he can express another side to his colonial
credence. He is an enthusiastic hunter: 'I shot seventy lions during the
five years I was in the Sudan' (35). Here is a glimpse at the world of
Thesiger: the privileged and macho life of the British military elite.
Back in Addis Ababa in 1945, he meets O. B. Lean, who is searching
for someone to head into the Empty Quarter to track locust
movements. Thesiger immediately proffers himself for the position:
'All my past had been but a prelude to the five years that lay ahead of
me' (38). With these words Thesiger concludes the opening chapter
with an enticing sentence that builds suspense and draws the narrative
onwards to the main event: the Empty Quarter. This technique of
foreshadowing, linking the past to a future as yet untold, though soon
to be narrated, is used throughout *Arabian Sands*.

Thesiger introduces some of his companions and their ways, such
as smoking a pipe or bread making, the daily routines and rhythms of
Arabian travel on a 'first journey on the fringes of the Empty Quarter',
merely a 'probation' (54) for later endeavours. There is a gradual
building of atmosphere as the nature of desert travel with the Bedouin
is explained in an easily digested manner. This is not the
anthropological focus of Thomas or the monotonous daily detail of
Philby, but practices are still being delineated for a Western readership.
Thesiger portrays the wonders of camel riding and local tracking skills
with a sincere sense of awe. Then the reader is shown Salim bin
Kabina. He is to become a central figure in Thesiger's travels in
Arabia. While other Bedu have had sketchy outlines, bin Kabina
receives a detailed description. He is first seen in homoerotic stance
'conspicuous in a vivid red loin-cloth, and with his long hair falling
around his naked shoulders' (69). Thesiger then offers a tender
portrait:

He was about sixteen years old, about five foot five in height and loosely built. He moved with a long, raking stride, like a camel, unusual among Bedu, who generally walk very upright with short steps. He was very poor, and the hardships of his life had marked him, so that his frame was gaunt and his face hollow. His hair was very long and always falling into his eyes, especially when he was cooking or otherwise busy. He would sweep it back impatiently with a thin hand. He had a rather low forehead, large eyes, a straight nose, prominent cheek-bones, and a big mouth with a long upper lip. His chin, delicately formed and rather pointed, was marked by a long scar, where he had been branded as a child to cure illness. He had very white teeth which were always showing, for he was constantly talking and laughing. (70)

When Thesiger returns from England the following year it is with plans to cross the Rub' al Khali over sands not visited by Thomas or Philby. It is October 1946. Bin Kabina will be his personal servant while tribesmen of the Rashid will be his guides and companions.

As the tale of his travels unfolds, there is a long digression during which Thesiger decants his thoughts on the nature of Arabia and the Bedu. The 'unchanging Bedu' of millennia have been irrevocably altered in the last forty years. Since the First World War, cars, aeroplanes and radio have opened the deserts to outsiders. Oil now offers an easy comfortable life:

> It seemed to me tragic that they should become, as a result of circumstances beyond their control, a parasitic proletariat squatting around oil-fields in the fly-blown squalor of shanty towns in some of the most sterile country in the world. (96)

Nostalgic expressions are a recurring theme in *Arabian Sands*. Thesiger decries the creeping modernisation and industrialisation of the desert. Earlier in the text, he reflects ruefully that 'the maps I made helped others, with more material aims, to visit and corrupt a people whose spirit once lit the desert like a flame' (82). Here is the obvious truth that his very presence there is a Westernising force. Worse, his mapping of the unknown lands has actively aided the oil-men. Thesiger may not wish to be a harbinger of change and indeed may argue his ethnographic role to detail the Bedouin culture before it is bastardised beyond recognition, yet he yearns for 'traditional' Bedouin society in that paradoxical position of 'mourning for what one has destroyed'.[20]

At the well of Khaur bin Atarit, there is a quiet moment of reflection for Thesiger. He is joined on the lip of a high sand dune by bin Kabina. While he strips his rifle bolt, he asks 'if I had met Thomas, the only other Englishman who had been with his tribe' (121). The question leads Thesiger into a reverie on those exploratory forefathers, Thomas and Philby, and their relative achievements. For the reader, the moment reinforces the sense that Thesiger is a late imperial explorer. His travel is not merely about crossing a desert land for the first time; it is also about his time with the Bedouin. The nature of Thesiger's relationship with his travel companions is central to the text. In the writing of Thomas and Philby the Bedouin are mere vehicles to guide and assist (or hinder) the progress of the traveller across the unknown sands. In *Arabian Sands* individual portraits and intimate relationships are essential elements.

Bin Kabina sleeps as Thesiger dreams of Thomas and Philby. When Bin Kabina wakes, Thesiger 'raced him down the dune face, floundering through the avalanching sand' (122) in another vibrant expression of their close friendship. They play together as if lovers: 'A little later bin Kabina tickled the back of my neck, and thinking it was [a] spider I jumped convulsively and upset my tea' (123). Yet the friendship is apparently nothing more. Two pages later Thesiger notes, 'homosexuality is common among most Arabs, especially in the towns, but it is very rare among the Bedu, who of all Arabs have the most excuse for indulging in this practice, since they spend long months away from their women' (125). If we are to believe Thesiger, it is a seldom discussed topic: 'Only twice in five years did I ever hear them mention the subject.' Bin Kabina 'thought the practice both ridiculous and obscene' (125). If Thesiger details his fondness for bin Kabina and others, he also recognises his own separateness:

> I was happy in the company of these men who had chosen to come with me. I felt affection for them personally, and sympathy with their way of life. But though the easy quality of our relationship satisfied me, I did not delude myself that I could be one of them. They were Bedu and I was not; they were Muslims and I was a Christian. (139)

He is distinct even if the empty world and tough life of the Bedouin appeals to him.

Though Thesiger may be the initiator of the expedition, al Auf is the true leader; he has already crossed the Sands twice, once only two years before. Thesiger asks who his companions were, to which he replies, 'God was my companion.' It is an 'incredible achievement' in Thesiger's eyes, who knows 'if I travelled here alone the weight of this vast solitude would crush me utterly' (142).

There are practical concerns. Thesiger is worried over the leaking water-skins: 'a drop falling on to the sand every few yards as we rode along, like blood dripping from a wound that could not be staunched' (142). Driven on by the wiry figure of al Auf, they trek up the face of a vast sand dune at a seemingly impossible angle. But they can only press on, for further east are the quicksands of Umm al Samim; to the west only more vast dunes. To return to Mughshin meant defeat; unthinkable. When they finally conquer the dune, Thesiger 'slumped down' believing that they had broken the back of their journey, that they had crossed the notorious Uruq al Shaiba region.

It is a short lived triumph. Al Auf soon puts him straight: 'Did you think what we crossed today was the Uruq al Shaiba? That was only a dune. You will see them tomorrow' (148). Dramatic suspense is again employed, drawing the reader through the emotive journey of Thesiger. Having experienced his terror and then triumph at this mere dune, the narrative tension builds as the true Uruq al Shaiba are anticipated. This winching-up of tension can then be increased as concerns over the camels and the dwindling supplies are further illustrations of the precarious plight of the expedition. They have 'only a few gallons of water left and some handfuls of flour'. The animals are 'trembling, hesitating' as they climb 'upward along great sweeping ridges where the knife-edged crests crumbled beneath our feet' (149).

When they reach the peak of one chain of dunes, Thesiger surveys the scene:

> There was no limit to my vision. Somewhere in the ultimate distance the sands merged into the sky, but in that infinity of space I could see no living thing, not even a withered plant to give me hope. 'There is nowhere to go,' I thought. 'We cannot go back and our camels will never get up another of these awful dunes. We really are finished.' The silence flowed over

me, drowning the voices of my companions and the fidgeting
of their camels. (149)

On they trudged through the sands; up and down dunes, refreshed
merely by a few drops of water rationed by al Auf. For two hours they
rested, then Thesiger woke to al Auf's assurance, 'Cheer up, Umbarak.
[Thesiger's adopted name] This time we really are across the Uruq al
Shaiba' (150). The culmination of the enterprise was upon him. It had
been two weeks since they had departed Khaur bin Atarit on the start
of their journey over two hundred miles of dense dunes:

> For years the Empty Quarter had represented to me the final,
> unattainable challenge which the desert offered. Suddenly it
> had come within my reach ... Now I had crossed it. To others
> my journey would have little importance. It would produce
> nothing except a rather inaccurate map which no one was ever
> likely to use. It was a personal experience. (154)

It is an odd comment, for Thesiger has already confessed his maps
proved valuable to later Westerners seeking to exploit the desert. Nor
is it the journey's end. With the achievement of this goal he returns to
Salala along the edge of the desert over the gravel plains of Oman to
the RAF base where he first made camp in October 1945: 'These
airmen were my fellow countrymen, and I was proud to be of their
race.' Yet there is an essential difference between them and him:

> They belonged to an age of machines; they were fascinated by
> cars and aeroplanes, and found their relaxation in the cinema
> and the wireless. I knew that I stood apart from them and
> would never find contentment among them, whereas I could
> find it among these Bedu, although I should never be one of
> them. (184)

The ambiguity of Thesiger's stance starts to explain his digressions into
nostalgic reverie. He is a divided soul, caught between these two tribes.
He is an outsider to each.

Thesiger's initial crossing of the Empty Quarter forms much of
Arabian Sands, though it is not the end to his travels. He was to cross
the desert once more, this time from the Hadhramaut to Sulaiyil and
then up to Laila and Jabrin, across the northern regions of the Rub' al

Khali to arrive at Abu Dhabi. Before this second crossing, he met
another Bedouin youth whose beauty seemed to transfix Thesiger:

> This boy was dressed only in a length of blue cloth, which he
> wore wrapped round his waist with one tasselled end thrown
> over his right shoulder, and his dark hair fell like a mane about
> his shoulders. He had a face of classic beauty, pensive and
> rather sad in repose, but which lit up when he smiled, like a
> pool touched by the sun. Antinous must have looked like this,
> I thought, when Hadrian first saw him in the Phrygian woods.
> The boy moved with effortless grace, walking as women walk
> who have carried vessels on their heads since childhood. (188)

Bin Ghabaisha is his name. That he is analogous to Antinous seems
to imply that Thesiger positions himself in the role of Emperor
Hadrian. There are clear parallels. Antinous accompanied Hadrian for
six years on his imperial travels. Perhaps their relationship is
comparable to that of the Roman lovers? The sub-clause of 'I thought'
hints at the reflective time which Thesiger has spent imagining bin
Ghabaisha. Kabbani observes that 'Thesiger sublimates any desire for
the boy into a purely literary attraction'. His sensuality evolves to
become 'double-edged' as his beauty becomes feminised.[21]
Alternatively, Thesiger's allusion to an ancient love affair may be a
means of expressing his own repressed feelings for bin Ghabaisha.
Aside from his youth and beauty, he is a good hunter. Thesiger hands
him one of his spare rifles. He is also a close friend of bin Kabina, who
promises, 'we will always be your men' (188). Expressions of
admiration for the Bedu punctuate the text but for bin Kabina and bin
Ghabaisha a special reverence exists: *Arabian Sands* was dedicated to
these two Bedouin youths.

The bond between Thesiger and his Bedouin entourage is potent.
There are powerful resemblances to the relations established between
T. E. Lawrence and his bodyguard of Ageyl tribesmen. The parallel is
more striking when comparing Thesiger and bin Kabina and bin
Ghabaisha with Lawrence and his two young Bedouin friends, Daud
and Farraj. There are also strong resonances with the Etonian culture
of 'fagging' in the relations with these boy servants. (Thesiger went to
Eton, though Lawrence did not). Certainly in Thesiger's work there
exists an expression of kinship between him and his Bedu entourage
that is not detailed by Thomas or Philby. In the descriptions of

Thesiger's interactions with his two young servants there is an additional emotional charge to their relationship.

When bin Kabina collapses unconscious the following dinner time, it seems Thesiger will lose one of his young guard. The sense of pathos and the reaction of Thesiger are unique in the text:

> His pulse was feeble and his body cold: he was breathing hoarsely ... I remembered with bitter regret how I had sometimes vented my ill-temper on him to ease the strain under which I lived, and how he had always been good-tempered and very patient. The others crowded round and discussed the chances of his dying, until I could scarcely bear it; and then someone asked where we were going tomorrow and I said that there would be no tomorrow if bin Kabina died. (189)

The future of his journey seems to rest with the fate of this boy. Thesiger carries him to the fire in his arms, wraps him in blankets and sits beside him 'hour after hour wondering miserably if he was going to die'. He nurses him back to life. It is a rare chance for the reader to see the gentler side to Thesiger.

*

The crossing of the Empty Quarter by Bertram Thomas in early 1931 was closely followed by the efforts of Harry St John Philby to explore the Sands more comprehensively. Wilfred Thesiger later enhanced those first explorations, criss-crossing the Rub' al Khali until his mapped journeys resembled 'string around a parcel'.[22] Thesiger enters the Empty Quarter only fifteen years after Bertram Thomas began his inaugural passage but he writes a very different type of travelogue. Gone is the language of scientific exploration which Thomas employs, so redolent of Victorian imperial travellers to describe unexplored corners of the globe. It has been replaced with a personalised vision of a new land and its people. A narrative of reflective experience fills *Arabian Sands*. Yet while Thesiger's work is only the third travel text on the region, he already writes as a belated traveller, bemoaning the loss of the true nature of those lands to the Westernising process. Nostalgia has rapidly succeeded scientific zeal in the Empty Quarter.

3

IMPERIAL WARS

It was my fortune once to witness from the air a battle of one tribe against another to the north of the Suwaikieh Marsh, a sideshow quite apart from the Turks or British. But it was an Englishman who led one side, one Englishman alone leading a wild savage tribe into fierce battle against Turkish friendlies on our right flank. The career of this Englishman may never be written, yet in the history of the world there is probably no romance that can equal it; most people have heard, and much has worthily been sung, of Colonel Lawrence, of Syrian and Hedjaz fame; the story of Colonel Leachman is perhaps even stronger. Before the war Leachman spent his time wandering over large tracts of Arabia, and when British forces went to Mesopotamia he was employed politically in the desert. His prestige was amazing, and his name known to every Bedouin from Aden to Mosul. He lived in that desert from January to December dressed as an Arab, and with his boy Hussein [Hassan] wandered about amongst the tribes, perhaps even behind the Turks, organising, compelling, acquiring priceless information. There was a price on his head, and he lived with his life in his hands, but he could shoot a tribesman dead for misdeeds in front of the tribe and no hand would be lifted against him. Occasional visits to G. H. Q., and he would be gone, riding out to the horizon on his little Arab pony with his long legs dangling nearly to the ground. Eventually he would return wizened and thin, with probably a severe dose of fever after months in the desert in the heat of the summer, living on Arab food and water. Throughout Eastern Arabia the people were under the impression that it was Leachman who commanded British forces, and even that he was the King of England. On special cards that were printed for flying officers, to produce in the event of coming down in the desert, was written his name in large Arabic letters. Such was the magic of his personality. When I left Mesopotamia two years later, I had not seen Leachman for several months; he was still in the desert.[1]

The passage was written by Lieutenant-Colonel J. E. Tennant, an air commander operating above Mesopotamia to support British Expeditionary forces as they fought their way from Basra to Baghdad during the First World War. *In the Clouds Above Baghdad* (1920) provides a vision of a lone Englishman leading a tribal battle in the desert north of Kut. It is a passing glance made from the skies above. There on the ground is Colonel Gerard Leachman, British military traveller, operating as though the sheikh of a Bedouin tribe, attired in the garb of the Arab, and fully accustomed to desert life. Tennant provides no date to tie down the glimpse of Leachman. It is a moment in 1916. When later airmen caught a sight of the elusive Englishman on his lone travels across Arabia they would dip their wings or roll the plane, receiving a wave of recognition in reply.[2]

While Tennant maintains 'no romance can equal it', the career of Leachman comprised a series of solitary expeditions in the waterless plains of Arabia. The romance is imagined, the reality far harder to endure. Before the war, he had travelled to regions never seen by European travellers before, and when war came, he spent even longer in the desert before returning 'wizened and thin'. His exploits in Arabia continued when the war ended, until he was killed in August 1920, at Khan Nuqta, near Fallujah, during an insurrection against British rule.

Tennant's passage on Leachman with its distant past tense could easily be seen as a eulogy to the recently murdered British colonel, but in fact at the time of publication, Leachman was still travelling the deserts of Arabia in the service of the British military. Yet Tennant's prescient words read as if taken from an obituary. His foreword to *In the Clouds Above Baghdad* is dated April 1920: merely four months later, Leachman would be dead at the age of forty. When Sir Arnold Wilson, the Civil Commissioner of Baghdad, wired the news of Leachman's death to the Secretary of State for India, he commented that 'his strong sense of duty and discipline, his courage, enterprise, and ability earned for him both among his countrymen and amongst Arabs a reputation enjoyed by no other Political Officer'. Wilson also noted that 'his death is a serious blow to our position [on the] Upper Euphrates'.[3] The statement illustrates just how much influence one British military traveller held over the tribal activities of Mesopotamia. Wilson was right to express his concern. The news of the death of Leachman soon spread; tribes rose so effectively against the occupation that, but for a stronghold at Fallujah, the British military lost control over Iraq.

The power which Gerard Leachman exerted over the tribes of Mesopotamia is testament to his undoubted ability to undertake solitary travels across Arabia, and to communicate with and influence tribal leaders to the betterment of British military interests. His desert journeys of 1910 and 1912 were certainly ground-breaking, and were recorded in two articles written for the *Geographical Journal*. However, these were the only accounts Leachman published of his travels. His exploits undertaken during the First World War were never made public by himself or any one else. When Tennant states that 'most people have heard ... of Colonel Lawrence' he is no doubt referring to the publicity given to Lawrence's adventures by the American journalist Lowell Thomas who had begun his popular illustrated lectures in 1919. At that time, though the activities of Leachman were well known to the British military and others concerned with Arabia, the wider British public was ignorant of his name. Leachman's story may have been 'perhaps even stronger' than that of Lawrence's but no-one had then told it. Leachman did not beat his own drum. He shunned praise for his travels and was reluctant to record his journeying, even when it was to serve British military intelligence purposes. The distinguished military historian and traveller Sir John Glubb (Glubb Pasha) wrote of Leachman more than fifty years after his death that: 'Unfortunately he [Leachman] was completely a man of action and scarcely ever put pen to paper. Even the government he was serving could never extract any reports or office returns from him. This has undoubtedly militated against his fame.'[4] While there are those such as Tennant who eulogise the saga of Leachman's desert travel, it is the dashing figure of Lawrence of Arabia who has remained in the public eye as the romanticised English desert traveller of the First World War.

In this chapter, I explore travellers' depictions of three imperial wars in Arabia waged by Britain over a forty year period. The romantic image of the British military traveller that emerged from the First World War was of a solitary Englishman travelling Arabia with a tribe of Arabs. By the Second World War, the nature of desert warfare had dramatically changed. In the third imperial conflict to be explored, the Suez War of 1956, British military control over matters in Arabia decisively slipped away. Though forming a coda to the chapter, the moment was a crucial one. This critical event in British imperial history in Arabia was recorded by James Morris in *The Market of Seleukia* (1957), his reflection on the war and the state of the Middle East at that time. The travelogue of war was no longer written by those involved in the conflict but by an observing journalist.

*

In the period prior to the First World War, imperial knowledge of the lands of Arabia remained patchy and insecure. For the British military, travellers' desire to cross these untracked deserts and provide valuable surveys of their geographies and peoples had to be weighed against concerns as to the reaction by local tribes to the presence of British travellers in their lands. In December 1913, an experienced Arabian traveller, Captain Shakespear, prepared to travel across the Arabian Peninsula. He held the position of Political Officer of Kuwait and intended to meet with Ibn Saud, an emerging figure in the power politics of the tribes of southern Arabia. An official telegram from Lord Hardinge, Viceroy of India, stated the case for accepting his proposed journey:

> He has received an invitation from Bin Saud, who is a personal friend, to visit him at Riadh, and proposes to proceed thence in the direction of Hail. Shakespear, who has long been preparing himself for such a journey, knows Arabic well, is personally acquainted with tribes as far as Nejd, and is thus exceptionally well qualified to undertake a tour of this description. There is at present peace amongst tribes on his proposed route, and we trust it may be possible, if the political situation allows, to grant him permission. His exploration would be most useful, both from military, political, and geographical points of view.[5]

The telegram illustrates just how intimately the travel plans of individual journeys across Arabia were tied to British imperial and military concerns in the region. The value of Shakespear's proposed journey is in the information it may supply, not only on the landscape, its waterholes and grazing but on the tribal structures as well as the relationship he can build with Ibn Saud. Travel is intricately linked to gaining knowledge of Arabia. Six months later, after his proposal has been accepted and Shakespear has completed the mission and is preparing to speak to the Royal Geographical Society about his journey, officialdom once more steps in to ensure nothing will escape uncensored. Britain is now at war and the wide field of Arabia is a potential battleground. A letter from the Foreign Office sent by the Under Secretary of State (dated 11 June 1914) notes: 'I am to state that Sir E. Grey [Foreign Secretary] would be glad to see in advance the text of any address which Captain Shakespear may propose to give in public.' The reply from the India Office (dated 13 June 1914) offered reassurance on that point, stating confidently that 'steps will be taken to ensure that any paper which Capt. Shakespear may propose to publish regarding his journey in Arabia will be submitted to Sir E. Grey before publication'.[6]

That proposed lecture never took place. Shakespear instead returned to the company of Ibn Saud. In January 1915, Shakespear stood with the 6,000 Bedouin of the Saudi army assembled to fight the Shammar. As battle began, he is said to have shouted: 'No white man has seen this sight before.'[7] When the mounted Arab tribesmen tore into one another, Shakespear was one of the victims. Yet the tale of his 1914 journey was eventually told. In 1922, Douglas Carruthers, another British traveller in Arabia, published 'Captain Shakespear's Last Journey' which detailed the momentous journey Shakespear had taken from Kuwait all the way to Suez, covering '1200 miles of unknown country'. Carruthers praises him for taking regular latitude observations and 'hypsometric readings for altitude, which give a most useful string of heights between the Gulf and the Hejaz railway'. [8] What his death meant, according to Carruthers, was that he 'was the first Britisher to sacrifice his life in a country which was destined to play a large part in the cause of the Allies, eventuating in the final overthrow of Turkey'. What Shakespear also provided is the prototype for that particular form of British traveller in Arabia who travelled as a lone military officer in the service of British intelligence.

In his opening address on the matter of Shakespear's 1914 journey, Carruthers stated:

> The full story of the part Arabia played in the war remains to be written. It will be a stirring tale, full of romance and of all the glamour of guerrilla warfare; it will also contain episodes of individual enterprise and resource on the part of a few Englishmen which will compare favourably with any in the long story of British achievement in Asia.[9]

During the First World War in Arabia a handful of British military travellers undertook missions to explore and chart those segments of the land and its peoples yet to be traced on War Office maps. That the First World War was a time of individual enterprise in Arabia is certainly true. Yet for Gertrude Bell, at least, the war was a time when lone exploration of Arabia was curtailed. Instead, the knowledge gained by her earlier travels was employed for intelligence needs. In early 1914, as Gertrude Bell had headed to Hayil, a Foreign Office telegram had stated that the government had 'disclaimed all responsibility in the case of Miss Bell'.[10] She was a lone Englishwoman travelling into a sensitive area of central Arabia and potentially a political embarrassment. But the information she gathered on the rise of Ibn Saud proved invaluable, and Gertrude Bell was soon welcomed into the fold of British intelligence as Britain rapidly shifted towards war later that same year. She settled into the role of Political Officer for Mesopotamia, based in Baghdad, and devoted her energies to the secret reports written for the Arab Bureau in Cairo. She never wrote another travel book after she completed *Amurath to Amurath* in 1910.

In 'A Tribe of the Tigris' (1917), Gertrude Bell presented an essay on the state of the region she had come to have considerable political influence over. The article begins:

> The Tigris is a river in Arabia. The merchant may regard it as a trade route, and the soldier as a line of communications, the geographer may score the map with names ancient and modern, but no other definition will satisfy the ethnologist or guide the administrator. The Tigris is a river of great tribal confederations, immigrants from the deserts of the Arabian peninsula. Names that ring through the heroic legends of Arabia – Bani Tamin, Bani Rabi'a – are to be found among

them, and historical record confirms their claim to such high ancestry.[11]

Rather than the kind of dry, factual account on the nature of the Tigris and its local tribal structures which might be expected from reports written for British military requirements, the article contains a lyrical element. Against the simplistic statement of the short initial sentence sits the layered second, splicing the nature of the river across a variety of viewpoints. Though written initially for the specific audience of British intelligence, Bell's commentary on the Arabian tribes contains a distinct flourish. The piece would be collated with others Bell had written on Mesopotamia to be published anonymously as *The Arab of Mesopotamia* by the government office in Basra.[12]

Gerard Leachman had written a 'Brief Note on Tribes of the Tigris Below Baghdad' for a report on tribes of Iraq, compiled in November 1916 by British military intelligence. It was Gertrude Bell who edited his work, altering the title to the strategically more significant 'Below Kut'. British forces under Charles Townshend had surrendered to the Turkish siege in April 1916. Less than a month after the report was compiled, a British offensive headed back towards Kut. The opening of Leachman's report is in a very different style from that which Bell would offer the following year:

> The Arabs of the lower Tigris are Shiahs, but show little religious tendency and do not appear to be fanatical to any degree. Although of ancient stock, they seem to have entirely lost the fine characteristics of the Bedouin, and the average Arab is influenced in most of his actions by money considerations.[13]

Instead of the lyrical form of Bell's opening sentences, weaving a variety of perspectives on the Tigris, Leachman's account is direct and unsentimental as is required of the official report. He has no desire to spend time writing on the people of Arabia when he could be off travelling those same lands.

The piece is worth comparing to the style of the reports T. E. Lawrence wrote for the *Arab Bulletin*. This was the official publication of the Arab Bureau, the intelligence organisation set up in 1916, based in Cairo, with a remit to oversee Britain's influence in the Arab Revolt. An article titled 'Military Notes' was also printed in November 1916 and similarly details an Arab tribal grouping, in this case the 'Sherifial forces' of the Hejaz:

> It would, I think, be impossible to make an organized force out of them. Their initiative, great knowledge of the country, and mobility, make them formidable in the hills, and their penchant is all for taking booty. They would dynamite a railway, plunder a caravan, steal camels, better than anyone, while fed and paid by an Arab authority. It is customary to sneer at their love of pay, but it is noteworthy that in spite of bribes, the Hejaz tribes are not helping the Turks, and that the Sherif's supply columns are everywhere going without escort in perfect safety.[14]

Lawrence is not only prepared to interpose his opinion into the paper but add a certain dash and flair to the writing. His sympathy is clearly with the tribes. While Leachman praises 'the fine characteristics of the Bedouin' he too appears to make what Lawrence sees as a 'customary ... sneer' at the drive of the 'average Arab' to 'money considerations'. The driving force behind the *Arab Bulletin* was D. G. Hogarth, Lawrence's old mentor from Oxford, and this certainly played a part in dictating that the *Bulletin* had 'from the first a literary tinge not always present in Intelligence Summaries'.[15]

Though written for a wider readership, Gerard Leachman's two earlier accounts of his travels have a very similar style to his military intelligence reports. His articles for the *Geographical Journal* outlined his journeys into north-eastern Arabia in 1910 and central Arabia in 1912. In 1910, he witnessed a tribal battle between the Roalla of the Anaiza and the Shammar but there is no aggrandisement of the battle in his description of the scene:

> In battle the Beduin thinks little of the fighting and much of the loot, but the Shammar are kept in hand till the enemy are beaten, and then only are they allowed to loot. Prisoners taken are beheaded, though sheikhs are often spared.

The excitement is held in check by the factual nature of the sentences. The incident is being reported, the aspects of the raid dissected for a British audience, yet Leachman does not add embellishments or colour to the action or comment on his involvement in the activity. Instead, what is provided is a rather skeletal outline of the battle. The factual nature of the fighting is offered without any romanticisation of the event.

The account of his 1912-13 mission down to Riyadh to meet Ibn Saud was published in 1914. The route took him through central Arabia to the wells of Leina, which he had earlier revealed to Western eyes, and then south to Riyadh. His intention had been to continue further 'into the totally unexplored country of the Great Desert of the Ruba-el-Khali to the south, but this eventually proved to be impossible'.[16] Only rarely is any personal aspect to the journey apparent. At Aghar, some 100 miles from the wells at Hazil, Leachman recounts how the local sheikh composed an ode in his honour: 'The poem was duly recited to me in a very cold and cheerless dawn, and I am afraid his reward did not come up to his expectations.'[17] The moment provides an insight into the nature of Leachman. He was not in Arabia for an exotic adventure. The presentation of a paean apparently cut no ice with Leachman. In the description of his remarkable expedition across central Arabia, there is little sense of a personal journey portrayed to the reader.

It is this aspect which makes Leachman's sparse writing on his travels in Arabia so different from that of T. E. Lawrence, whose own self is a pivotal focus of any report on travel in Arabia. Nowhere is this made more vivid than in *Seven Pillars of Wisdom* (1926). On the opening page of the Introductory Chapter, Lawrence addresses the matter, stating of his text: 'This isolated picture throwing the main light upon myself is unfair to my British colleagues.'[18] The placing of an apologia so soon may acknowledge the bias in the work but it does little to shift attention away from Lawrence who remains central to his tale of the Arab Revolt. Rather than the passive observer which Leachman presents, Lawrence writes with a far greater sense of rhapsody. Both are serving British officers, but for Lawrence the writing up of his experiences offers a vast expanse over which his literary desires can wander. As he is absorbed into an Arab fighting force so Lawrence is also transformed by the very environment of Arabia:

Some of the evil of my tale may have been inherent in our circumstances. For years we lived anyhow with one another in the naked desert, under the indifferent heaven. By day the hot sun fermented us; and we were dizzied by the beating wind. At

night we were stained by dew, and shamed into pettiness by
the innumerable silences of stars. (8)

Lawrence and his fellow travellers are distilled to a basic essence, an
existential core, by a process of weathering in their harsh world. The
epic vision of the narrative sees only a collective 'we'. They have been
physically welded together by the desert environment. His unity with
the Bedouin has displaced his identity as a British political officer.

As the collection of tribesmen gathers under Emir Feisal just north
of Yenbo on the Red Sea, Lawrence adopts the garb of the Arab
sheikh and rides beside the leader of the Arab Revolt:

> The march became rather splendid and barbaric. First rode
> Feisal in white, then Sharraf at his right in red head-cloth and
> henna-dyed tunic and cloak, myself on his left in white and
> scarlet, behind us three banners of faded crimson silk with gilt
> spikes, behind them the drummers playing a march, and
> behind them again the wild mass of twelve hundred bouncing
> camels of the bodyguard, packed as closely as they could
> move, the men in every variety of coloured clothes and the
> camels nearly as brilliant in their trappings. We filled the valley
> to its banks with our flashing stream. (103)

The scene is one dripping with colour and romance: the lone
Englishman travels wrapped in his borrowed robes, riding upon a
camel through the desert, and surrounded by the flamboyantly
adorned horde of 1,200 tribesmen. Lawrence has become one with the
Arabs. Together they present the reader with a wild and exotic
gathering. The assembly is a quite glorious one, and in the centre is a
serving British officer.

With these examples, the narrative wealth of *Seven Pillars of Wisdom*,
its richness, scale and complexity, can at least be sampled. Unlike the
more objective description of the lands and peoples of Arabia offered
by the writings of earlier military travellers such as Shakespear and
Leachman, in *Seven Pillars of Wisdom* the narrator turns the spotlight on
to his own experiences. Leachman and Shakespear may have travelled
wider across Arabia and mapped unknown regions but Lawrence
offers a far more intense exposition of the adventures of a British
officer. The fleshing out of his narrative persona becomes a key
feature of the travelogue.

Circumstance and personality dictated that it would be Lawrence who would be the eponymous figure of British Arabian travel to emerge from the First World War. The mythologising publicity of Lowell Thomas coupled with the epic text of *Seven Pillars of Wisdom*, and its abridgement *Revolt in the Desert* (1927), created a public vision of a flamboyant and extraordinary British military traveller in Arabia under the soubriquet of 'Lawrence of Arabia'. A comparison of Leachman and Lawrence goes some way to explain the nature of their legacy and why it is not 'Leachman of Arabia' who is remembered. The two Englishmen met in 1917 at Wejh on the Red Sea, sharing a meal alongside Feisal and Captain Bray who recorded the event:

> Lawrence, in full Arab robes, richly embroidered, a gold dagger at his waist, speaking as softly as Feisal, carefully choosing his words and then lapsing into long silences. Leachman, clothed in faded khaki, inscrutable, with that puzzling smile of his lurking at the corners of his mouth, but straightforward and decisive in speech. The contrast between the two Englishmen was patent: Lawrence, acting the Arab and maintaining his prestige through the medium of his magnificent clothes. His servility to Feisal and his seeming unreality form a picture which still lingers in my mind.
>
> Leachman on the other hand was so obviously and unashamedly the Englishman, and a masterful one. His sufferings and hardships were mapped on his lean visage and pride showed behind the curtains of his eyes. He had endured five years of toil and danger, and three more still harsher years were in store for him ... Whereas all the world outside Arabia has heard of Lawrence; yet by a strange trick of fate, comparatively few Arabs have heard that name, yet the name of Leachman is still borne by countless sons of a warrior people and among them is still the synonym for gallantry and loyalty.[19]

Lawrence and Leachman represent two vastly different imperial agents: Lawrence is dressed to the nines in another's garb, actively adopting the clothes and manners of his Arab hosts; Leachman is more comfortable in his worn British Army regulation uniform, unwilling to fracture his identity as an Englishman and a soldier. There is no disguise, no cultural dressing up for Leachman. Meanwhile,

Lawrence is enthusiastically wrapping himself in the accoutrements of Arabian culture suitable for a prince. He is compared to Feisal, the true Arabian prince, indirectly in dress and directly in speech. He is 'speaking as softly as Feisal'. The Englishman is mimicking the Oriental; as Bray would have it, Lawrence is 'acting the Arab'. By 1936, when Bray's work was published, 'all the world outside Arabia has heard of Lawrence', but in 1917 when the two figures meet, 'Lawrence of Arabia' had not been born. According to Bray, a British military man far more in the mould of Leachman than Lawrence, it is Leachman not Lawrence who is remembered in Arabia as the greater traveller.

Just as Leachman offered few words to detail his travels, he was equally taciturn on the subject of Lawrence. According to Lawrence, Leachman 'was first and foremost a bully'.[20] In 1929 when Lawrence was commissioned to write a reader's report on the biography of Leachman which Harry St John Philby had written, he was unequivocal in his criticism:

> He was a ruffian, actually: a long, lean, ugly jerking man, with deliberately bad manners, a yellow, jaundiced eye, harsh-tempered, screaming and violent. He was always lifting his hand to hit. He came to our side of the desert, as Philby says: but not for a holiday with Mark Sykes. He was to have joined our show, he being fed up with Mesopotamia. In five days he had twice beaten his servant, a poor worm he had brought with him from Bagdad. We couldn't afford those sort of morals in our camp. So off he went. A very savage was Leachman. I suppose all conquerors have to be of that rather hard grain. He had no conception that beauty existed. His passion was for mastery, and for activity, sane or insane, directed, misdirected, or aimless.

Though other military voices have chosen to downplay the stern and sometimes violent nature of Leachman's approach to the Arab population, Lawrence clearly abhors the thought that he and Leachman shared any common ground. Where Philby's biography draws parallels between the two, Lawrence notes, 'some inconsistencies in the comparison'. The two figures may have operated under the same British imperial command in Arabia but their approach to matters military derived from very different schools of thought. To Lawrence, Leachman represents the worst form of British rule:

> I think his life is a very eloquent sermon, to empirials, of what to try to avoid in dealing with brown races. To think yourself so much better than mankind is surely to be so much worse? He made me a little ashamed to being (nominally) English.[21]

Philby's *The Legend of Lijman* did not get accepted for publication. The weight of Lawrence's report was no doubt a contributing factor, arguing as it did for considerable alterations to much of the early sections of the text. Unfortunately, all other correspondence between the publisher Stanley Unwin and T. E. Lawrence (then T. E. Shaw) has been lost. It would not be until seven years later in 1936 that Bray's biography of Leachman was published. By then Lawrence too would be lost to the world.

Lawrence had first privately published *Seven Pillars of Wisdom* in 1922, printed by the *Oxford Times*, creating just eight copies of his work. In 1926, a subscriber's edition was printed to a run of two hundred and eleven copies.[22] When the text became available for general circulation following Lawrence's death in May 1935, 110,000 copies of *Seven Pillars of Wisdom* were prepared in the first year of its publication by the publisher Jonathan Cape.[23] The phenomenon of Lawrence of Arabia which had commenced with the vision created by Lowell Thomas in 1919 was now complemented by the epic adventure tale of this exotic Englishman, a serving British officer dressed as an Arab prince, traversing Arabia either by camel or car and battling both the Turkish enemy and his personal demons on the way. Whatever the nature of the text, the enthusiastic reception by the British reading public ensured that the book became an instant bestseller.

Even before the circulation of the text to the general British public in 1935, *Seven Pillars of Wisdom* had exerted an influence over the travel literature of Arabia. Douglas Carruthers's jaunty tale of travel in search of the fabled Arabian oryx was published that same year. In a postscript he laments the news of Lawrence's death. Carruthers had been given a section of nine chapters from the *Oxford Times* edition. In *Arabian Adventure* there is much in the narrative style which mirrors Lawrence's writing. When Carruthers heads out into the desert on the pretence of hunting gazelle with the Bani Sakhr he experiences an emancipation born of the open space which Arabia offers:

We were free! A boundless beautiful country lay ahead of us, a
rolling desert, with lovely soft contours, already green with the
flush of spring ... We acknowledged no master, we obeyed no
rules – except those most intricate ones of the desert.[24]

The tone of Carruthers's ecstatic proclamation is closely akin to that
found in Lawrence's text. There is that same semblance of fusion
between the lone English military traveller and his Bedouin
companions into a collective force. Once more, it is the land of Arabia
which has welded them together and created the sense of glorious
existence. This united 'we' knows only the desert as its master.
Compare the section to one from the Introductory Chapter to *Seven
Pillars of Wisdom*:

We were fond together, because of the sweep of the open
places, the taste of wide winds, the sunlight, and the hopes in
which we worked. The morning freshness of the world-to-be
intoxicated us. We were wrought up with ideas inexpressible
and vaporous, but to be fought for. (4)

Not only are the evocations of a spiritual ecstasy strikingly similar but
so too are the expressions of a cross-cultural amalgam of Englishman
and Bedouin. Lawrence's work clearly exerted a recognisable influence
on Carruthers's style.

The publication success of *Seven Pillars of Wisdom* renewed public
interest in the activities of British military officers in the Arabian desert
during the First World War. In the preface to *Steel Chariots in the Desert*,
Rolls notes that 'a friendly passage in the foreword to T. E. Lawrence's
book *Seven Pillars of Wisdom*' was the incentive to write up his war
diaries into a more readable form.[25] On the back of the sales success of
Lawrence's text in 1937, Jonathan Cape published the war memoirs of
Rolls, his driver in Arabia, just two years after they had released *Seven
Pillars of Wisdom* to the British public.

The following year, 1938, Douglas Glen and his companion
Dawson set off from England to trace Lawrence's footsteps through
Arabia some twenty years earlier. This produced the first true homage
to Lawrence's travels. After hardening themselves up in the Libyan
desert, the two acolytes begin their particular pilgrimage tracing the
journey from Jidda to Akaba, though Glen reveals an important
distancing from the trek of Lawrence:

Although our route would be much the same as his, there was
to be a vast difference in the means employed; he having
ridden Sherif Ali's own camel whilst we should enjoy the
luxury of a Chevrolet car.[26]

The two set off for Akaba in some refined and mechanised mimetic
process. They copy the journey of Lawrence, but only in the route
undertaken, not in the method of transport. Yet there is no
recognition that their trail is made less authentic by the use of the car
rather than the camel.[27] Glen and Dawson are happy enough to head
off in their Chevrolet, meeting Bedouin in the desert and asking them
if they remember 'El Auruns'.

*

The Second World War presented a radically altered form of conflict
in Arabia from that which British military travellers had experienced
during the First World War. Rather than journeying across uncharted
desert with Bedouin tribesmen, such a facet to the experiences of
Lawrence, Leachman and Shakespear, war in Arabia now consisted
chiefly of mechanised battles on a massive scale. Tanks had replaced
camels as the vehicles of combat. The sense of romance which had
accompanied many of the adventures of British officers in the earlier
Arabian campaign was replaced by a gritty reality in the experiences of
thousands of troops sent to the western desert of Egypt. It is perhaps
not surprising then that the literature produced by the war experiences
of British writers travelling across Arabia during the Second World
War contains little of the sense of exotic adventure to be found in
depictions of the 1914-18 war. Certainly there emerged no figure to
compare with Lawrence of Arabia, nor any single travel text like that
of *Seven Pillars of Wisdom*. It may well be the contrast between the
conflict of the Second World War and the nature of warfare in
Lawrence's text which helps to account for the notable rise in sales
during the years 1939-45. A reprint of *Seven Pillars of Wisdom* in two
volumes for World Books and the Reprint Society had a print run of
close to 90,000 during 1939-40 even though only 2,000 copies of the
book were produced during 1938. The return to war refreshed a public
thirst for Lawrence's tale. Indeed, production figures of a cheap
edition (first produced in 1940), show a significant rise to 35,000

copies between June 1942 and February 1943, a period which reflects the battles of El Alamein.[28]

In Robin Maugham's *Nomad* (1947), both Lawrence and *Seven Pillars of Wisdom* are recurring motifs. The book opens in a field hospital in 1941 which consists 'of long rows of single-storied huts sprawled in the desert between Cairo and Suez'.[29] Maugham is one of the many war-wounded. When he is eventually moved to a convalescence home in Jaffa he scans the books in the library:

> Idly I looked at the titles until I saw *Orientations,* by Sir Ronald Storrs. During the long voyage around the Cape I had read *Seven Pillars of Wisdom* for the second time, and I remembered Lawrence's description of Storrs ... I had been thrilled by the Seven Pillars. But the peoples and events seemed of another world, heroic and refined, which had few points of contact with the bit of Levant we had known. Lawrence seemed too god-like, too remote from those few things of the East an ordinary soldier could see, too unattainable. (29-30)

The distinction is clearly drawn between the two world wars in Arabia. Lawrence and his text are from one 'heroic and refined' and quite distinct from the present conflict. The process which has converted Lawrence into Lawrence of Arabia in the years since the last imperial war in Arabia has been one akin to deification, his experiences as a soldier utterly removed from those of current British servicemen. The nature of war has radically changed. Images of open desert raids belong to a bygone era.

In Beirut, Maugham runs into the tensions that exist between the English and the French in Arabia. He meets a 'tipsy French lieutenant' (38) who states the French case:

> 'You have only just come here. You wait. You will see. The English work against us with the Arabs. They want to take our place.'
>
> He swayed and steadied himself against the bar.
>
> 'Chaque Anglais se croit un petit Lawrence,' he said, and stumbled to the door. (39)

Once more the ghost of Lawrence returns to haunt Maugham's remembrances. In French eyes each Englishman apparently sees himself as a little Lawrence. Maugham seems either unable or reluctant to shake the spectre. He calls on Colonel Stirling who served alongside Lawrence in Arabia. Indeed, Maugham has extensive contacts within the British imperial hierarchy and procures meetings with other significant figures. He meets John Bagot Glubb (Glubb Pasha), stays with Freya Stark in Baghdad and then visits Winston Churchill in Damascus. When forced to return to England, invalided home due to his head injury, he is invited by Churchill to spend the weekend at Chequers to discuss the situation in Arabia. Maugham collapses and is forced to spend the next three years recuperating, devoting himself to 'learning about Arab things' (135).

When he finally returns, Maugham rejoins Glubb and journeys to the ruined fortress of Jafer where Auda Abu Tayih, the colourful leader of the Howeitat, had been based. Maugham drifts into a reverie about the tribal leader he has met only via his depiction in *Seven Pillars of Wisdom*:

> Suddenly a tall, strong figure in a flowing burnous stood before me. I stared fascinated at the fierce black beard, the large eloquent eyes, and the powerfully hooked nose. It was Auda to the life. The man spoke.
> 'What do you wish here?'
> I stammered an explanation.
> 'You have heard of Auda Abu Tayih? I am his son. I am Mohammed Pasha, the son of Auda Abu Tayih'. (181)

Once more Maugham is stepping in Lawrence's footprints. Captivated by the apparition of the Arab leader, Maugham is transfixed, only just able to find his words. He has returned to the world of his imperial forefather as a figure from Lawrence's adventure appears to materialise before him.

Mohammed offers his British visitor a 'snow-white' baby camel as a welcoming gift, but Maugham is more interested in the souvenirs and memories which Auda's son has of an earlier Englishman in Arabia. He enters Mohammed's tent only to discover a 'tattered, dusty copy of *Seven Pillars of Wisdom* which Lawrence had given his father'. Though 'only a child', Mohammed recalls 'his smallness and his gentleness.... But what I admired most was the endurance of his camel rides. He rode from Tobeik to Jafer in one day' (200). The remembrance of Lawrence is reverential in tone. Though he has been dead only eight years or so, he has become mythologised in the narrative depiction of him. He lives on, aided in the process of deification with the retracing of his world by the next generation of British travellers to Arabia keen to live in the romanticised desert landscape he apparently inhabited. Most experiences of the Second World War in Arabia were in fact constructed from a far bloodier reality. In *Nomad*, Maugham commences his narrative in a field hospital and dedicates his book to 'those who were wounded and lived, but cannot tell their tale'. Yet he strives to turn away from the world of El Alamein to one in which Lawrence still holds sway.

*

In *Alamein to Zem Zem* (1946), Keith Douglas provides an account of his war travels centred on the reality of mechanised conflict. Douglas had already emerged as a respected young poet during his time at Merton College, Oxford where he had studied under the tutelage of Edmund Blunden.[30] In the narrative form which Douglas employs to detail his experiences in the battlefields of North Africa, the poetic sensibility is never far away. In October 1942, six days after the artillery salvo had signalled the commencement of the battle of El Alamein, Douglas ignored orders and headed away from a training camp to rejoin his regiment and take command of a Mark III Crusader tank.

Much of his narrative concentrates on the routine and regimen of being a soldier. There are powerful insights into Douglas's life as he prepares to enter the war:

> I lay down to sleep in my clothes, covered with my British warm [army officer's overcoat] and blankets, for the nights were already beginning to be cold. Perhaps betrayed by the spectacle of the stars as clear as jewels on black velvet into a mood of more solemnity, I suddenly found myself assuming that I was going to die tomorrow. For perhaps a quarter of an hour I considered to what possibilities of suffering, more than death, I had laid myself open. This with the dramatic and emotional part of me: but my senses of proportion and humour, like two court jesters, chased away the tragic poet, and I drifted away on a tide of odd thoughts, watching the various signs of battle in the lower sky ... The moon, now

grown much greater than when a week or two ago she had inspired me to write a poem on her ominous pregnancy, presided over a variety of lesser lights; starshells, tracer of orange, green, blue, and a harsh white, and the deeper colours of explosions. We were still at an hour's notice.[31]

The style concerned with exposing the inner self of the narrator is reminiscent of *Seven Pillars of Wisdom*. The elements of the native environment sit beside the clashing colours of the war. There is a poetic sense to the scene painted by Douglas, one that echoes the war narrative of Lawrence. The moon with its 'ominous pregnancy' sits as a goddess of war, as Athena over the silent battlefield of tomorrow, and over a narrator whose divided selves battle to rule the mind. In the manuscript of *Alamein to Zem Zem*, there exists a single-sentence foreword that echoes this notion of the moon as a symbol of war: 'I look back as to a period spent on the moon, almost to a short life in a new dimension.'[32] The 'tragic poet' competes with the 'court jesters'. In a similar manner, these two forces vie to control the feel of the narrative. The style of the 'tragic poet' who details the moon in her colourful bower of tracer shells contrasts with the blunt truth of the final sentence.

Alongside such musing on the possibilities of being killed, Douglas creates an authentic representation of the soldier's life. Daily processes are given significant focus, such as the ritual of the making of tea:

The immense moral satisfaction and recreation of brewing up was one I never realized. As soon as the permission is given, all crews except those of tanks detailed for look-out duties swarm out of their turrets. The long boxes on the side of the tank are opened: tins of bacon or M. & V. [Meat and Veg.], according to the time of day, are got out, while someone is lighting a fire in a tin filled with a paste of sand and petrol. A veteran, blackened half of a petrol-tin, with a twisted wire handle, is unhooked from some extremity of the tank and filled with water for tea. Within five minutes a good crew has a cup of immensely strong and sweet hot tea and sandwiches (for example) of oatmeal biscuits fried in bacon fat and enclosing crisp bacon. (26-7)

With the detail of the soldiers' domestic arrangements comes the sense of routine, of the commonplace activities. But the peace is soon shattered as Douglas and his tank crew head into action:

> As we approached another trench, I was too late to prevent the driver from running over a man in black overalls who was leaning on the parapet. A moment before the tank struck him I realized he was already dead; the first dead man I had ever seen. Looking back, I saw he was a Negro. 'Libyan troops,' said Evan. He was pointing. There were several of them scattered about, their clothes soaked with dew; some lacking limbs, although no flesh of these was visible, the clothes seeming to have wrapped themselves round the places where arms, legs, or even heads should have been, as though with an instinct for decency. I have noticed this before in photographs of people killed by explosive. (34)

Douglas infuses his narrative of battle and personal journey with the same poignancy and depth of feeling which Lawrence achieved. In its detailed depiction of life in the forces *Alamein to Zem Zem* is comparable to *The Mint* (1955), Lawrence's account of his days serving as an apprentice in the RAF.[33] But *Alamein to Zem Zem* is chiefly a powerful account of a bloody, mechanised war in Arab North Africa. Close to Galal railway station on the Mediterranean coast, Douglas comes across an abandoned Italian M13 tank. He lowers himself into the turret searching for a Biretta to loot. Instead, he finds the remains of the tank crew:

> They lay in a clumsy embrace, their white faces whiter, as those of dead men in the desert always were, for the light powdering of dust on them. One with a six-inch hole in his head, the whole skull smashed in behind the remains of an ear – the other covered with his own and his friend's blood, held up by the blue steel mechanism of a machine-gun, his legs twisting among the dully gleaming gear levers. About them clung that impenetrable silence I have mentioned before, by which I think the dead compel our reverence. I got a Biretta from another tank on the other side of the railway line. (66)

The scene is horrific for the reader but described with the emotionless detail of one immersed in the reality of modern warfare. Douglas makes no comment on his personal reaction to the sight of the dead Italians, merely of the 'impenetrable silence' which held them. The poetic sensibility hears that deathly peace which serves to 'compel our reverence'. Douglas does not disturb the dead in his search for a gun. The mundane tone of the final sentence returns the reader to the expediency of war. He gets his Biretta. It is in this fashion that the narrative serves to convey the experience of Alamein, of mechanised war across the Sahara in 1942. The juxtaposition of visions of mutilated bodies with the brewing of tea operates to illustrate the daily life of the soldier. It is a world away from the open deserts of *Seven Pillars of Wisdom*. In *Alamein to Zem Zem*, the desert becomes a place scattered with the detritus of shells, bodies and all the debris associated with two massed ranks actively engaged in modern warfare. Rather than Lawrence who travels with Malory's *Morte D'Arthur* and recreates a sense of medievalism in his battling quest through the Arabian desert, Douglas's account of war is of a distinctly twentieth-century world. He travels not by camel but by tank; he reads not of chivalrous knights but a variety of novels from *Alice in Wonderland* and *National Velvet* to a pilfered German copy of Nietzsche's *Also Sprach Zarathustra* in spare moments when not sharing biscuits and bully beef with his compatriots.

In the advance on Tripoli, Douglas was wounded in nine places by shrapnel from a mine. He found himself in another sector of the war, a dressing station; soon to be followed by a Casualty Clearing Station. As he recovered from the injury in Tunisia through 1943, he wrote up his experiences on the pages of a desk diary and provided a work 'unique in the literature of its period, in that no other British poet of Douglas's quality had battle experience'.[34] Though he had created the finest account by a British soldier serving in the battle of Alamein, Douglas never saw the work published. He was killed in Normandy on 9 June 1944 at the age of twenty-four.

*

The account which George Rodger provided of the Second World War he describes as 'more a saga of travel than a chronicle of war'.[35] Rather than being in Arabia to fight, he is there to report on the fighting for *Life* magazine. As a journalist and photographer Rodger journeys overland in 1940 across Africa from Cameroon to Chad, then to the oasis of Kufra in southern Libya before reaching Sudan, Ethiopia and Eritrea. In June 1941, he heads to Syria where the Vichy French forces are being attacked by the combined might of British and Fighting French troops. Outside Damascus, Rodger finds the truck he is travelling in a target for Vichy aircraft:

> The planes were flying in line, very low, only about 200 feet up, and were using light bombs. Each plane that passed over dropped a load on us. I lay flat on the ground with my nose in the sand and I was almost winded as the ground thumped up each time the bombs hit. Stones thrown up by the explosions showered around us ... I prayed. I guess we all did. I thought we were all as good as dead, and my mouth went horribly dry. But I thought I might as well get some more pictures of our finale and decided to leap up as the next plane went over the top and grab a quick picture as it flew away. (101)

The war reporter is defenceless against the onslaught. Yet rather than attempt to hide, Rodger risks his life for the chance to capture the moment on film. The narrative is from the distinct perspective of the journalist. Rather than a vision of a battle such as Douglas offers of Alamein, *Desert Journey* is the experiences of a journalist. His is an account of war from outside the conflict. Unlike the stance of a soldier, Rodger's position is one step removed from the battlefield.

Rodger arrives at Damascus merely an hour after it has fallen. Later that day, accompanied by a British captain, he takes a drive around the city in an 'ancient horse-drawn vehicle' and receives a welcome reception from the locals freed from Vichy control:

> People leaned from balconies which overhung the narrow streets and dropped coins and cigarettes into our open carriage. Children grabbed the bridles of the horses and led them through the crowds which surged into the street before us calling 'Shallom!' – God be with you. Women, girls, and even old men clung to the carriage and fervently kissed our hands. (105)

It is the kind of victory parade reserved for conquering heroes. Showered with the grateful praise of the people of Damascus, Rodger and Captain Ingram have little right to such an effusive tribute. Neither of them have taken part in the action to free the city but instead have rather gate-crashed the celebrations. They eventually feel the prick of their consciences and head away from the jubilant masses; for, as Rodger notes, 'over 2,000 men had suffered death or disablement to win this battle – we had only been observers' (105). The guilt at pretending to be one of the soldiers who freed Damascus grows too great. Rodger returns to the life of the war correspondent; he heads off to the comfort of his hotel, the best in town.

*

In the same vein of being a 'saga of travel rather than a chronicle of war', James Morris (now Jan) offers his take on the third imperial war to be considered: the Suez War of 1956. In *The Market of Seleukia* (1957), Morris provides a memoir of the war from the eyes of one sent there as a war correspondent for *The Times*. Britain increasingly ceded influence in the Arab world after 1945. The Suez War can perhaps be viewed as the tempestuous tantrum of an imperial power that was losing its hold on lands which it had once had firmly in its grasp. In January 1952, Cairo rioted, targeting British-owned businesses for burning. Six months later, on 26 July 1952, the coup by the Free Officers including a young colonel, Gamal Nasser, left Egypt in the hands of a military elite about whom the British knew little. American influence over British foreign policy was amply recognised in the warning by the State Department that any response in the form of a British military operation 'would be disastrous'.[36] Almost exactly four years later, Nasser announced the nationalisation of the Suez Canal. Yet even American pressure could not stop Prime Minister Anthony Eden leading Britain into an imperial war in Egypt, this time with the allies of France and Israel. Suez would be the last time British forces acted to secure an imperial possession in Arab lands. Later conflicts, such as Aden in 1967, were significantly part of a British desire to withdraw.

The Market of Seleukia is centred on that 'decisive moment' when 'the Tricolour and the Union Jack flew side by side over the Suez Canal, and the Israelis were masters of Sinai from Gaza in the north to Sharm el Sheikh at the southern tip'.[37] Morris acts as the voice of an interpreter, who travels the Middle East region at this crucial moment when 'the world waited in an awed hush to see what would happen next' (18). He begins his tale as though a storyteller recounting his travels to an expectant audience around a fire:

> One day in November, 1956, I stood beside a road in the Sinai desert with a colonel of the Israel Army. A troop of French-built tanks had stopped nearby, and the young Israeli tank-crews were sprawled on their turrets or eating sandwiches in the sand ...
> All around us, as we stood there talking that afternoon, there lay the debris of a defeated army. There were smoking and blackened trucks; burnt-out tanks; guns destroyed in their emplacements; boots and tents and rifles and ammunition boxes; and a multitude of papers, paybooks and orders and letters home, littered among the tentage or blowing fitful and forlorn across the desert. (17)

Morris sets his scene in the Sinai with a poetic, layered depiction of a war zone that finds resonance with the visions drawn by Douglas in the Sahara during the last war on Egyptian soil. There lies scattered the same detritus of disabled and abandoned tanks as sat amidst the sands of El Alamein. Yet now it is an Egyptian army which sits defeated.

As a witness, a reporter for the British public, Morris stands in 'the aftermath of a cataclysmic battle' unsure what the action of that afternoon would mean. Here he is as the amalgam of the traveller and the war correspondent who finds himself unstable in his footing at the end of the battle rather like George Rodger before him in Damascus. Instead of heading to his hotel room, Morris turns to those around him, the men of war, to explain just what it is that he is witnessing:

> It was a crux of the twentieth century, in which the future of the world hung in balance, and more than one proud Power faced ignominy or disaster; and in particular it was a turning-point for the Muslims of the Middle East, who stood breathless and aghast all around us.
> 'And what's going to happen now?' I asked the colonel, who was drinking warm orange juice out of a bottle. He wiped his mouth and smiled, not without a trace of satisfaction. 'God knows,' he said, 'but I can promise you this: after this little lot, the face of the Middle East will never be quite the same again.' (18)

As Morris rests beside the 'breathless' and defeated Egyptians, it is the Israeli colonel who commands a clear voice on the state of the Middle East. It is just as it should be. For Israel, it is a day of victory. Though Britain and France may believe at that moment that they too should celebrate, the rejoicing would not last long. For Morris, the occasion of standing that day in November 1956 in the sands of the Sinai, listening to the words of that Israeli colonel is a stepping off point. His experiences of the Suez War form merely the introduction to *The Market of Seleukia*. Yet that instant is central to a work which he considers 'a picture of the region as it was that day, frozen for a moment in all its varied attitudes, before the hot breath of history melted the tableau' (18). It is the final time Britain can still believe that it, rather than the USA, is the chief imperial player in Arabia. After Suez, 'the pretence that Britain could take the lead was abandoned'.[38]

So much had changed in forty years. The First World War figures of Leachman and Shakespear, who had provided the model of a lone Englishman travelling into tribal worlds before the more widely publicised exploits of T. E. Lawrence, were now long forgotten. The appearance of *Seven Pillars of Wisdom* in 1935 had rejuvenated public perceptions of the romanticised nature of Lawrence's war journeys in the open landscapes of Arabian deserts so sharply contrasted with the trenches of France and Belgium. It seemed a handful of valiant military travellers had apparently won the deserts of Arabia for Britain during that conflict. On the battlefields of El Alamein, Lawrence remained popular reading for British troops now fighting a mechanised tank war. Though the reality of that war was quite different, as Keith Douglas's work demonstrated, Britain had once more secured victory on Arab sands. Yet by the time that the dust of Suez had settled, Britain's position in Arabia had become irreparably fractured. No longer were there stirring accounts of desert battles written by military travellers enwrapped in the fray. Now it was down to a journalist to report on the Suez War, and to tell of the time when Britain started to lose its imperial footing in Arabia.

4

MODERNISING ARABIA

It was thus my good fortune to travel by the Rayak-Hama branch of the *Damas Hauran et Prolongements* Railway. I arrived at Rayak about 1.30, not more than an hour late, and there prepared to board the Hama train; this conveyance was filled with people, some frantically mounting, others excitedly descending from the cars. At one third-class carriage three native porters were wildly endeavouring to cram a Turkish officer, a Saratoga Trunk, a little Boy, and some Loaves of bread into a compartment which already contained three Mohammedan Women, a Fruit-seller, a Zaptieh [Turkish policeman], a Barber, a Prisoner, a Native mission teacher, the Zaptieh's saddle-bags, a Sword, Two umbrellas, a Bandbox containing a Sewing Machine, the Fruit-seller's Stall, and one hundred and fifty Oranges in a cloth; the cloth had burst and the oranges streamed through the chinks in the door not occupied by the porters wrestling with the officer; the Mohammedan ladies explained in brief that there was 'no Majesty and no Might save that of Allah, the Glorious and the Great'; the Zaptieh, who had not paid his fare, roared explanations over the Officer's shoulder; the porters thrust the Officer; the Officer pushed the fruit-seller; the Fruit-seller cast aspersions on the religion and ancestors of the Oranges; the Barber cried 'Shame!' on all for having so little self-control, while the Mission Teacher, on whom he was sitting, was too overcome to make any comment. Truly there was no engine on the train, nor was there any likelihood of its immediate movement; but it must not be supposed that orientals are never in a hurry; on all occasions of departure or arrival,

confusion, violence and strife reign supreme; fatalism is
forgotten, and it is every man's duty to heave, to punch, to
kick, to curse and swear, until the train, steamer or caravan has
started.[1]

It is November 1902. Mark Sykes details a comedic vision of the train
at Rayak railway station, Lebanon. He is a rich, young Englishman,
fresh from Cambridge University. He looks on to a scene of chaos.
There appears to be utter disorder. An amalgam of peoples and their
possessions battle for seats and space aboard the third-class carriage.
Sykes possesses the only island of sanity amidst the conflagration. It is
from this oasis of calm, the mind of the English gentleman, that the
reader may view the hilarity of train travel in Arabia. The clinical
dissection of the scene serves to delineate its foreignness. As each
element of the train carriage from the fare-dodging Zaptieh to the
Saratoga trunk is brought into focus an exotic mosaic gradually
emerges. Train travel is a raucous riot as each passenger cries out over
the others. Only the mission teacher is silent. It is a world away from
the polite, orderly scenes of the imperium at Paddington, King's Cross
or St Pancras.

Mark Sykes would become a chief political advisor on British affairs
in Arabia during the First World War. Elizabeth Monroe describes him
as 'infectiously enthusiastic and optimistic; he was rich, travelled, gay,
alert and companionable'.[2] He has been aptly labelled 'a late edition of
the Victorian "Travelling Gent"'.[3] His name is best remembered not as
a traveller but as the British signatory of the secret Sykes-Picot
agreement of 1916 that partitioned the Ottoman dominions between
Britain, France and Czarist Russia. The assurances given to the Arab
Revolt concerning independence stood incongruous to plans drawn up
between the imperial powers. The following year, as the details of the
agreement came to light, Sykes's name would become infamous within
Arabia. In 1919, while in Paris to attend the Peace Conference, the
brief and eventful life of Mark Sykes was ended by the influenza
epidemic which swept Europe after the war.

At the turn of the century, the train was the first wave in the
modernisation of travel in Arabia. In 1900, Sykes had completed his
first travel book, a light comic romp across Ottoman lands.[4] His mode
of transport had been by the traditional method of the mule. The birth
of the French-built railway systems in northern Arabia offered
travellers a novel form of transportation. A short line was built from

Jaffa to Jerusalem in 1892, and a 1.05 metre gauge line connected
Beirut to Damascus and on to the grain producing areas of the Hauran
by 1895.[5] The Rayak to Baalbek branch line opened in June 1902.[6] Just
five months later, Mark Sykes was to witness the scenes at Rayak
station. In Egypt, a line had been built from Alexandria to Suez via
Cairo as early as 1856. The Hejaz railway opened in 1908, offering
pilgrims the chance to travel from Damascus to Medina. The line was
the 'crowning material symbol of Pan-Islam ... financed by private
subscriptions from Muslims throughout the world and was thus free
from the taint of European investment capital'.[7] It was by this route
that Arthur Wavell made his surreptitious way to the cities of Islam in
1912. For centuries, the camel, horse and mule had provided the only
alternatives to walking. This chapter details how in the short period of
one generation, there emerged two technological advancements in the
mode of transport available: the train and the motor car. In the 1870s,
when Charles Doughty had travelled with the hajj, it had been in a
train of animals. Forty years on, locomotive trains now carried faithful
pilgrims to Mecca, and Ford cars could be seen darting over the flat
plains of the desert. Later, the arrival of aircraft would once again
radically alter the nature of travel in Arabia.

*

Donald Maxwell came to Arabia at the end of the First World War as
an artist commissioned by the Imperial War Museum. He travelled
throughout Iraq, providing an account of his adventures in *A Dweller in
Mesopotamia* (1921), written in a light narrative style somewhat
reminiscent of Sykes. In Chapter 6, entitled 'Arabian Nights 1919',
Maxwell presents a vision of the future for Arabian travellers:

> Somewhere in Mesopotamia, in the desert country that lies
> between the Euphrates at Felujeh and the Tigris, and in the
> neighbourhood of a walled-in group of buildings known as
> Khan Nuqtah, in the month of February of this year, and on a
> singularly miserable and rainy afternoon, there might have
> been seen a dark object moving very slowly across the
> uninteresting field of vision. At a distance it would not have
> been very easy to make out the nature of the thing, and a
> newcomer to the scene, with no local knowledge of
> circumstantial evidence to guide him, would have hesitated

between a buffalo or a hippopotamus and finally given it a vote in favour of it being some slime-crawling saurian that we came across in pictures of antediluvian natural history.

A closer view, however, would have made clear to him that it was no animal, but some species of tank, coated and covered with mud, accompanied by three similarly encased attendants, probably human beings, staggering and skidding about in its immediate vicinity. From time to time, one of these three would mount on the head or fore-part of this object, with the effect of causing it to slide and plunge forward for a few yards to stick again and again, snorting and panting and unable apparently to make any further progress.

A detective, equipped with a certain amount of motor knowledge, might have been able to discern that the mud-encrusted monster was a Ford car. A tailor, whose technical training would help him to penetrate the disguise of thick slime, might have been able to recognize by the cut of their clothes that the first of the three figures was an R.A.F. driver and the other two were naval officers. As a matter of fact one of these forlorn representatives of our boasted sea-power was Brown, and the other one, although I think he would have hesitated to swear to his identity at the time, was the unfortunate writer of these chronicles.

There was no doubt about it; we were done.

'At the present rate of progress we shall reach Baghdad in about ten days,' said the driver, 'and it's getting worse.'

A few more hours' rain and no power on earth would move the car an inch.[8]

The opening vision of a 'dark object' traversing a rainy desert emerges by degrees into something more definable. Maxwell tests the acuity of his readers' sight, imagining an alliterative 'slime-crawling saurian' and a 'mud-encrusted monster'. When the figure of a Ford motor car finally materialises from the murky atmosphere, it has transmogrified from being some ancient creature of a bygone epoch into a mechanised construct of the modern world. Yet it is a beast that cannot survive on the muddy plains of Mesopotamia. The Ford car is transforming once more, this time from a means of traversing the lands of Arabia faster than any being has achieved before, into a stolid, stationary heap of metal. For all its engineering and innovation, the car must be abandoned to the dictates of the desert. The triad of British travellers is saved from the quagmire by local Arabs and the clean-up entails 'scraping each other down with a ruler, so that we could see which was which'.[9] They manage to find a train heading to Baghdad on the branch line from Dhibban by stumbling across some tracks and so are rescued from their plight by another mechanical beast recently arrived in Arabia. Though they were not to know it, their timing was fortuitous. The line was to shut the following year.[10]

Mark Sykes and Donald Maxwell both detail the experience of travelling Arabia by modern methods, offering depictions which emphasise the comic moments which the arrival of mechanised transport can bring. Both portray the breaking down, the disabling of these modes of travel. At Rayak, the train due to carry Sykes to Baalbek is immobile. For Maxwell, the Ford is no match for the mud of Mesopotamia. While the period of time between the two travellers has seen the emergence of the motor car as a novel means of transport in a changing Arabia, it is seen as comically ineffective as a vehicle to cross the desert. When Maxwell emerges from the mud, it is the train which provides his means of escape; one generation of mechanised transport acting as saviour from the next.

In fact, the motor car had already proved its worth in one key arena. The first substantial deployment of the motor car in Arabia took place in the First World War. The tale of its appearance in 1917 is told by a driver of those prototypes of four-wheeled travel. In *Steel Chariots in the Desert* (1937), S. C. Rolls offers a travel text centred on his experiences of driving T. E. Lawrence during the Arab Revolt.[11] His book was only begun late in 1935, stimulated by the publication of the general edition of *Seven Pillars of Wisdom* in which Rolls was favourably portrayed. It is a tale of when the car first emerged as a means of journeying through Arabia.

Rolls was sent to Libya at the end of 1915, where he was involved in the development of 'war-chariots' (22) for desert use. These were built of a Rolls-Royce chassis mounted with a steel cylinder which heated up so much that men were 'in danger of being cooked like rabbits in a saucepan' (23). A Vickers-Maxim gun was fixed on the turret while various holes in the armoured plating allowed a rifle to be used. They were mainly used as two-man vehicles, preferably two short men. After an initial spell in the Libyan desert in 1915 in a campaign against the Senussi, the armoured car unit reached Akaba 'late in

August 1917' (148). Lawrence rapidly recognised the value of these steel chariots to the desert campaign and chose Rolls as his driver:

> I was delighted that Lawrence had singled out my tender for his own use, and from that time until the end of the campaign we travelled together something like twenty thousand miles. Until then he had ridden the length and breadth of northern Arabia on camels, outstaying the Bedouins themselves in his disregard of hunger and fatigue. But there was no comparison between Ghazala and a Rolls-Royce in the mind of a man who the quicker he could shoot himself from end to end of the desert like a weaver's shuttle, the better he would be pleased ... There were still times when Ghazala or her sisters could be of use to him, but very largely from this time onwards the Rolls-Royce, later aided by an occasional aeroplane, took her place. (164-5)

The car has replaced the camel as the standard for Lawrence's travel through Arabia. The declaration from Rolls details the transition from the romanticised image of Lawrence, white-robed upon his faithful Ghazala, to journeying aboard the war-chariot of the revamped Rolls-Royce. Yet the more enduring image is of Lawrence upon four legs rather than four wheels.

In *Seven Pillars of Wisdom*, Lawrence enthusiastically embraced the possibilities which steel chariots offered. From Guweira, north of Akaba, the cars raced over mud-flats ('their speedometers touched sixty-five') with the knowledge that 'it was nearly impossible to break a Rolls-Royce'.[12] In the expediencies of war, the practical value of the car outweighed the camel. Alongside their speed and durability was the protection they afforded from gunfire: 'Armoured car work seemed fighting de luxe, for our troops, being steel-covered, could come to no hurt' (363). It was only when the cars drove into the beloved old castle of Azrak that doubts surfaced over the appropriateness of mechanised beasts from the West in deepest Arabia: 'I felt guilty at introducing the throbbing car, and its trim crew of khaki-clad northerners, into the remoteness of this most hidden legendary place' (447). The moment is short lived. Lawrence spends far more time rejoicing at the value of the car: 'A Rolls in the desert was above rubies', he states lyrically. 'Great was Rolls and great was Royce! They were worth hundreds of men to us in these deserts' (474-5). According to *Steel Chariots in the*

**T. E. Lawrence arrives at Damascus in a Tin Lizzie
(October 1918).**

Desert, Lawrence found the camel 'was not only less bruising, but also gave better opportunities for sleeping on the march'. However, steel chariots had speed on their side; exemplified on the plains of Jefer when the car 'shot away more smoothly and swiftly than an electric train' (256). Of course, there were certain dangers with using cars. When refuelling at night with a candle for light, Rolls causes a 'terrific "Woof!" or muffled explosion' (257) as the petrol tank catches violently aflame. But the chariot is saved.

The advantages of the car over the camel were not only accepted by British individuals employed in the battle with Ottoman forces. Auda Abu Tayih, the fabled leader of the Howeitat tribe of northern Arabia, had spent much of his life upon horses or camels. When he travelled with Rolls in a steel chariot, he had the option of a cushioned front seat but chose instead to sit on some boxes of gold behind. From there, 'amused by the unaccustomed motion of car-travelling, he permitted his handsome old face to show a good-humoured smile'. As the car lurched across rutted ground, Auda, 'clapped his hands in juvenile delight and nodded to me as a sign of his approval of my great skill as a driver' (192). Feisal, the Hashemite leader of the Arabs, had his own vehicle, a Vauxhall, nicknamed the 'Green Linnet' (255). During the triumphant entrance into Damascus in October 1918, it was in this car that Feisal paraded around the ancient Arab city, 'sat calmly' with 'horsemen racing one another, or galloping in wide circles round the green Vauxhall and its escorting cars' (281). Here is the confluence of the old and the new in the moment of victory. The traditional vehicles of desert travel swarm in joy around the metal frame of mechanised mobility in which their leader sits.

Just as the motor vehicle provided a pivotal innovation in the enterprise of imperial warfare in Arabia so it emerged in the 1920s as a central aspect to a number of travel texts. Rosita Forbes covered some 430 miles by car from the oasis of Siwa to Alexandria in the final section of her journey through the Sahara but employed more traditional methods of travel when venturing to the oasis of Kufra.[13] In *The Diabolical* (1934), H. H. McWilliams details the journey made in 1933 by a group of American and British archaeologists from Tel Duweir, some thirty miles south-west of Jerusalem, back to England. 'The Diabolical' of the title is a reconditioned Ford station-waggon thought by the Arab workers on the dig to possess 'some kind of magic which would drive it through the worst quagmire and the deepest river'.[14] The narrative style is informal, concerned with the intricacies of the travellers' relationships and the state of 'The Diabolical', yet illustrates the appearance of the motor vehicle as a central component of the travel experience. Some fifty years later, *Juggernaut* (1987) told the tale of a journey made in the opposite direction, from England to Arabia.[15] It too is a narrative where a truck is both the means of transportation and a key character in the adventure.

The arrival of the car enabled the British imperial administrators in Arabia to keep more efficient control. When the British Army departed, following victory in the First World War, they left behind their 'Tin Lizzies', as the early Fords were named. They could be useful for some journeys over gentle desert terrain, though for longer journeys the old method of the camel was still required. Major Jarvis, writing of his time in 1920 as a colonial overseer in Egypt, laments the necessity of the camel to visit the far-flung populations of Baharia and Farafra.[16] A decade later, he states:

> At the present time the general reliability of cars and the amount of work done by the Egyptian Government in improving tracks and erecting sign-posts has made desert travel a comparatively safe and easy undertaking, so that ordinary motorists who possess a slight knowledge of what is happening under the bonnet may journey into the deserts without hardship or risk.[17]

Jarvis then offers a series of car routes across the Sinai desert for the traveller. He is a more than adequate guide, being the holder of the imperial title 'Governor of Sinai'.

In other parts of Arabia, though less developed for road transport, there were similar signs of change. Harold Ingrams, alongside his wife Doreen, travelled widely across southern Arabia throughout the Aden Protectorates. Working for the Colonial Office, they met local leaders and forged what became known as 'Ingrams' Peace' in the years 1936 to 1939. In October 1934, the Ingrams headed to the Hadhramaut, arriving at Mukalla by boat. They toured the town in a car lent with driver by the Sultan of Mukalla. It was an Essex Six that raced at 'fifty miles an hour' along the shore, 'scattering crabs and gulls in all directions'.[18] In order to travel into the interior of the Hadhramaut, they had to turn to the donkey and the camel, though from Seiyun to Tarim the Ingrams were driven in a car borrowed from local dignitary

Seiyid Bubakr who had an ambitious road-building plan to link the town with the coast at Shihr. For ten years, he ploughed money and manpower into the project, lifting a road up the heights of the Wadi Hadhramaut though his enthusiasm for car travel was not shared by all:

> We frequently had to diverge slightly from the track in order to avoid large stones placed on the road by beduin who maintain an active dislike of modern methods of transport. The tribesman's prejudice against the motor car is not simply mere conservatism but a dread that motor transport may oust the camel and thus deprive him of his livelihood.[19]

The tensions of a modernising Arabia were tangible. In 1934, change was apparent even in the isolation of the Hadhramaut. In the town of Tarim alone there were some sixty cars and when the Ingrams returned in 1936 merely forty miles remained to complete the road linking Tarim to the coast.

As early as 1922, two New Zealanders, the Nairn brothers, had established a motor link between Damascus and Baghdad. The enterprise offered travellers a swift route over 500 miles to the newly acquired British dependency of Iraq by 'taking the Nairn'. Acting as a mail service, the Nairn bus provided vastly improved communication between British controlled Iraq and London. Gertrude Bell, writing to her stepmother Florence Bell from Baghdad in September 1923, shows her enthusiasm for the possibilities the service may offer:

> Here's an interesting experiment: I am going to post this tomorrow by the overland mail, i.e. by car to Damascus. Will you tell me how many days it is on the way, for if it proves a success I shall write to you weekly instead of fortnightly.[20]

Elsewhere in Arabia, mechanisation was making its mark. By 1926, Ibn Saud had control of the Hejaz and the Holy Cities of Islam 'just as the transportation revolution swept over Arabia. Motor cars, and especially Ford cars and buses, were appearing in the most unlikely places in the Kingdom.'[21] At the forefront of this revolution was none other than the explorer and entrepreneur Harry St John Philby, who acted as chief advocate for the advancement of motorised pilgrim traffic. By 1934 he had 'secured a monopoly on the import of Fords' into Saudi-controlled Arabia.[22] The development of the car as a means of transport offered Philby opportunities to head into the southern reaches of Ibn Saud's kingdom, neatly fitting with the King's own designs to extend his influence over the Yemeni border and into the Hadhramaut.

In May 1936, Philby began a motorised adventure from near Mecca to Abha and on to Najran. In two cars, with a force of eight Saudi soldiers, Philby headed for Shabwa, 'skirting the western edge of the Rub'al-Khālī', then into the Hadhramaut where he finally halted at Mukalla awaiting a replacement for a broken axle.[23] No British traveller had made such a journey before, though British authorities were less than enthusiastic at Philby's accomplishment. He had marched into the lands of the Aden Protectorate with armed Saudis and 'endeavoured to impress upon everyone he talked to the benefits of living under Ibn Sa'ūd's rule'.[24] The Colonial Office asked him to leave, which he did, taking a gentle wander back through undemarcated Saudi-Yemeni border regions upsetting both local tribesmen and the Imam of Yemen.

*

If travel within Arabia had dramatically altered with the introduction of the motor car, the journey into the region also radically changed as aircraft routes were established. In the late nineteenth century, the usual method of journeying to Egypt was by steamer. The account by Robert Barr is typical. Also known as Luke Sharp, a Scottish popular fiction writer, he sets off from Manchester aboard the steamer *Creole Prince* for a two-month voyage. Travelling via Malta, Barr arrives at Alexandria, and then heads on to Cairo. The package aspect of Barr's travel means he is a passive tourist, making observations as he moves around the East, though largely unable to dictate his direction or destination. The *Creole Prince* docks at Beirut. Barr and fellow passengers have the chance to take the train to Baalbek. It is the same journey Mark Sykes will take a few years later. Rather than detailing disorder, Barr explains how his 'summer garments' are inappropriate as snow beats against the window panes of his train carriage.[25]

For H. Rider Haggard travelling in 1900, the journey commenced by train from Charing Cross to Italy, from where he wound his way round to Cyprus and, in time, sailed from Limasol at night for Beirut aboard a Cook steamer.[26] Norman Lewis made two voyages down the

Red Sea for a thwarted attempt to travel into Yemen in 1937, one on board a sambuk and one in a cargo steamer. His experiences of the steamer are nightmarish:

> On the steamer the white men were only semi-human. The captain was so mean that he had never been known to go ashore when the ship was in port, for fear of spending money ... The passengers, other then ourselves, consisted of a half-crazy lighthouse keeper, a gun runner who had just disposed of a consignment of defective weapons, and a French merchant who dismissed every issue, every topic of conversation, life itself, with a gesture of weary loathing, 'dégoûtant mon ami, je vous assure, c'est dégoûtant'.[27]

If Lewis found his fellow passengers on board ship somewhat disagreeable, by the 1930s there was another means for travelling across Arabia. Imperial Airways had been launched in 1924, originally with 'plodding biplanes and flying-boats' which 'sailed the skies with a distinctly maritime dignity'.[28] Within years, Imperial Airways were operating services all over the Middle East. In August 1927, King Feisal of Iraq flew from Baghdad to Gaza, a route that traced the path of the recent oil pipeline and motor road.[29] Developments in transport ran parallel with the growing thirst of Western powers for Arabian oil.

Aeroplanes had first appeared in Arabia during the First World War. They provided T. E. Lawrence with powerful support in routing Turkish forces camped at Abu el Lissan. The bi-planes would fly low, 'at about three hundred feet', taking the Turks by surprise and then once they had dropped their bombs 'the lightened machines soared up and home to El Arish. The Arabs rejoiced: the Turks were seriously alarmed.'[30] Twenty years later, when Norman Lewis was boating down the Red Sea to southern Arabia the aeroplane was 'now a familiar feature of the South Arabian sky, which is reserved for intervention in serious tribal warfare ... villages of certain continually warring tribes in the neighbouring province of Hadhramaut have been bombed'. The aeroplanes are a potent sign of strength to enforce 'Ingrams' Peace' in the Aden Protectorate. Lewis notes how traditional methods for warding off evil cannot cope with the emergence of aircraft as an imperial force: 'Casualties are the consequence of a too complete faith on the villagers' part in the protective value of the Fatihah – the opening chapter of the Quran – which is read ceremonially as an anti-aircraft measure.'[31]

Freya Stark owed much to the presence of an imperial air force in southern Arabia. She details her dramatic rescue in 1935 from deep in the Hadhramaut when struck down with a mystery illness involving fever, exhaustion and heart palpitations. Stark is offered the medical advice that 'there is nothing so good for fevers as a sudden shock like falling from a car'. She turns instead to a more modern transport solution. Messages are sent to Aden requesting a doctor and Stark is rescued by the arrival of four RAF bombers: 'their aluminium shining in the sun, more beautiful to my eyes than any aeroplanes that I had ever seen'.[32] From the seclusion of a hidden town far from Aden, in the recesses of the Hadhramaut mountains, the aeroplane offers a lifeline. In a letter written from Shibam to Venetia Buddicom, dated 15 March 1935, she expresses her amazement at the power of this transport means: 'It seems incredible that tomorrow night I shall be in an English hospital in Aden.'[33] In gratitude, *The Southern Gates of Arabia* (1936) was dedicated to 'The Royal Air Force, and especially to those in Aden who made the writing of it possible by carrying me to safety from Shibam'. For some British travellers, the arrival of the aeroplane in Arabia was a godsend.

*

The modernising of Arabia occurred not merely through developments in transport. As trains, cars and airplanes provided the traveller with swifter means by which to explore the region, another factor was fast emerging as a driving force of change across the region: the discovery of oil and the realisation of its value to Western imperial powers. British interest in oil evolved at the end of the nineteenth century. For Charles Marvin, writing in 1889, the empire's petroleum reserves were underexploited. Prophetically, he noted of the 'neighbourhood of Kerkook' that 'the Oil from this region might become of great commercial importance, as it is inexhaustible in quantity, and even without a railroad, transportation is easy by way of the Tigris and Persian Gulf to Bagdad, Bussorah, India and beyond'.[34] Eight years later, Captain Maunsell would make similar claims concerning sites at Mosul and Kirkuk.[35] Donald Maxwell, the war artist already seen in a Ford stuck in the mud of Mesopotamia, arrived at Abadan in 1919. The refinery had only been open since 1912 when production from oilfields at Masjid I Sulayman in south-west Iran began under the freshly formed Anglo-Persian Oil Company.[36] The mechanics of the oil business were firmly in place. Maxwell drew the refineries, pipelines and British military guards overseeing the local workers. The vast metal stanchions of the oil works had already taken on a sinister, monstrous property. It was a messy business. His light-humoured advice to travellers was 'dirty your face and you might walk about Abadan without attracting notice'.[37]

Britain's desire for oil was closely linked to both military and political thinking. By 1912 the British Admiralty stated that oil needs to fuel the navy 'were to be met extensively from Middle East resources, and the Foreign Office was left to translate Admiralty demands into foreign policy'.[38] During the First World War, motorised transport in the form of lorries, cars and motorbikes altered the way battles were fought. All needed oil. 'All the Great Powers were now well aware of the critical role that petroleum played, in both modern warfare and, increasingly, the modern economy.'[39] As recognition of the need for oil grew in Western minds, so the era of oil diplomacy was born.

In 1933 the right to drill for oil in Saudi-controlled Arabia was being sought by both British and American-based companies. Harry St John Philby had just completed his exploration of the Empty Quarter. His special relationship with King Ibn Saud enabled him to negotiate both a lucrative deal for himself as middleman and the oil concession for the American company Socal (Standard Oil Company of California). Philby had not only solved 'his problems of household debts and school bills', he had 'vastly enjoyed his resultant sense of importance'.[40]

The renovation of Arabia was rapid. In Hasa region, 'all the paraphernalia of the oil industry was beginning to pile up on the Saudi shore. There were pipes and cranes, girders and drums, wrenches and dies, cars and lorries'. With the thirst for Saudi black gold, the old ways were soon being replaced. As the mechanised oil industry moved into Arabia, traditional scenes and lifestyles found themselves outdated: 'By and by a whole new civilization had been created where, but a few months previously, there had been nothing but a few mud huts, the camels and the sea for as long as men had been there.'[41]

Wilfred Thesiger found the transformation of his beloved Arabia difficult to bear. His travels across Arabia in the 1940s were by camel and covered some ten thousand miles. In the Introduction to *Arabian Sands*, he expressed his sense of nostalgia and bitter distaste for the mechanisation and modernisation of Arabia that had occurred since his earlier explorations:

> If anyone goes there now looking for the life I led they will not find it, for technicians have been there since, prospecting for oil. Today the desert where I travelled is scarred with the tracks of lorries and littered with discarded junk imported from Europe and America. But this material desecration is unimportant compared with the demoralization which has resulted among the Bedu themselves.[42]

The dual evils were mechanised transport and oil exploration. Both were responsible for the wounds inflicted upon the desert and its peoples. Thesiger wrote the original Introduction in the late 1950s. In 1977, he returned to Arabia. For three weeks he travelled across Oman and the Trucial States as never before, using 'aeroplanes, helicopters, cars and even a launch' such that he covered 'distances in an hour that previously had taken weeks'. In the preface written to detail this final voyage through Arabia, he narrates scaling the Jebal al Akhdar with his old companions bin Kabina and bin Ghabaisha only to find 'here, too, was an airfield with jet planes and helicopters landing and taking off'. The climb had been a feat that Thesiger had been desperate to achieve previously. Now he found no exaltation at its accomplishment, only a deepened sense of loss. His Arab friends 'had adjusted themselves to this new Arabian world, something I was unable to do'. His nostalgia is clear. He wants the Arabia of a pre-industrialised, pre-mechanised world which he knew in the 1940s. Abu Dhabi is now 'an Arabian Nightmare'. [43] Everything has changed.

When James Morris (now Jan Morris) arrived in Oman in 1955, Thesiger had only been gone five years. Morris was a correspondent for *The Times*, there to travel with the Sultan of Oman, Said bin Taimur, on a modern voyage through south-east Arabia. The journey through Oman is 'the last of the classic journeys of the Arabian peninsula'. However, Morris would not travel for endless days as Thesiger did. It would be a modern expedition, 'attended by few of the hardships and dangers of its terrible camel-back predecessors, for it was undertaken by motor convoy'. Yet the journey would venture through lands never visited before by a British traveller. As such, it was comparable with the greater British Arabian explorations 'of the Burtons, the Doughtys, the Philbys and the Thesigers' in setting a 'travellers' precedent' and opening another window onto the world of Arabia. It would be a drive through the 'gravelly hinterland' of Oman, 'concerned essentially with oil, that irresistible agency of change'.[44]

Elsewhere in Arabia, Britain had lost much of its imperial status but in Oman ties were still firmly secured. For Morris, there was a sense of playing a fading colonial role: 'Though I was the only European in those trucks, still the adventure smacked perceptibly of the open cockpits, Rolls-Royce armoured cars, proconsuls and spheres of influence of the Pax Britannica' (11-12). It is a voyage that will reshape the political landscape of this region of Arabia. The Sultan of Oman is keen to draw the border of his country. It is a vexed issue. Tribes in the interior, particularly those of the Ibadhiya, an Islamic sect, consider themselves as a separate state, aligned more closely to Ibn Saud of Saudi Arabia than British-backed Oman. For Britain, it is a matter of oil. Any oilfields within Oman would offer concessions to a British company while demarcation within a Saudi Arabian-controlled region would send any oil to an American company.

Morris narrates the episode in a tone reminiscent of a fairytale: 'So one day the Sultan, the British government and the concessionary oil company ... decided that the time had come to settle the matter once and for all' (20). There is a sense of anticipation. The mood is one of a story unfolding, perhaps one retold from *One Thousand and One Nights*. It is an old tale with modern players: an Arab prince, a fading imperial nation and a powerful business corporation. The Sultan has agreed to Morris travelling with the entourage on this journey of national definition. Morris waits at Salala in the same RAF base where Thesiger stayed in the 1940s. The imperial linkages between the Sultan and Britain are extensive. As they commence the journey, the Sultan produces a map created by Bertram Thomas when wazir [political adviser] of Oman in the 1930s.

The convoy consists of seven 'American trucks, all identical, piled almost to overturning with stores and bags'. With high excitement, 'a champagne feeling in the air' (43), they prepare to leave. The trucks rapidly cover the 600 miles across the Jeddat al Harasis from Salala to Fahud where the eyes of the oil prospectors are focussed. For now at least, there is none of the nostalgia for a pre-mechanised, pre-oil Arabia expounded by Thesiger. Instead, Morris pronounces that, 'places inhabited by oil companies, however intrinsically prosaic, always manage to develop a peculiar opulent magic' (63), and that 'I have never felt this hygienic mystique more strongly than I did at

Fahud' (64). He is invited to join the oilmen in their camp and heads happily for their newly built quarters. They are air-conditioned and designed to accommodate all the possible requirements of the Western world transposed into the Arabian desert. There are spotless rooms with 'bedside lamps, rugs, white sheets', hot showers, 'a limitless supply of such things as beefsteaks and butter' and, more radically, 'large quantities of beer' (64-5). He has already witnessed the scene in Kuwait where 'big highways tore through its old buildings and pierced the mud wall built (only thirty years before) as a defence against raiding tribesmen' (69). Changes come rapidly, soon eroding traditional ways. Morris now sees the arrival of oil as a 'coarsening process' whereby the 'acid of money corroded those new oil societies' (70-1).

The Sultan's mission of national definition proceeds with Morris detailing the progress of the convoy. There is little enthusiasm for the Sultan from the countryside peoples. Nizwa is the 'key-point of the national history, at once the Hastings, the Westminster and the Canterbury of Oman' (94). Then it is on to Ibri and the Buraimi oases. Beyond, in the hills, Morris draws parallels with idealised images of English countryside. Just as Oman and Britain are closely tied politically, so Morris sees more imaginative links between the two countries. A scene of greenery beside a spring has a 'Constablian air' such that 'you expected to see Salisbury spire rising among the hills, or hear the jingling of harness brasses' (121). This rifling of English Arcadian visions is a device used throughout the text to stabilise British readers' sense of Arabia within familiar constructs. Earlier, the Qara mountains were 'for all the world like some unspoilt English downland. Housman would have felt at home here; Hardy, if he had strayed to Dhufar, might well have expected some pungent Dorset countryman to appear over the next ridge' (45). The effect is to create an Arabia full of the innocent trappings of rural England. Just as that world was fouled by the fumes of modernisation, so the gentle unspoilt worlds of Oman will be sullied by the process of oil exploitation.

The journey ends in Muscat with success for the Sultan in uniting his country for the first time. For Morris, the tale of a remarkable tour concludes with a sombre note on the weakening role of Britain in Arabian affairs. The postscript, added for the reprint of 2000, is labelled 'Envoi'. This lamented leave-taking is for the pre-oil world of Oman, as, 'sure enough, oil was found at Fahud' (157). The idyllic Omani landscapes depicted were obsolete to a new-fangled nation built from oil money. Even the Sultan would no longer be required; shipped off to die in England in 1972. The journey which Morris had participated in and publicised became the catalyst of change for Oman. With that motorised jaunt, the borders of Oman could be drawn, the concessions and preparations for oil production undertaken by British-based companies. Writing at the end of the twentieth century, Morris notes, 'the past had vanished like a dream: and like a painted dream, half a lifetime on, does our own progress across Oman seem to me today' (158). The final words echo the nostalgia which Thesiger expressed on returning to that same region of Arabia in 1977, a quarter of a century after he had last journeyed there. He saw *Arabian Sands* (1959) as a 'memorial to a vanished past, a tribute to a once magnificent people'.[45] Both Morris and Thesiger had glimpsed the future of Arabia and both could only lament the loss of the past. In a matter of years, lifestyles consistent for millennia underwent seismic shifts. For the traveller, this was an Arabia that needed redefinition.

*

In *Arabia: Through the Looking Glass* (1979), Jonathan Raban traces his path to discovering this modern, mechanised and oil-rich Arabia of the 1970s. He commences his journey on the Earls Court Road in London. He has read of the Arabs from the 'classic "British Arabists"' but now searches in vain for them, struggling 'to pick out Doughty-Arabs or Lawrence-Arabs or Thesiger-Arabs among the new nomads of the Earls Court Road'.[46] Instead, what Raban observes are:

> People who looked as if they might have stepped out of Thesiger, but who wore cufflinks and wristwatches which together would have accounted for a year's substantial English salary ... they were a people whom the English thought they knew, and who had suddenly turned into bewildering strangers. (16)

Raban sets out to rectify matters. He tries to learn Arabic, goes to a new Arabic nightclub and, finally, heads off for the Gulf.

In Qatar, oil money has brought a 'wailing six-lane highway' beside which rests a muddled modern detritus of 'crushed Pepsi cans, discarded Frigidaires, torn chunks of motor tyre, cardboard boxes, broken fan-belts lying in the dust like snakes, the building rubble, polystyrene packing-blocks, and a rather long-dead goat' (70). Raban recognises it as a product of the 'careless absentmindedness of the very rich. No one leaves more squalor in his wake than a passing millionaire' (71). The remnants of the past are just about visible amidst the mess: 'A very pregnant, yellow, vulpine bitch - a degenerate descendent of the Saluki family - bared its teeth at me from the heap of rubbish which it was defending' (71). The creature may have an honourable ancestry but is now a mutant variant of that family, devoid of its once proud heritage and left to scavenge scraps discarded by a fast-developing Doha.

In Doha museum, Raban finds a vestige of Qatar's cultural past: a Bedouin tent. Everything is arranged as though a family still lived beneath the camel hair. Their clothes, muskets and household utensils rest as they should: 'The coffee-pot stood over the ashes of a fire' (81). Yet the Bedu themselves are absent. It is as though the inhabitants of this lost world have been relocated, leaving their home and its contents to the eyes of modern Doha. It is a popular exhibition; a glance at the world before oil, before cars and money. In a section on Bedouin customs, Qatari families gaze at mirrored counterparts. Raban observes the visitors:

Fathers went on ahead with their sons, busy with explanations. The masked women and their daughters were left behind with time to gaze and dawdle. They stood absorbed in front of waxwork figures who looked exactly like themselves. From the illuminated glass cabinets the same masked faces stared back; they wore the same gold necklets and bracelets, the same black robes and shawls. *Women in Typical Qatari Costume. A Bedouin Wedding. A Sheikh's Family.* Their own everyday bangles had been laid out on beds of black velvet and softly backlit. (81-2)

The distinctions between the old and the new are subtle. In the blink of an eye, those who once lived nomadic lives in the desert have been transplanted into the city, pampered with modern accoutrements. They glance back into the homes which their ancestors inhabited and see people who look like themselves. Yet the tents, the desert, have been abandoned. If it were not for the petrodollar, the Qatari families would not be visitors to a museum gazing at a lost lifestyle but still living it. Elsewhere in the museum are more mechanical exhibits. There are two 1940s Cadillacs and a British army truck. Though only thirty years old, the vehicles are such distant cousins to the cars which race along the highways of the Gulf that they deserve their positions in the exhibition. They are simply the past, just as the Bedu tents are. The fact that they are from a past so recent means nothing to a land and people undergoing such rapid and profound change: 'In Qatar more or less anything that happened before 1950 belongs to legend' (83).

When Raban heads to the desert he mistakes a Bedouin encampment for a 'used-car lot' (101). The sight is far removed from the idealised example of Bedouin life he witnessed in the museum. Undaunted, Raban draws on the romantic depictions of previous British travellers: 'Remembering Lawrence and Thesiger and the legendary hospitality of the bedu, I stopped the car. From somewhere inside this great scrapheap, dogs set up a ferocious yowling, and a young man waved his fist and shouted at me to go away' (101). The Bedu beloved by a past generation of travellers have been replaced with a modern version: a bastardised and brutalised collection of people who have missed out on the oil wealth. Instead of tents, they now have new homes: 'the carcasses of old automobiles had been hammered together to make temporary shelters' (101). They now carry out a marginalised existence, living literally within the discarded metal cages of the modern age. Though Raban does not make the comparison, these Bedouin can be seen in the same way as the dog on the rubbish heap beneath the motorway. Just as the creature is a 'degenerate descendent' of a saluki, so these modern day vagabond Bedu are the vestiges of once venerated desert tribesmen.

Away from the museum, Raban meets another side of cultural life in Doha. Abdel Rahman is *the* Qatari playwright. His play *Umm Ziin* charts the loss of traditional Qatari life to the ways of the West and the emergence of the oil industry. It offers the modern Qatari audience 'a romantic explanation of their present boredom and sense of disconnection' (117). They were children of the petroleum age, and they had already begun to eschew the financial advantages it had brought them. The lives of their grandparents were seen 'with more or less unqualified nostalgia' (117). Raban is quick to recognise that the vision is not new:

If Wilfred Thesiger had ever written plays, he might have been the author of *Umm Ziin*, and I found it sad that a Qatari audience should subscribe so readily to this (I had thought peculiarly Western) mythology of their own loss and corruption. (117)

Both Thesiger and a Qatari theatre audience depict Bedouin life in romanticised and idealised frameworks. The recognition that the Bedu had survived by eking out a bare existence from the desert lands is clouded with heroic images born of modern opulence. Raban comments that, 'it is one of the privileges of the rich to idolize poverty from a safe distance' (117). It is a charge laid at the feet of both Thesiger and the Qatari audience.

In Abu Dhabi, Raban sets off once more to discover the Bedu. He follows the footsteps of previous travellers but into the modern day dwellings that have replaced the tents: 'All over the emirate, the nomads who had been the companions of Thesiger, Philby and Bertram Thomas now lived on new breezeblock estates in the desert' (134). At Al Ain, a town on the border of the Empty Quarter, he enters an unprepossessing house that appears 'no bigger than a slab-sided concrete garage' (138). Inside, he finds a spacious courtyard with a garland of trees. The wooden home is raised from the ground, carpeted and bathed in splashes of sunlight: 'Vines and acacias, set against white stucco, formed a kind of living wallpaper' (138). Raban is quite taken with the graceful beauty of the modern Bedouin abode. The old man of the family explains how life has dramatically altered in six years: 'They had been very poor; there had been no television, no motor cars. Now – he praised Allah and Sheikh Zayed [ruler of Abu Dhabi] – they had this fine house; they had "a.c."; life was very good; they wanted for nothing' (140). Raban will not leave them at peace with this idyllic experience of modern existence. Were they not afraid that the evils of the cities, of the urban world, could come to Al Ain? Raban talks of 'thuggery, isolation and family breakdown' (141). The men and boys of the family listen politely:

Nothing like that, they assured me, would ever happen here. It was obvious that they thought I was telling improbable travellers' tales. Yet they had come much further than I had. Six years away from being desert nomads, they were talking confidently about careers in engineering and medicine ... they gave every sign of having adapted gracefully to a life in which Modern Tissues, the Range Rover, the twin-tub washing machine, two televisions, floral Thermos flasks, air travel and the local Hilton were taken perfectly for granted. (141)

These Bedouin emerge not as figures lost in a modern Arabia but as a people glad to accept the vital improvements in their living conditions. Their homes and their lives have been stabilised with the comforts that petrodollars have provided. In a few years, the nomadic realities of hunger and hardship have been replaced with the possibility of life away from the Arabian sands. While Thesiger may despair at the changes wrought so rapidly over Arabia, these Bedu celebrate. Their vision of a pre-oil Arabia is far less tainted with nostalgia. Their memories of desert life recall a more impoverished existence, a far tougher reality.

5

WOMEN IN ARABIA

On returning to the raft we heard that an English Pasha had just ridden into the town and that he was coming to visit us. He had met Hassan, who had been buying supplies in the bazaars, and the following conversation had ensued, which Hassan now repeated for our benefit.

ENGLISH PASHA. Who are you?
HASSAN. I am a cavasse. [guard]
ENGLISH PASHA. Who is your Pasha?
HASSAN. Victoria Pasha.
ENGLISH PASHA. Where is he?
HASSAN. She is sitting on the raft.
ENGLISH PASHA. What is she doing here?
HASSAN. She is floating to Baghdad.
ENGLISH PASHA. Where did she come from?
HASSAN. She came out of England.
ENGLISH PASHA. Is she alone?
HASSAN. No, she has a friend, who is not her sister, neither is she her servant.
ENGLISH PASHA. Give the ladies my salaams and say that I will call upon them.

X and I looked at one another. The meeting of an Englishman under such circumstances is no doubt, in one sense, an excitement; so would it be to meet a tiger in an English country lane. In a jungle, now, one expects a tiger, and being prepared for his attack, does not resent it. In the same way one is prepared to meet an Englishman on common ground in England, but, in an Asiatic wild, one is not prepared for the onslaught and one is therefore taken at a disadvantage. It was ten days since we had seen ourselves, as the Man would see us, in a glass (and then it was only a missionary's glass), and we had lost nearly all our hairpins in the crevices of the raft.

'Is my face as red as yours?' said X.

The question was evidently the outcome of the thoughts which assailed her mind during the few moments' silence in which we had gazed at each other, wondering whether we really looked like that too.

'Your face is all right,' I said, 'it's only red in patches; but your hair is disgraceful. How's mine?'

'It's all right,' said X, critically, 'it's only coming down in patches. But there is no time to do anything; here it is; we must brazen it out.'

A young Englishman was boarding the raft; he was spick and span, shaved, brushed, a clean collar, and polished boots.

'You must excuse me for calling upon you in this dishevelled manner,' he said as we shook hands, 'but travellers have to come as they are; I daresay you can sympathise,' and he glanced round at our *ménage*.

X laughed. 'Oh, as far as that goes,' she said, 'we are all in the same boat.'

'Raft,' I corrected in a nervous flutter.

The Young Man looked at me and smiled. I realised that he thought I was trying to make a cheap joke, such as one might have been capable of in the country lane.

'I must introduce myself,' he went on. 'I am Captain T----- of V-----. I am on my way there now. It's strange you should just have arrived to-day as I was crossing the river ...'

I murmured something about tea and fled into the men's hut, where Arten was boiling the kettle.

'Arten,' I stammered out in broken Turkish, 'the English Pasha will have tea with us. You must bring the cups clean. The English never have dirty cups.'[1]

It is 1904. Louisa Jebb and Victoria Buxton float down the Euphrates towards Baghdad on a raft constructed from 260 goatskins. *By Desert Ways to Baghdad* (1908) tells of their journey over Ottoman lands. They travel as independent women, with a hired Turkish guard and cook. They know little Turkish and no purpose but adventure. They are neither spinsters nor colonial wives, but single women in their early thirties. Up river, they have already faced armed Kurdish bandits only to draw their own revolvers and escape. Yet the appearance of an Englishman requires that they return to Edwardian social niceties. The Englishman leaves after 'about half an hour' for his camp. As soon as he has departed, the women revert to their self-assured ways. They deride the captain for having a 'five-course dinner' awaiting him and 'a looking-glass hung on the wall of his tent, and hot water and a clean towel'. Life for the colonial forces is all laid on. Not so for the traveller. As a final dig, the narrative of the scene concludes: 'And that's what a man calls roughing it!' (214). It is Jebb and Buxton who really rough it in Arabia.

This shifting of gender roles creates confusion. In the opening conversation between Hassan and the Englishman, the statement by Hassan that his Pasha is 'Victoria' goes unheard. Not expecting to hear of a woman travelling in such parts, the Englishman replies 'Where is he?' It is the first and only time that the name of X is mentioned in the text. In the chaos of the moment, the narrator has accidentally inserted her companion's forename. Why Victoria Buxton should feel the need to disguise her identity can only be guessed at. Perhaps she felt her role as an independent woman traveller through Turkey and Arabia might damage her character or name. There is a further complication to the scene in the dialogue between Hassan and the Englishman. It is a conversation recounted to the reader third-hand, apparently passed down from Hassan to Louisa Jebb and subsequently to the reader. The process introduces a sense of fictionality. Were the words actually spoken as recorded? The dialogue seems a construction, one fashioned from the actuality of the meeting between Hassan and the Englishman.

As the two women compare states of dishevelment, the Englishman arrives. He is confronted with two wild women. They are free travellers in Arabia, unlike himself who is there with British military forces. When Jebb declares to the cook Arten, 'the English never have dirty cups', she refers only to the English visitor, not herself and X. By using dirty cups previously on the voyage they have shed something of their national self, but with the arrival of an Englishman for afternoon tea, the cups must be clean. As independent travellers, neither woman need adopt the model of the Edwardian woman as a preserver of standards of respectability. Yet the arrival of the English Captain signals an enforced return to the social norms of their home society: with comical alarm the women scamper to replace a facade of gentility and domestic decorum. The two women have been liberated by the process of travel, able to ignore the requirements of behaving like English ladies. For ten days, they have been freed from social constraints. They have not looked in a mirror, nor spent time on their hair or facial appearance. The presence of Hassan and Arten has not necessitated a concern for maintaining 'correct' dress: the Oriental male does not demand a feminised self from the two travellers. Their sense of gender returns with distinct suddenness only with the unannounced appearance of the unnamed and unwelcome Englishman.

This depiction of two unmarried, strong-minded English women travelling through Arab lands in the early twentieth century makes the text remarkable. Sara Mills envisaged reading certain women travel writers as 'proto-feminist' whose texts 'have strong narrators and where narrative incident is the focus of attention'.[2] Louisa Jebb's travelogue certainly meets these criteria. Jebb and Buxton had met at Newnham College, Cambridge. Coming from the upper reaches of British society may have offered the financial freedom to travel, but few women travelled with the independent spirit which they showed. However, Cheryl McEwan has stressed the need to 'avoid celebrating proto-feminist heroines ... forsaking a critical understanding of the part they [women travellers] played in imperialism and the production of imperial knowledge'.[3] While Jebb and Buxton may have actively avoided the imperial world of the British during their time in Arabia, *By Desert Ways to Baghdad* was republished by Nelson in 1912 as a one shilling pocket-edition which proved a popular read for British troops stationed in Mesopotamia during the First World War.[4] The tale of two young Englishwomen not only raised a smile amongst those soldiers, it served to encourage them. If two lone Englishwomen could cope with Eastern ways, then surely a serving British soldier can? Even apparently independent travelogues such as *By Desert Ways to Baghdad* have a degree of colonial connection.

The field of women's travel writing began to receive attention in the 1970s with Virago reprinting earlier travelogues, allowing a process of rediscovery to get underway. Since then, some critics have looked to define a style of women's, as opposed to men's, writing, with little success. A number of anthologies which have been valuable in illustrating the quantity of women travellers have also reinforced the stereotype of the eccentric spinster, doing little to explore the nature of women's travel writing and merely recycling various unconventional travellers.[5] Women travelled to Arabia, as they did elsewhere, for a wide variety of reasons. Some, such as Louisa Jebb, travelled independently; others had more defined roles as colonial wives, missionaries, travel writers or archaeologists. What can be stated is that the existence of a British imperial network in Arabia enabled and assisted British women travellers, as well as men, to explore the region.

This chapter examines the ways in which women travellers related to that British imperial presence in Arabia. Many lived within the structures of that world, actively supporting and strengthening its hold in Arabia. Others, like Jebb and Buxton, chose to travel separately, beyond those confines. Their imperial associations are slight when compared to the distinctly colonial travellers Gertrude Bell and Freya Stark. Each travelled independently, yet both actively supported British imperial intelligence. Then there are those travellers that who can be termed colonial wives. Unlike most wives, the figures of Mabel Bent, Violet Dickson and Doreen Ingrams travelled alongside their husbands into Arabian lands rarely seen by European eyes. They helped provide valuable information to the process of imperial governance. After having traced the theme of the colonial connection between women travellers and their voyages into Arabia, I will examine various depictions of the harem and the women's quarters, where women travellers have exclusive access. The chapter closes with a view of the one writer who holds the distinctive position of having travelled as both a man and a woman in Arabia: James/Jan Morris adds a unique perspective to any discussion of the role of gender in travel writing.

*

When Margaret Fountaine began travelling with her sister, Rachel, around Europe in the 1890s her interest was in butterflies and men. Her collection of lepidoptera and amorous relationships expanded as she ventured further from the rectory in Norwich where she grew up. By 1901, she had moved beyond Europe and was alone in Beirut. On a carriage from Beirut to Damascus she met a young Syrian who offered to be her dragoman to the city. His name was Khalil Neimy. Together they explored Damascus and its surrounds, heading up Mount Kassioun where Fountaine 'found a very good form of the fiery red *M. Didyma*'.[6]

On the journey to Baalbek, Neimy kissed Fountaine 'repeatedly on [her] hands and arms'. Being in a '"loose" mood', Fountaine made no action to halt him and the next few days were filled with 'blind entreaties and mad infatuation' (125). Soon after, Fountaine recognised her duplicitous role as an English woman with an Arab lover:

> Later that afternoon I found myself talking with Miss Stowell, the English missionary here in Baalbek, and for the first time I began acting that double part which I kept up so well during the whole rest of time that I was in this country ... And as I sat talking to Miss Stowell I was again a high-minded, honourable, Englishwoman; the thought that on the previous day I had almost sunk to the level of being the mistress of my dragoman could not live in the pure atmosphere of the British Syrian School House. (126)

The notions of being an Englishwoman and in love with an Arab are irreconcilable. Fountaine is the guest of British missionaries in Baalbek. Miss Stowell is part of a growing number of women who are arriving in Arabia engaged in religious and educational work for evangelical organisations. The two women are linked by their nationality, but that is all. Fountaine is soon engaged to marry a Syrian man. She is thirty-nine; he is twenty-four.

Her travel is extraordinary in that she journeys as a lone Englishwoman with a Syrian lover. The frankness of her diaries about their embraces, detailing how they kissed and how she struggled within herself to hold from having sex with him is part of what makes them unique. In Jerusalem in 1901, she tells how 'we went very near the brink' and though she 'longed to give him the delight he sought from me', she asked him to go away (139). These sentiments, expressed to the secluded confession of the diary, read as strikingly overt for a middle-aged Victorian lady, daughter of a clergyman, particularly as they concern a man so socially and culturally removed from her own world. The narrative is distinctly a personal confession, not written for an audience. Fountaine agrees to marry but then discovers Neimy is already married. When English friends hear of her feelings for Neimy, they illustrate what life would be like as his wife in English society whether it be at home or abroad. Mr Segall, a missionary in Damascus, tells of an English woman who married a Syrian and later turned to the British Council 'for protection' only to be refused 'as she was no longer a British subject' (144). The amorous wanderings of Victorian ladies were not to be supported. Fountaine sees the matter as 'merely another incident of the injustice of the laws concerning women in this world' (144-5). She may have begun her life in Arabia closely affiliated with the world of the British evangelical movement, but she is forced away by her relationship with Neimy. An Englishwoman cannot marry an Arab, even if he is a Christian. It is British colonial society which has propped up her independent explorations into northern Arabia in search of butterflies, yet that society swiftly shuns her when she chooses a native as a lover.

Fountaine's diaries tell of a woman who is born to a respectable English rural life and who spends most of her days travelling the world with a Syrian dragoman fifteen years her junior and many rungs beneath her on the social ladder. They had 'escaped the cares and worries of matrimony' (155). In the pursuit of butterflies she had an excuse to continue to travel the world and she did so with Neimy for some twenty-seven years. Her travels only became known with the opening of her diaries in 1978, one hundred years after they were begun. She had stipulated that period of delay before the twelve volumes, 'each roughly the size and thickness of a London telephone directory' (14), could be opened to the public eye.

For Rosita Forbes, there were no such concerns over self-publicity. Twice married to British army husbands, Forbes changed her name from the simple, homespun 'Joan' to the more exotic 'Rosita' and embarked on a life of travels and travelogues beginning in 1920 with her trek through the Sahara desert of Libya and Egypt to the oases of Kufra and Siwa.[7] In *The Secret of the Sahara* (1921), Forbes charted the journey made alongside the Egyptian Ahmed Hassanein. Divorced from her first husband, Forbes travels as an independent Englishwoman disguised as a local. While it is Hassanein who guides them through the desert, it would be Forbes who later took the praise for enduring a gruelling thousand mile journey. By the end, both are desperate to leave the sand behind:

My nails were broken, my nose blistered. My only European dress had been hidden for months at the bottom of a sack of bully beef tins, yet I was sincere when I echoed Hassanein's vicious 'Civilization, hamdulillah!' as he stuffed his kufiya into a corner of his knapsack and pulled out a fez![8]

In these final words of the book, Forbes's concern for her appearance
contrasts with the achievement of crossing vast expanses of the desert.
In cheerfully sincere manner, Forbes presented herself as a glamorous
Englishwoman who had ventured into the unknown regions of Arabia
for the joy of the experience. The style proved a success. Through the
1920s and 30s her later books sold well, though never rekindling the
sales of *The Secret of the Sahara*. Her fame brought Forbes into contact
with the elite echelons of British colonial Arabia.

It is a pattern which can be seen repeated in other independent
women travellers in Arabia. With the success of their first travel text,
the travellers become accepted by organisations such as the Royal
Geographical Society, and so known across the network of imperial
nodes which spanned the region. Gertrude Bell and Freya Stark are the
best-known examples of this process. Geographical and political
knowledge of Arabia in the 1920s and 30s was gained by travellers as
well as by those specifically in the pay of the British government. As
Forbes found celebrity with her Saharan travels, she came into the
sights of British diplomatic circles. In the secretive build up to
Forbes's 1922 journey to the south-west of Arabia, she ignored orders
that the region was off limits. But it was not only British officials who
found her difficult; at Sabya in Yemen the Emir Idrisi needed nine
hours to persuade Forbes that no stranger was permitted to head
further north.[9]

While the British establishment was uncomfortable with her
activities, Forbes had become a traveller whose escapades provided a
good deal of invaluable information.[10] In 1924, Forbes was attempting
to team up with Harry St John Philby in a venture to cross the Rub' al
Khali. Though the plan never materialised, it serves to highlight some
similarities between the two writers. By that time both were operating
beyond the grasp of British authorities. In Aden, with their proposed
travel known to officials, Forbes was forced to abandon the venture
and headed for Abyssinia. When she wrote to Philby in 1925, she
noted that 'it will be very difficult for either you or me to get into
Arabia "agin the Govt". We are too well known.'[11] While Forbes did
not take Philby's dramatic path of renouncing allegiance to Britain, she
was certainly not averse to working against the grain of the
establishment in order to reach her own designated destination. Unlike
other successful, single, female travellers, such as Bell or Stark, she did
not fall happily into the embrace of establishment figures across the
region. That she ventured 'agin the Govt' makes her exceptional

Rosita Forbes as a 'Beduin Sheikh'.

amongst British women travellers to Arabia. That she did so, however, does not deny the fact that she exploited her position as a traveller free to explore colonised lands with relative impunity, charting an unknown part of the world and documenting its peoples and places for the imperial readership back in Britain.

Rosita Forbes travelled in a manner that few women had done before. With lipstick and charisma, she was an attractive, distinctly feminine traveller through 1920s' Arabia. Forbes's emergent form of independent woman traveller was not celebrated by some Arabists, as it was by her British readership. On reading *The Secret of the Sahara*, Gertrude Bell questioned not only the depicted role of Hassanein but Forbes's abilities in Arabic.[12] If Forbes represented a novel form of women traveller, born from an evolving female identity in the 1920s, Bell was a distant cousin, more closely related to the Victorian travellers. Bell and Forbes were of different eras; if from the same higher echelons of English society, they had been born a generation apart. More significant was the relationship they established with colonial governance. As the secret plans emerged of Forbes's abortive attempt to cross the Empty Quarter with Philby, Bell 'voiced the general government frustration', being as strident in her condemnation as other British officials.[13]

*

In *The Desert and the Sown* (1907) Gertrude Bell had established her reputation as a travel writer. The book drew acclaim, detailing the journey of a lone Englishwoman in her late thirties traversing the plains of the Hauran and Greater Syria. Bell was an accomplished scholar and linguist, who moved amongst the peoples of Arabia not in disguise but openly as an Englishwoman, dictating her needs in precise, immaculate Arabic to both the locals and the collection of men who formed her entourage. She fitted easily into the ancestry of British travellers who had made their way across Arabia. She even secured the use of Mikhail, the cook who had accompanied Mark Sykes on his adventures only a few years before.[14] A contemporary reviewer of the book noted that 'women make the best travellers' in that they avoid presenting a threat to natives. According to Professor Lane-Poole, Bell 'went proudly as an Englishwoman, and she had no cause to regret it in a land which was ringing with the praises of Lord Cromer's splendid work in Egypt and of longings that his rule might be extended over Syria'.[15] Bell would certainly have endorsed such sentiments concerning British imperialism in Arabia.

Her interest in archaeology distinguished her as a woman traveller who ventured away from home not for health or adventure but the manly pursuit of scientific endeavour. Bell was in Arabia to explore meaning to the monuments and structures of the past, as well as to map the peoples of the present. This trespass on to the traditional grounds of the male traveller was not accompanied with the feminine manner of someone like Rosita Forbes. Indeed, Gertrude Bell appears as a distinctly masculine form of Englishwoman in Arabia, striding singly across the desert without a husband or a local amour to accompany her. Instead, she had her dragoman, cook and other servants. It may well be the vision of Bell as the intrepid traveller heading alone into the vast wilds of the colonial world that made her appeal to certain English male travellers. Wilfred Thesiger is said to have considered her 'the only true female explorer of the Middle East'.[16] It may be fairer to state that Bell was a female explorer of Arabia whose only choice at that time was to travel in the form dictated by male forefathers. That meant stepping on certain toes. Mark Sykes described her as a 'silly chattering windbag of conceited, gushing, flat-chested, man-woman, globe-trotting, rump-wagging, blethering ass!'.[17] Much of the diatribe may refer to Bell's personality, but it is her gender which also grates on Sykes. In preparing to venture into Arabia alone, she was crossing defined societal boundaries. A woman could partake in exploration as the partner of a man, as Lady Anne Blunt or Isabel Burton had done, but Bell was forging a trail single-handedly. Yet as a woman stepping on to a male-designated track, she was certainly not a rebellious or antagonistic newcomer. Her family credentials were first-class, as was her degree from Lady Margaret Hall, Oxford. Her support for British colonial policy in the Middle East was always secure, as was her belief that women should not be given the vote.

Amurath to Amurath (1911) secured Bell's position as a female traveller extraordinaire. The text is a record of a journey that starts at Aleppo and ends back in Konia, Turkey. From Aleppo, Bell heads to the archaeological site of the Hittite capital at Carchemish, then travels along the left bank of the Euphrates down through Mesopotamia to Baghdad. From Baghdad she traces the Tigris upstream to Mosul, meandering across Asiatic Turkey to arrive finally in Konia. The preface takes the form of a letter to Lord Cromer of Egypt offering unqualified support and praise for his imperial policy. Bell has just travelled through the provinces of a distinctly dying Ottoman Empire at a time when the Young Turks movement has sparked into life. She sees her book as a chronicle of five months 'suspense and even of terror' as she travelled through a land where 'constitutional government trembled in the balance and was like to be outweighed by the forces of disorder, by fanaticism, massacre and civil strife'. Instead, in Egypt she sees a very different state of foreign occupation, as will a future reader of her text, who: 'Remembering that the return of prosperity to the peoples of the Near East began with your administration in Egypt, [...] will understand why I should have ventured to offer it, with respectful admiration, to you.'[18]

By 1924 and the publication of the second edition, Bell had moved from being a lone female explorer of Arabia to an essential element in British colonial administration. The transition from traveller to imperial agent was not such a dramatic one. Bell was born to the class from which the Empire drew its (normally male) leaders. During the First World War, she was appointed to the role of Oriental Secretary to the High Commissioner, initially based in Cairo and subsequently in Mesopotamia, under Sir Percy Cox. The position was no doubt helped by the personal letter of recommendation from Lord Cromer:

> Miss Gertrude Bell who is a great friend of mine is about to go to Egypt ... she is the daughter of Sir Hugh Bell, who is well known in English politics and is a great iron-master in Middlesbrough. I have known her for many years and she knows more about the Arabs than almost any other living Englishman or woman.[19]

Once secured in the British administration of Iraq, Bell was soon writing intelligence reports on the nature of the Arab tribes of the region. When a collection of essays entitled *The Arab of Mesopotamia* was anonymously published in 1918 by the Government Press in Basra, it was generally assumed to be the work of a select band of unnamed colonial males. In fact it was entirely penned by Gertrude Bell. Her glee at this gentle deception is apparent from a letter written to her stepmother, Florence Bell: 'Why, yes, of course I wrote all of the Arab of Mesopotamia. I've loved the reviews which speak of all the practical men who were the anonymous authors, etc. It's fun being practical men, isn't it.'[20] Bell's position as a high-ranking colonial administrator was entirely anomalous with her being a woman. That her work was read as the efforts of 'practical men' is hardly surprising considering she was the only woman to be in such a position within imperial governance. For Bell, the moment was a proof she had transgressed the societal boundaries imposed on Georgian women. She too could be of genuine, practical value serving Britain's imperial project in Arabia.

Her elevation in the imperial ranks was smoothed by a journey made to Hayil in central Arabia between 1913 and 1914. Though initially the Foreign Office opposed the expedition on the grounds they could not be responsible for her safety, the trip provided the British government with up-to-date intelligence on the state of Rashid and Saud tribes. Bell was held virtual prisoner by the Rashid in Hayil for almost two weeks. The fact that she was a woman actively worked to her advantage as 'during her short imprisonment at Hayil (where only women could visit her) she obtained highly valuable information from a Circassian woman who had been a concubine to the last Emir'.[21] As a woman, Bell drew less suspicion than a male traveller and so gathered information on the region with impunity. Women travellers were not seen as political agents but as something of a novelty. Bell was held not because she was a threat but because she was trespassing. As a female traveller deep in central Arabia, Bell could operate as a far more effective imperial spy than any man could. She was swiftly rewarded for her enterprise, the mission gaining acclaim for her explorative abilities and respect for her expertise on the region. She was not shy of making her achievements or political opinions known. On her return from Arabia in 1914, she wrote to *The Times* concerning the matter of Captain Shakespear's latest journey, adding an account of her own adventure to Hayil:

> The Shammar capital had not been visited, so far as my knowledge goes, by any European since 1893. In the interval the political conditions had undergone considerable alteration ... My belief is that Ibn Saud is now the chief figure in central Arabia, although the Ottoman Government was still pursuing its traditional policy of subsidising and supplying arms to the Rashid.[22]

As usual, Gertrude Bell's instinct on Arabian affairs was right on the mark. The Saud tribe rose in power in the region, finally defeating the Rashid in 1921 and establishing Ibn Saud as ruler over much of Arabia.

Bell never published a full account of her expedition to Hayil. Her time was concentrated on her position within the politics of Arabia rather than on travel writing. In Cairo, she worked alongside T. E. Lawrence, cataloguing in precise detail the information she had collected on the Arab tribes. Her travel knowledge was destined for British intelligence sources rather than the general public. When the true story of that adventure to Hayil emerged, it was presented not by Bell but by her old friend, the archaeologist D. G. Hogarth, in a lecture to the Royal Geographical Society in April 1927. Bell had died some nine months before, in Baghdad, due to a deliberate overdose of barbiturates.[23] In his lecture, Hogarth presented a factual, scientific account of her journey to Hayil noting the latitude observations she had made. One footnote to the published transcript of the lecture comments: 'Miss Bell carried a 3-inch transit theodolite, in whose use she had been instructed at the R.G.S. Judged by a subsequent observation at Hayil, which, when computed, agreed with another obtained by Charles Huber, her latitudes may be relied upon.'[24]

It seemed that Bell had been presented with the greatest possible accolade in that she was now accepted as a traveller in the mould of a man. Her accurate use of scientific equipment was the final benchmark. *The Times* reported the lecture the next day, again noting the scientific nature of her work: 'She had kept her bearings and times of marching continuously, taken several latitude observations, and recorded systematically the readings of barometer and thermometer. These are no mean achievements of a solitary woman in a dangerous land.'[25] It is as though Bell was being praised for being manlier as a traveller than could be hoped for; she had finally managed to throw off the yoke of her gender. The adoption of a scientific approach not only provided detailed geographical information for British imperial needs but drew Gertrude Bell closer to contemporary male travel writers.

*

From the very beginning of her travels in Arabia, Freya Stark seemed to follow a path beaten by Gertrude Bell. In 1928, she travelled by donkey with her friend Venetia Buddicom south from Damascus into the Jebel Druze, on a route that mirrored one taken by Bell in 1905.

Stark had read Bell's *The Desert and the Sown* (1907), no doubt using the account to plan her own adventure. Stark never acknowledged the fact, nor the value of the role model which Bell offered as a woman traveller in Arabia, but the parallels in the careers of the two women are clear.[26] Freya Stark emerged as a successor to Bell once her travelogues of journeys into southern Arabia in the 1930s became widely read and admired.

Like Margaret Fountaine, Stark found her introduction into Arabia as a guest of Protestant missionaries. She arrived in late 1927 at Broumana, a small Christian enclave situated above Beirut, and spent four months there working on her Arabic and preparing for the adventure into Druze country planned for the following year.[27] Stark was a thirty-four-year-old single woman. In 1928, when French military police discovered Stark and Buddicom in the Druze village of Shabha, so began the first phase of her life as a traveller operating beyond the realm of the establishment. In that first instance, it was French authorities who found Stark as a peculiarly eccentric adventurer in their midst. For Stark, the experience provided the material with which to begin her life as a travel writer. She wrote up her time in the French garrison for the *Cornhill Magazine*.[28]

Two years later, Stark travelled to Baghdad, where she found herself an outsider to the British colonial community which had established itself in the Iraqi capital. She gained a reputation as a woman who preferred the company of men to that of the colonial wives, just as Bell had done a few years before. In *Beyond Euphrates*, Stark defines a stance quite distinct from the world of British colonialists:

> The general official attitude in Baghdad seemed to be that everyone and everything ... could be classified into a street of some sort, and an unhygienic one if Oriental. The Civil Service lived in a residential area, and thought it a poor sort of taste to enjoy anything outside: and if their 'man in the street' attitude towards the lovely and variegated world surprised me, it was nothing as to the astonishment with which I became aware of the British official attitude towards women.[29]

By the time that Stark wrote the second volume of her autobiography in 1950, she was firmly established as both a writer and traveller. In 1930, in Baghdad, she was very much an unknown figure, though one gaining a reputation as a daring and audacious woman. She

had compared herself to Gertrude Bell in an earlier letter to Herbert
Young, noting that Bell's enterprise to the Jebel Druze in 1905 was
accompanied by 'three baggage mules, two tents, and three servants'
and so declaring her own venture 'the more adventurous'.[30] Bell's
stature as a female traveller and Arabist could not be ignored. In
Baghdad, her legacy included the Archaeological Museum she had
founded. Yet Stark continually denied the influence of Bell, even
turning down an offer from a publisher to write Bell's biography with
the comment she was 'not very fascinated' by Gertrude Bell's life.[31]

The Southern Gates of Arabia (1936) confirmed Freya Stark's standing
as an accomplished travel writer. She had already received success and
praise for *The Valleys of the Assassins* (1934), but it was the tale of her
time on the incense routes of Yemen and the Hadhramaut which
captured critics and readers. Yet ultimately the tale is, as she herself
confesses, 'a record of failure'.[32] Stark was rescued by the RAF when
illness prevented her reaching the ancient town of Shabwa and
becoming the first European to set foot there. The tale of her
adventure certainly involves many mentions of her health problems; as
she enters deeper into the lands of the Hadhramaut, away from the
control of Aden, so the narrative is dominated by a depiction of her
diminishing strength. In Do'an, Stark meets a mother with a child sick
with measles. Never having had the illness, Stark knows she will catch
it. She duly does and is visited in her sick bed by a procession of local
faces: 'slaves and mistresses, beduin girls round-faced and healthier
than the townswomen, and old men and women in need of medicines'
(139).

The emergent theme of Stark's sickness ensures that the narrative is
concerned less with the lands which she is exploring than the people
who help to pass her days. This is a very different focus from the
Introduction which offers a brief survey of the region and a history of
its exploration, and from the opening chapters which detail the nature
of the landscape, offering longitude and latitude markers and scientific
details of the temperature and air pressure. In Chapter 10, Stark notes:
'At eleven-ten we reached the Murabba'a of Sarab and camped for
lunch. The temperature was 70° in the shade, the aneroid 24.1' (102).
The shift from matters exterior to those domestic is something
peculiarly Starkian. She incorporates a scientific approach into her text
while at other times focussing on areas where women have unique
access: the harem or women's quarters. Her strength as a lone

Englishwoman travelling in forbidding lands contrasts with her illness and need for rescue by the imperial might of the RAF.

Stark operated as a flamboyant and feminine traveller in Arabia for many years. Photographs abound of her in floral hats and dresses amidst numerous incongruous scenes. As her reputation grew, so Stark became less of an independent figure operating under the radar of British imperial considerations in Arabia. Instead, she aligned herself with colonial policy and was recruited to work with British intelligence in the Ministry of Information as a 'Middle East expert' at the outbreak of the Second World War. Her presence and the reaction to her work had a significant effect not only in shifting views on women's involvement in the region but in actually shaping the 'British imperial outlook'.[33] The evolution of Freya Stark from a figure independent from the colonial whole to one who is working with British intelligence demonstrates that relations between women travel writers and imperial concerns were well maintained by the 1930s.

*

By the end of the Second World War, there were other imperial matters for women travellers to consider. Eileen Bigland journeyed to Egypt soon after 1945, as a professional travel writer. Most of her time was spent in the various British-affiliated clubs of Cairo. Her inability to understand the 'thorny Palestine question' did not endear her to those Arabs she did meet. When Bigland suggested that a local woman was exaggerating the situation in Palestine, she was told: 'You English writers are all the same. You come to the Middle East, you see nothing, you are half asleep all the time, you go home and write nonsense – absolute nonsense!'[34] The same could be said of Barbara Toy and her escapades across Saudi Arabia a decade later. She was apparently keen to see the effects of oil on the lands and peoples of Arabia. What she in fact spent most time doing was travelling by Land Rover visiting English expatriates such as Philby and Violet and Harold Dickson.[35]

When Ethel Mannin travelled across the region in the early 1960s it was with a very different political outlook. As she stated to Hasim Jawad, the Iraqi Minister for Foreign Affairs: '... all my adult life I had been opposed to imperialism and had worked against it, and that I preferred this word to "colonialism" which had replaced it in recent years and which, I thought, tended to give a veneer of paternalism to the basic exploitation'.[36] Being from a working-class background and an active socialist, she sits distinct from the vast majority of her fellow women travellers. Mannin vehemently opposed British imperial rule in Arabia. She dedicated her book *A Lance for the Arabs* (1963) to the Palestinian refugees, her work intended to 'present to the West a general picture of the Middle East, with special reference to the Palestine tragedy' (17). This is no romantic jaunt through the desert. Mannin's work is an emotionally charged polemic on the state of the Palestinian people as she finds them scattered across the region. Her sincerity and sympathy drive the narrative. At Shatilla camp near Beirut she meets another dispossessed Palestinian:

> I asked that he be told that I knew my country was responsible for the creation of 'Israel', but that some of us had always been against it, always opposed Zionism, and that that was why I was there; that my intention was to write a book which would set forth the monstrous injustice which had been done to the Palestine Arabs. (211-12)

As an independent woman traveller to Arabia, Ethel Mannin stands alone and largely unknown. While Bell and Stark actively worked to support British imperial rule, Mannin raised a rare voice of dissent.

*

For the colonial wife, being an Englishwoman in Arabia generally meant something quite distinct from that of the independent traveller. As the experiences of Freya Stark in British Baghdad illustrate, wives of imperial administrators often took very little interest in native matters, and indeed strived to create in Arabia a world as English as possible. Violet Dickson arrived in Arabia in 1919 as the young wife of a British captain. She was soon to meet the imperial gang, initially staying with the Philbys in Baghdad for a few weeks and later living next door to Bertram Thomas in Hillah, south of Baghdad. When Gertrude Bell threw a dinner party in their honour there was a less generous welcome: 'The other guests were five senior Arab officials, and most of the conversation was in Arabic, but Miss Bell did make one loud remark in English to the effect that it was such a pity that promising young Englishmen went and married such fools of women.' Not only 'aloof and unprepossessing', Bell was 'not interested in women's conversation'.[37] So the colonial wife meets the intrepid female explorer. While Violet Dickson spent much of her time in the duties of housekeeping in Arabia, she also travelled with her husband, a political officer, meeting the tribes which Harold was to keep an eye on. She went on to spend over half a century living in Arabia, becoming a greatly respected figure in Kuwait where she remained even after the death of her husband.

The figure of Doreen Ingrams offers another example of an adventurous colonial wife. In the 1930s, she too travelled with her husband Harold, a political officer, visiting the tribes of the Hadhramaut while preparing the ground for what would become known as 'Ingrams' Peace'. Doreen Ingrams breached the divide between colonial wife and traveller, prepared to head off alone without fear for her safety. As such she was distinct from the colonial community who 'had no interest in the "natives", did not attempt to speak a word of Arabic, and were astonished if a compatriot did not conform to their way of life – bridge, tea parties, the exclusive British club'.[38] The practical matters of travelling as a woman in open desert lands are made plain. Sanitary towel disposal was 'always a problem', dealt with by scratching a hole and covering with stones: 'These memorial cairns were to be found all over the deserts of the Hadhramaut' (94). As for other toiletry issues, Doreen Ingrams 'followed the example of the ostrich and, having walked a good distance from the camp, turned my back on it, satisfied that if I could not see the bedouin they could not see me' (94). Though travelling with an adopted local girl and a young baby, the Ingram family climbed the ten-thousand-foot high Jebel Sumara when exploring Yemen. The children provided 'no deterrent for they could be carried in wooden boxes slung on either side of a mule' (121).

The format of husband and wife travellers had strong precedents. In the 1870s, Isabel Burton had followed her husband Richard to a life in Damascus. During the same period, Lady Anne and Wilfred Blunt explored vast areas of the northern Arabian desert together. Lesser known are the figures of Mabel and Theodore Bent, who travelled across much of southern Arabia in the 1890s. Theodore died of malaria four days after their return to England in 1897. Over the following years the account of their travels was written up by Mabel Bent, compiled from 'some lectures he had given before the Royal Geographical Society and the British Association', the notes of her recently departed husband and her own 'Chronicles' of their journeys.

In the preface, Mabel Bent noted the 'imperfect' nature of the book.[39] The implication is that Theodore would have written a better travelogue. Yet *Southern Arabia* was extremely well received. Providing up-to-date information on a relatively unknown area of Arabia, the work also had political value. In 1901, the work was recommended as useful reading for Percy Cox, then British Agent at Muscat, before he headed out to assess the range of the Sultan of Oman's territorial reach.[40] The Bents' exploration had actually been initiated by matters imperial. In 1893, the British government had 'suggested to them that "a survey of the Hadhramawt by an independent traveller would be useful"'.[41] By taking up the challenge, Mabel Bent became the first European woman to travel into the region.

*

Whether travelling as a wife or independently, the British woman traveller to Arabia was able to explore one arena barred to the male traveller. The opportunity to enter the harem of a household, the quarter reserved for women and children, provided a focus for many travelogues. By drawing on the true nature of the harem, much of the literature on the subject broke with the vision of an imagined, sensual world drawn by male artists and writers. Women had access to this place of male-generated myth. Lady Cobbold, who had converted to Islam, made a pilgrimage to the Holy Cities in 1933. She took time out from her record of that journey to address the nature of the harem. She notes: 'it is a sanctuary, but far from being a prison. Neither is it crowded with wives and ladies of easy virtue, as is so often imagined.'[42] Instead, the harem provided an environment where women travellers could find themselves as the observed rather than the observers. When Doreen Ingrams stopped at Hureidha in 1937, she found the household intrigued by her shoes, if disappointed at their lack of stature. Ingrams is told Freya Stark 'had much higher heels. In the name of God most high and the religion He glorifies, you couldn't walk in them they were so high'.[43] The uninhibited environment of the harem offered the chance for conversation on matters more personal than merely shoe height. Doreen Ingrams comments that she 'got used to being asked all sorts of intimate questions about my life with Harold'.[44]

Not all women used the opportunity to expel entrenched myths concerning Arabian households. In a collection of tales referring to the more exotic moments of her travels, Rosita Forbes details her meeting with a white slave. Searching for the British Consulate in Jeddah, Forbes relates how she accidentally arrived at a house where she took tea and heard of a girl who is described to her as 'white as your sister'. When questioned as to whether she is a European wife, she is informed the woman is a slave:

> 'But preferred of my master. She is very beautiful-----' and at that moment, the curtains parted and a girl who might have been born anywhere north of the Mediterranean, north even of the English Channel, came into the room. She had a clear, colourless skin and light brown hair. She looked tired. There were smudges under her eyes. Showing neither surprise nor interest, she came across to us and sank on to the divan. A couple of Ethiopians busied themselves about her comfort.
>
> The girl drooped against her pillows. She looked young and illogically dissipated, but when her eyes met mine, they were full of content. Clear gold they were. I've never seen anything quite like them.
>
> She wore only a transparent muslin corselet which left her breasts bare, and a length of silk, blue and rose, wound about her hips.[45]

The depiction of the slave girl is the same sensualised vision which nineteenth-century Romantic painters such as Jean-Léon Gérôme or Eugène Delacroix had painted. It is a particularly masculine vision of the harem, complete with a shocking image of a beautiful white girl trapped into a life of sexual servitude and captivity. The retelling of the event is dramatised by the sudden appearance of the girl, who emerges just as she is being described. The girl is suitably laconic; stripped down to an erotic tincture of dress to emphasise her sensuality.

*

Just as the harem offered an insight unique to women travellers, so the work of one writer has allowed an exclusive insight into the role of gender. James Morris wrote a number of travel texts on Arabia from the late 1950s up to 1972 when he underwent a sex change operation in Morocco, emerging as Jan Morris. Describing her as 'probably the greatest woman travel writer of the twentieth century', Susan Bassnett notes that in Morris's work 'assumptions about travel writing and gender are most seriously challenged'. If there are distinctions to be drawn between the writing of men and women as travellers then surely they should be apparent across the spectrum of Morris's output. However, 'reading the books written before and after 1972 it is impossible to distinguish markers of gender other than occasional references to clothing'.[46] The narrative of Morris's travel writing appears to be unaltered by her change of sex. The only variance which may be evident is a 'sense of liberation' which Morris has felt since 'becoming Jan' and which 'some critics have claimed to find apparent in my writing'.[47]

When she returned to Cairo in 1978, a place she had lived and explored as James, it was to write an essay for *Rolling Stone* magazine. There is no discursive difference to recognise that it is her first exploration of Cairo since her sex change. If a distinctly novel feeling exists to the city now, it may be put down to the inauguration of President Anwar Sadat as a more Western-leaning leader: 'Cairo has a dazzle to it now: a fairground dazzle, perhaps, with hustlers and red lights.'[48] Of course, the sense of being dazed and overwhelmed could also be due to her travelling the city for the first time as a woman. When Jonathan Raban meets Jan Morris during that stay in Cairo, he is keen to discover whether she has found the city any different. Morris thinks that the people seem 'much happier ... *much* brighter and more hopeful than I remember them'. Raban wonders if this new look to the people of Cairo isn't an indication of the 'difference between the temperaments of James and Jan' rather than a transformation by the city.[49] Cairo hasn't changed; Morris is merely more comfortable in her new gender.

In the world of Arabia, the role of British women travellers can best be assessed not merely by searching for reflections on a subjective positioning based on gender. Instead, the identification which individual women writers held with respect to the overarching aims of British imperial policy, and their attitudes to, and relationships with, the people and places of Arabia, provide a more fertile background for exploring their work as travel writers. The figure of Gertrude Bell stands out not only for the vitality of her travel narratives but for the fundamental role that she played in imperial administration. No other woman played such a decisive role in British imperial politics in Arabia. There are many other women travellers who helped create the structures of British colonialism, particularly the more intrepid colonial wives such as Violet Dickson and Doreen Ingrams. The anti-imperial stance of Ethel Mannin is a lonely one. Just as with their male counterparts, for much of the twentieth century, British women travellers found that a colonial network existed across the Arab world. Many, like Freya Stark, made extensive use of these imperial connections. The example of Louisa Jebb and Victoria Buxton seen eschewing the demands of Edwardian society illustrates how travel provided some women with a freedom from domestic dogmas. To a certain degree women had the greater potential to roam; while women travellers could explore the reality of the harem, men merely fantasised. But the unique example of Jan Morris perhaps offers the truest tenet on the issue of the traveller: it is the individual nature of the traveller and not their gender which dictates how they will travel.

6

BAGHDAD AND BEYOND

Nearly midnight. Iraqi Airways Jumbo Jet flight No. 238 from London is over the mountains of Turkish Kurdistan and tilting its nose towards Baghdad. 'One hour more,' says the air hostess, and raises a champagne bottle over my glass. I sip at it and slip back comfortably into the dream I have been enjoying since we flew over Istanbul – a dream that is evidently a bizarre mixture of two very old movies, *The Thief of Baghdad* and *A Thousand and One Nights*. In it, I float in a gleaming technicolour city of towering walls and arched gates, golden domes and minarets like sticks of candy. An unnaturally spangled crescent moon hangs in the sky. I am, as any dedicated filmgoer will tell you, in Baghdad, the City of the Caliphs, and the man in charge at the moment is the great Harun al Rashid.

That cruel-faced, thin-lipped man in robes and a green *burnous*, surrounded by hard-eyed courtiers and slaves bearing scimitars must be, surely, the mighty Harun himself – though he looks remarkably like the actor Conrad Veidt. A beautiful girl in see-through Oriental trousers belly-dances to the sound of tambourines, flutes, harps – and a few incongruous jazz saxophones. When she spots me her huge black eyes grow larger over her veil. Suddenly – uproar. Harun's slaves rush towards me, scimitars raised. Too late – but no! The girl is pulling me through a hidden doorway. I hear her voice – the voice of the fabulous Maria Montez – low and urgent in my ear. 'Queeckly,' she hisses ... We flee through the streets of Baghdad. Beyond the city gate (fortunately unbarred) a large expanse of water – and an island, gleaming under tinsel stars.

Thank God: a refuge! Vain hope. 'Zat is ze Forbeeden Island,' Miss Montez is breathing in my ear. 'You may not go zere.' 'Why not?' I scream. She looks at me in amazement: 'Because eet is forbeeden!' (The actual line, believe it or not, that Hollywood scriptwriters foisted upon her.) I jerk awake to find a large, kindly man with four gold rings on his uniform sleeve standing over me. 'I am Captain Saudi, your captain,' he says, smiling stolidly. The dream – and it is surely everyone's vision of Old Baghdad – self-destructs into the no-smoking section of Iraqi Airways flight No. 238.[1]

Gavin Young heads towards Baghdad accompanied by the luxurious accoutrements of air travel. It is 1978 and twenty-seven years since Young first came to Iraq to work in the shipping world of Basra. Now, as he returns once more to the region of Arabia he has come to know so well, the dreams that fill his comfortable journey are those born of technicolour wonderings. Young may have seen the streets of Baghdad many times before, but in his dreams the city is one cast from the Oriental imaginings of Hollywood. The detail of this vision of Baghdad consists of elements collated from a fantastical mediaeval landscape. There are 'golden domes' and 'minarets like sticks of candy' past which Young glides beside an 'unnaturally spangled crescent moon'. It is a surreal world where *The Wizard of Oz* meets Harun al Rashid; where 1940s Hollywood meets *Arabian Nights*. Young slips gently into this cinematic Arabia where nothing is quite true. The actress Maria Montez leads him by the hand from the scimitars of Harun's slaves through the alleyways of Baghdad. Yet Young is himself confused in plotting the elements of his dream. He sees it as a 'bizarre mixture of two very old movies, *The Thief of Baghdad* and *A Thousand and One Nights*' but Maria Montez was in neither of these films and the actor Conrad Veidt played Jafar, not Harun, in *The Thief of Baghdad*. Young has a contorted and disorientated version of matters. Montez did play Scheherazade (as a dancing girl, rather than storyteller) in *Arabian Nights*, another 1940s' technicolour fantasy. Perhaps that is where his heroine appears from. The blurred distinctions between the real and unreal that Young experiences aboard his Iraqi Airways flight end with the appearance of the pilot. The dream of Baghdad that has entertained Young since Istanbul has vanished in a puff of smoke, even within the no-smoking section of the airplane. It is, Young maintains, 'surely everyone's vision of Old Baghdad'. Even in an age of swift, modern, air transport.

In this chapter, I examine the *Arabian Nights* vision of Baghdad which British travellers hold and how that image is altered by their arrival in the city. The thoughts of those travelling in the late nineteenth and early twentieth centuries are contrasted with impressions of Baghdad once it has come under British occupation in 1917. In the second half of the chapter, I look at travel in the marshes of southern Iraq. Wilfred Thesiger headed there in 1950, eventually recording his travels in the district as *The Marsh Arabs* (1964). He was not always a lone travelling Englishman. Both Gavin Maxwell and Gavin Young travelled with Thesiger through the marshes for varying periods of time. Together their accounts form a triumvirate of texts on this unique quarter of Iraq in the 1950s. It is a collective vision of a part of Arabia that has largely vanished in the half century since they lived in its watery world.

The title Iraq, 'well-routed country', officially replaced the term Mesopotamia on the coronation of King Feisal on 23 August 1921.[2] Zaki Saleh states: 'Mesopotamia is the name the Greeks used for the land of The Two Rivers, but the inhabitants of the land have always called it Iraq.'[3] The term Turkish Arabia was employed before the First World War, though all three terms cover the same region of the three vilayets of Mosul, Baghdad and Basra defined by the Ottoman Empire. British colonial staff and travellers used the term Mesopotamia or 'Mespot' during the war. The region offered an overland route to India, with Basra being crucial for shipping and oil. Such was its strategic importance, British troops had taken the city as early as December 1914. Post-war, the value of Iraq to the imperial cause ensured the country became a British Mandate under the terms of the San Remo conference held in April 1920.

A new batch of British travelogues on Mesopotamia was published following the First World War, reporting directly on the new addition to the Empire. Many of the authors had been involved in the campaigns in the region and noted the changes brought about by British administration. Alfred Vowles's account is typical, being compiled from diaries written during his service in Mesopotamia as a British soldier. *Wanderings with a Camera in Mesopotamia* (1920) is intended to 'give readers a *good general impression* of this new acquisition to the British Empire', for 'it must be remembered that matters, as they concern health and sanitation, have greatly improved since the

British occupation'.[4] Donald Maxwell who travelled the region at the end of the war as an artist for the Imperial War Museum, diverted from his normal jocular style when it came to imperial matters. He solemnly noted that 'should our sphere of influence be withdrawn from Mesopotamia things will revert back to chaos'.[5] Clearly, certain travel writers were not averse to stating the imperial line: British involvement in Iraq had only been beneficial to the country.

Edmund Candler had also fought in Mesopotamia and found little to endear him to the country. He could not forget the siege of Kut from 1915 to 1916 in which over 20,000 British and Indian soldiers had perished. In *On the Edge of the World* (1919) the only mentions of Mesopotamia are of escaping from it:

> The Kut experience sealed any prejudice one may have had for the bare, hot, uncompromising delta. It was a country of one mood. Its treelessness, stonelessness, and monotony were associated with stagnation and death, and the impression is not likely to fade.[6]

This vision of Mesopotamia was by no means singular. Gertrude Bell travelled the region before the war chiefly concerned with exploring the past glories of the region. Her view of the desert landscape around Babylon echoes that of Candler:

> It was a very barren world, scarred with the traces of former cultivation, and all the more poverty-stricken and desolate because it had once been rich and peopled; flat, too, an interminable, featureless expanse from which the glory had departed.[7]

While the lands of Mesopotamia afforded an uncomfortable sight for many British travellers, the capital of this barren world filled most with preconceived notions of an Oriental land of wonder. British travellers approached Baghdad with swirling images of Caliphs and genii filling their thoughts. Whether arriving by boat, on horseback or by airplane, they imagined a city built of golden domes and steep minarets, and peopled by colourful, exotic figures drawn from the pages of *One Thousand and One Nights*. The reality was quite different.

When Gavin Young's feet hit land, he declares Baghdad 'not a city of stately majesty'. It is 'a water colour, not an oil painting. It is flat and dusty ... an ancient city struggling awkwardly to be modern' (28). Baghdad is 'a melting-pot' and its inhabitants 'a vivid mixture of fire and sweetness' (39). It seems the vision of a magical mediaeval city has been supplanted by the reality of modern Baghdad. Expensive cars fill the streets. The petrodollar and Western cultural influences have transformed the city in the space of half a century. Yet though physically tied to the present, Young is not beyond returning to the romantic allure of the past. As darkness falls, he drops once more into his earlier reverie:

> During the clear, cool Baghdad nights, the full magic works. The moon glints on the golden teardrop of the dome [of Kadhimain]. Then you can really feel you are in what Flecker, in *Hassan*, described as the Caliph's 'dim-moon city'. (44)

The perfumes of the past remain intoxicating. Gavin Young falls under their spell like a narcoleptic slipping once more into a dream world. Baghdad is transformed. On this occasion, the medium is not the fantasy of Hollywood but the words of a favoured romantic conjurer of imagined Arabias: James Elroy Flecker, whom T. E. Lawrence called 'the sweetest singer of the war generation'.[8]

*

While Gavin Young headed to Baghdad by the easy convenience of air travel, Ely Soane's journey from Constantinople in 1908 took him overland to Baghdad. Soane travelled under the pretence of being Persian through those regions of northern Mesopotamia largely unexplored by the British, at a time (just before the First World War) when knowledge of the area would be very favourably received in London. He had spent five years in Persia, working in banking and honing his skills to pass as a Persian. In 1905, he had converted to Islam.[9] If eccentric, Soane, 'was in many ways typical ... of the kind of gentleman traveller who provided information to the British government'.[10] His disguise consisted of simply wearing a fez:

> It is strange what a simple exchange of headgear can do. Here was I, by the mere fact of wearing a fez, isolated, looked down upon by types one would pass unnoticed in London, audibly commented upon as 'quite a civilised-looking Turk,' exciting

wonder as to "'ow many wives 'e's got,' and such traditionally
Oriental questions.[11]

Soane's route is to travel from Beirut to Aleppo and then ford the
Euphrates, heading for Kurdish lands before doubling back and
returning by the Tigris to Baghdad and Basra. The final leg of his
adventure takes him out of Mesopotamia to Shustar in Persia. By the
time he reaches Diarbekr, Soane has been worn by travel and the
weather to create a more complete cloak to his true identity:

> I was darkened by wind and sun; nine day's black beard
> scraped the chest left bare by a buttonless shirt. My trousers
> were muddy and torn, and I wore a long overcoat, very much
> like the robes of any of the myriads of Turkish subjects who
> affect a semi-European dress. (58)

He meets a 'Baba Kurd' called Haji Vali who is returning from his
seventeenth hajj to Mecca. They both wish to travel down to Mosul
and so arrange a *kalak* [raft of skins and poles] to take them. The craft
is described as 'two hundred inflated goatskins arranged in the form
ten by twenty ... bound to a few thin transverse poplar trunks above
them' (72). By the time Soane approaches Baghdad, he has turned his
attention once more to his own appearance:

> I began to think how I might enter Bagdad as a European, for
> I wished to go straight to the only hotel, and appear the next
> day among the Europeans, with some of whom I had affairs,
> and some acquaintance. (364)

Soane dons 'a suit of white clothing', socks and 'a soft felt hat, much
squashed and battered – but still a Ferangi hat – ready in a
handkerchief' (364). He arrives at the lone hotel in Baghdad which is 'a
humble house kept by a Christian' (365). Dropping his disguise has its
drawbacks:

> I felt stranger and more lonely than I had ever done before.
> Gone was the coffee-house and the bazaar, of the multitudes
> of which I was one, and equal, with whom I spoke and
> laughed, and fought and wrangled. They were far away, and I
> must learn to look upon them as upon strange and inferior

beings, if such were now possible, and taking place again on the platform of Western birth, once more go on my way affecting to ignore their joys and sorrows - which had so lately been my own. (365-6)

Soane experiences the strains of adapting back to his English persona. In the garb of the local Iraqi, Soane has felt the warmth of being *as if* a Baghdadi. There is no sense of anticipating a fantastical world born of the imaginings of *Arabian Nights* as Gavin Young did. Soane arrives at Baghdad concerned only that he will make a decent return as a European to what is apparently the solitary hotel in the city. Unlike most British travellers, he details no enthusiasm for finding a 'City of the Caliphs'.

Soane's unromantic arrival in Baghdad in 1909 when few British or European travellers made such a journey is paralleled by the narrative of David Fraser who makes a similar expedition across Mesopotamia, arriving in Baghdad in the summer heat of 1908. Fraser aims to follow the proposed route of the Baghdad railway, an ambitious project of German imperialism or perhaps a 'shared Turco-German imperial strategy' designed to link Berlin with Baghdad.[12] The implications for British interests in Arabia were obvious to Fraser:

The maker of the line is Germany; by its means Germany is to colonise Asia Minor, reduce Turkey to vassalage, absorb Mesopotamia, oust Great Britain from the Persian Gulf, and finally to extend the mailed fist towards India.[13]

He arrives in Constantinople by steamer, heads across Asia Minor by the Anatolian Railway to Konia, then journeys on to Eregli in southern Turkey by the existing section of the Baghdad railway. Fraser sees his mission as 'to endeavour to discover what Germany has to gain by construction of the railway, and what England stands to lose' (31-2). He passes through the Cilician Gates then down to Tarsus and Adana. With his Greek servant Socrate beside him, Fraser travels to Aleppo where he hires a guide and six horses and seeks the 'deserts of Mesopotamia' (124). It is December 1907. Rain falls as they head off. They reach Carchemish and thoughts remain on the Baghdad railway: 'Jerablus sits fairly on the western bank of the Euphrates, and here the Baghdad Railway will essay the first crossing of the great river' (129). When Fraser crosses the river into Mesopotamia, he soon finds himself in trouble. An Arab horseman appears who starts to load his rifle, a Martini carbine. Fraser is shot in the left hand and right arm as the horseman turns robber. He flees to the village of 'Aktchi-Kaalah' for help, sending for a European doctor from Urfa, but in the meantime suffers the attentions of the local 'hakeems'. His servant Socrate faints at the sight of the changing of the bandages. Some five weeks later, nursing a broken radius and minus a finger, Fraser retakes the four-day trek to Aleppo. There he rests, taking seventeen weeks to recover, before heading off once more, now unable to ride a horse so taking a 'three-horsed vehicle' (177) as transport.

Such tribulations coming so soon into his time in Mesopotamia apparently did little to dent Fraser's ardour. When he finally approaches Baghdad his narrative portrays his excitement at reaching the city:

> Baghdad has its charms for the traveller. The narrow streets, the quaint houses, the iron-bound doors giving glimpses of shady courtyards and splashing fountains, are redolent of the East and all that it means to those unsatisfied souls who adore the picturesque and ache continually for touches of imagery in a world of materialities. Memory and imagination, too, are faithful genii easily summoned, and they will conjure for you from the pages of the Nights the most gorgeous palaces, the most impregnable castles, and the most beautiful gardens, all alive with running water and singing birds, coloured like a dream, and languorous with the smell of roses. (234)

For Fraser, as for Young, Baghdad is a city that ignites dreams of an Oriental wonderland. Fraser, too, acknowledges that the reality is quite different. In the next sentence he declares: 'But the city of Haroun al Rashid is no more' (234). Baghdad is 'of mushroom growth and mean appearance, remarkable only as the capital of a remote province of the Turkish Empire' (235). There is a remarkable echo from Fraser's Baghdad of 1908 to Gavin Young's description of 'the small shabby capital of a mere Turkish province'.[14] David Fraser approaches Baghdad in the punishing heat of July 1908 disfigured from his traumatic travails in northern Mesopotamia, while Gavin Young journeys to the city seventy years later, sipping champagne in the luxury of an airliner. Yet both find their imaginings of Baghdad to be the mere hallucinations of romantic sensibilities.

Gilbert Hubbard arrived in Mesopotamia as the British secretary of a Delimitation Commission set up to define the Turko-Persian boundary. His text is a personal record of a 1000 mile journey undertaken from the Persian Gulf to Mount Ararat, surveying the frontier. In April 1914, Hubbard accompanied the sickened chief of the Commission, Mr Wratislaw, to Baghdad. Hubbard's initial vision of the city is of a mirage:

> It was a strange ethereal city which gradually took shape before our eyes, for the haze obscured the lower half of each building, leaving its upper portion floating in the sky ... But the vision was fleeting, and disillusion followed close at heel. The dream-city soon became a solid thing of brick and mortar, and the nearer we came to it the less ideal it appeared.[15]

Hubbard warns the prospective traveller against expecting too much from the city: 'the traveller who arrives there, primed with memories of the Arabian Nights and hoping to find himself again among their scenes, is doomed to bitter disappointment.'[16] The unfolding of the image of Baghdad echoes that of both Fraser and Young. Each traveller finds that the dream-like apparition of the city of the Abbasids, and of *One Thousand and One Nights*, melts upon meeting into a place of stark, urban reality. The Baghdad of the imagination which helps to conjure the initial visage of the city cannot be maintained once the true nature of the city assaults the senses of the traveller.

By contrast, when the archaeologist E. A. Wallis Budge travelled to Baghdad by the Tigris in the 1880s, he found much to please him. Though finding a hatred of Christians, Budge is remarkably upbeat on the nature of Baghdad, a trait which he recognises as unusual:

> Though many travellers to Baghdâd have found the city dull and uninteresting, I must confess that I found many places and things in the eastern part of it well worthy of examination. At first the bazârs seemed most unattractive, but as I made the acquaintance of one dealer here and another dealer there, I discovered that the shopkeepers did not put their best things on exhibition.[17]

Budge meets a dealer named 'Alî the Kûrd' and marvels at the extent of his collection of Persian and Sassanian antiquities. Budge is an accomplished archaeologist, and is in Baghdad not merely to savour the city, but as a representative of the British Museum hunting Mesopotamian antiquities. He discovers a great many Babylonian tablets for sale, being 'astonished to see such large collections of tablets, for most of them numbered many hundreds' (234). Budge sets about buying up the tablets from the various dealers in the bazaars, then packing them into wooden boxes and clandestinely stowing them aboard the British steamer *Comet* under the cover of night. The Ottoman authorities track Budge's movements, aware he is apparently preparing to export the tablets without declaring them to customs. A tense game of cat and mouse sees Budge successfully shipping the boxes of tablets to Basra and away by mail steamer to the safe-keeping of England:

> The news of this little bit of successful smuggling soon went from one end of the Persian Gulf to the other, and the British communities at Bushire, Muscat, etc., rejoiced that a valuable collection of Babylonian antiquities had been secured for the British Museum. On my return to England I found that the news had already reached London, and those who were not my friends, as well as some who were, criticized my action severely, and openly accused me of 'stealing' tablets which were the property of the Turkish Government ... But I had a perfectly clear conscience about this bit of smuggling and besides this, I felt that I had only done what anyone would have done who had the welfare of Babylonian and Assyrian Archaeology and his employers' interests at heart. (239)

By 1917 no such subterfuge was necessary as British troops had overthrown Ottoman control. Baghdad had a new imperial ruler. Serving the regime were a number of travellers who had rested their wings in Baghdad. Ely Soane, who had been captured by Turkish forces at the start of the war, was enlisted to the Expeditionary Force in 1915 before spending 'a brief period of tuition in the Intelligence Department' and becoming editor of the government run *Basrah Times*.[18] Gertrude Bell was by 1919 assistant to the Civil Commissioner, A. T. Wilson, and directly influencing British policy through works such as her *Memorandum on Self-Determination in Mesopotamia*.[19] By 1920, the city boasted a collection of British political officers administering British imperial policy in recently acquired Mesopotamia. Baghdad had a variety of new attractions for the well-connected British traveller. Bertram Thomas detailed the scene:

> The early months of 1920 passed pleasantly enough in Baghdad. For instance, there were the Pleasant Sunday Afternoons of Miss Gertrude Bell, after the usual Sunday morning ride, often taken with that eager, distinguished woman herself. These 'P.S.A.s', as they were called, were held in Miss Bell's garden, and the political intelligentsia of Baghdad were invited - a gathering of those whose brothers for the most part were in the Sharifian camp with the Amir Faisal in Syria.

Those involved included 'a stream of officials on leave or returning to their Divisions – personalities such as Leachman and Soane, men with an unrivalled knowledge of the land and the people they had made their life study'.[20] Things had come a long way in a short period. It was merely eleven years since the same Ely Soane arrived in Baghdad to stay in the only hotel available for European guests.

By the time that Freya Stark published *Baghdad Sketches* in 1937, she was part of a significant British community in the city, writing the bulk of her sketches for the *Baghdad Times*. Stark, like many British travellers both before and after her, finds the initial sighting of Baghdad unappealing:

> What you first see of the Caliphs' city is a most sordid aspect; a long low straight street, a dingy hybrid between East and West, with the unattractiveness of both. The crowd looks unhealthy and sallow, the children are pitiful, the shops are ineffective compromises with Europe; and the dust is wicked, for it turns to blood-poisoning at the slightest opportunity, and bears out the old Babylonian idea of an atmosphere inhabited by Demons.[21]

Though there is the reference to 'the Caliph's city' there are none of the fantastical dreams that Gavin Young is to experience some years later. Gone is the enthusiastic glorifying of the city that David Fraser has decried. In Stark's portrait, Baghdad has nothing to offer the traveller. While many who have painted the wonders of the imagined world of mediaeval Baghdad have noted the less than astonishing true nature of the city, Stark's vision is the least enticing. In her eyes, Baghdad has turned from the place of Arabian dreams to a Stygian nightmare peopled by a 'sallow' population and where friendly genii have transfigured into 'Demons'.

*

A vast expanse of marsh and swamp, almost treeless, in which the roads are water and the village streets water; miles on miles of rustling reeds and long horizons; a watery desert; home of millions of mosquitoes. Who would believe that such a place could be chosen as a place of human habitation? Yet many populous villages exist in the great swamps which reach from Tigris to Euphrates in Lower Mesopotamia, and there are people who have never been beyond the confines of the marshes, and, like water-birds, know little of dry land.

The houses of these villages and townlets are not built of brick, stone, or even mud. They are built entirely of reeds, which shine golden in the sun against the blue water and ever green rushes, and to go from street to street or village to village the inhabitants use primitive canoes, daubed over with bitumen, which they pole deftly through the canals, over the wide expanse of flooded rice-land, or through the tall world of reeds.

There is something of the water-bird in their nature. Merry as water-wagtails, quick to see a joke, fond of laughing and singing, they are as much at home in the water as they are on dry land. Children can swim almost as soon as they can walk. In summer men are in and out of the water all day long, and even in winter their clothes are scanty. Little boys and girls run about the villages stark naked, and as for wet feet, no mother of the marsh-villages ever worries about that. Hardy little savages, reed-children grow up wiry and strong, and one rarely sees diseased eyes or wasted limbs as one does in the big towns.[22]

This idyllic world of the Marsh Arabs was painted by Ethel Stevens in the early 1920s. She was the wife of a British administrator and a resident of newly formed Iraq. Her vision of the country is filled with hope and enthusiasm. The population of the marshes are 'like water-birds'; fluttering, gentle creatures living out an enviably simple life in their nests amidst the reed beds. In Stevens's eyes, their children are 'hardy little savages' who run around or swim all day in the sun to ensure they become 'wiry and strong'. This is the vision of the primitive savage which has haunted so many European travellers' perceptions of indigenous populations. Stevens notes no individuals, meets no single dweller of the marshes but instead sees merely the swarming masses of these happy-go-lucky amphibious creatures as they dive in and out of the waters.

The marshes of southern Iraq consist of a vast area of some 6,000 square miles centred on the town of Qurna which marks the meeting of the Tigris and Euphrates rivers and the start of the Shatt al Arab. Its population of Marsh Arabs, or Madan, have developed a distinct identity recognised by both Iraqis and British travellers. The environment is a haven for enormous numbers of migrating birds; the wildlife of the marshes being cited by all travellers to the region. Incredibly skilled at carving canoes, reed building, fishing and harvesting the other resources of the marshes, the Madan have evolved a unique way of life. Yet aggressive policies of dispersion and drainage have now destroyed much of the watery world that Ethel Stevens saw in the 1920s. Following failed uprisings against Saddam Hussein in 1991, the marshes became a safe haven, as they had for refugees from the Iran-Iraq war that raged through the 1980s. In the 1990s, as a Shia tribal people, the Madan, 'were subjected to prolonged persecution' involving 'an economic blockade and repeated bombardment by the Iraqi army' and the destruction of great areas of the marshes by diverting key rivers.[23]

Of those British travellers to depict the Marsh Arabs in the first quarter of the twentieth century, Stevens was almost uniquely sanguine. Most were far less flattering in their depictions. Visiting in 1908, David Fraser talks of the 'riverine Arabs' as 'a villainous lot in appearance, very dark-coloured, dirty, and ragged ... Laziness is their chief characteristic, and robbery their favourite diversion.'[24] G. E. Hubbard was just as dismissive in late 1913, describing the marshes as a 'mostly dismal-looking swamp'. They offer 'a lifeless scene' containing merely 'occasional flocks of wild-fowl' and a scattering of 'naked riverain Arabs up to their waists in water cutting reeds, which they use for fish-traps'. They are not people to be trusted, being 'river vermin' with a 'love of piracy'.[25]

These sentiments were echoed by Alfred Vowles, who had met the Marsh Arabs while serving as a British soldier. He sees them as 'semi-civilised' and 'expert thieves and raiders ... their marsh haunts and hiding places making excellent places of retirement in times when punishment is due'.[26] In *Alarms and Excursions in Arabia* (1931), Bertram Thomas detailed his experiences of the military campaign in 1918 to control the Muntafiq marshes, in particular one 'troublesome' sheikh, Badr bin Rumaiyidh or 'Old Badr'.[27] The women of the marshes were another matter entirely:

> Washing their garments over a tiny stream are black-eyed matrons and young virgins, the latter disporting gay-coloured clothes to distinguish them, and, if they be *ma'adan* of the marsh, unveiled, the hussies! Their laughing moon faces, their hair plaited with coloured beads, their large flashing eyes and dazzling teeth, and their firm young bodies, straight as an arrow and full of grace, are things goodly to behold.[28]

When Stuart Hedgcock and his wife Monica decided to write a book on the Marsh Arabs in the 1920s, it was at the suggestion of Gertrude Bell. As a serving British political officer in the region, Hedgcock used the pseudonym 'Fulanain' when *Haji Rikkan* was published in 1927. 'Fulanain' provides the narrative voice, though the work is centred on the world of 'Haji Rikkan', a simple trader in the marshes. This vision is one created by an English wife and husband, whilst serving in an occupying army. Hedgcock's political remit is to know and understand the ways of the Marsh Arabs in order to control them. His creation of *Haji Rikkan* is, in a sense, an expression of this act of espionage.

In Chapter 12, the English narrator 'Fulanain' heads deep into the marshes. The little travelled world of the marshes is introduced as a place of innocent beauty where 'the tiny marsh flowers were at their loveliest, gleaming like jewels on the surface of the water, or half hiding their delicate pinks and yellows in the shadow of the reeds'.[29] At a lonely marsh hamlet, Fulanain meets a blind old woman who on discovering he is a *'farangi'* [European] hands him 'a flat packet wrapped in cloth that might once have been white', mysteriously stating: 'This was his command, that I should give it to a *farangi*, to another of his kind' (251-2). The parcel contains a calf-bound book which, though badly damaged by age and damp, contains the title 'Personal Narrative of Travels in Babylonia, Assyria, Media and Scythia, in the year 1824, by the Major the Hon. George Keppel, F.S.A.' (252).

When questioned, the old woman tells the remainder of the tale. On that distant day the tribesmen were bewitched by the *tantals*, or evil spirits of the marshes and after capturing the Englishman, set fire to the reed hut in which he was tied up. She had crept to his rescue, cutting him free but in the process catching aflame so that her sight was lost. Fulanain, recalling the words of the blind woman, states 'the strange story, corroborated as it was by the witness of the book, was evidently true' (265). He muses as to whether that English traveller of the nineteenth century had managed to escape 'the dreadful death prepared for him' or whether 'escaping from one death, he had found another in the endless mazes of the marsh?' (266). He heads home with the book in his hand.

The tale of this lost Englishman in one of the dark places of the marshes is reminiscent of a Rider Haggard novel. There is the colonial adventurer who has ventured too far and discovered the evil that may lurk in uncivilised lands. Fulanain tells the story with all the elements of a colonial gothic short story: an Englishman lost in a distant corner of the world; vile, malevolent spirits; a blind old woman; and a battered, ancient book that holds a terrible secret.

*

When Wilfred Thesiger first developed an interest in exploring the marshes in 1950, *Haji Rikkan* was the only work he could find on the subject.[30] Thirty years had passed since Hedgcock had created his legend of the Marsh Arab. Thesiger headed to southern Iraq after a brief sojourn with the Kurds. He had previously spent five years with the Bedouin covering thousands of miles of Arabian desert as an observer of their changing world. After eight years in the marshes, Thesiger emerged as the self-declared, last Western witness to the Marsh Arab way of life. Yet there had been two other British travel writers who accompanied Thesiger for varied periods in the marshes. Both Gavin Maxwell and Gavin Young were to write up their experiences of the marshes and their time with Thesiger. Many of the same Arab characters feature in each travelogue, and many of the same episodes and adventures are reported, if through separate travellers' eyes. Together, their texts provide a complex narrative on the marshes in the 1950s.

In the Introduction to *The Marsh Arabs* (1964), Thesiger declares:

> Recent political upheavals in Iraq have closed this area to visitors. Soon the Marshes will probably be drained; when this happens, a way of life that has lasted for thousands of years will disappear. (13)

The book begins with this wave of pessimism for the future survival of the very peoples the book sets out to focus upon. As such, nostalgia is developed for the ways of the Marsh Arabs even before they are illustrated to the reader. It is an emotion relentlessly expressed throughout the text, just as it is in Thesiger's earlier work, *Arabian Sands* (1959).

In the opening chapter, 'A Glimpse of the Marshes', Thesiger approaches the marshes on horseback, accompanied by a friend, Dugald Stewart, who is British Vice-Consul at Amara. They are both of a certain distinctive British class. It is 1950. Though the British Empire has clearly started to wane, there is something resolutely imperial in the appearance on the horizon of two Old Etonians on horseback, heading for unexplored territories. Six months later and Thesiger is back, now a lone white man with the Marsh Arabs. He relishes the prospect and suggests his travel role is unique: 'I was probably the first outsider with both the inclination and opportunity to live among the Madan, as one of them' (59). Or rather, *as if* one of them.

Thesiger heads for the house of Falih bin Majid, sheikh of the Al bu Muhammed tribe, on the edge of the marshes. He briefly outlines his own upbringing in Abyssinia and his own tastes:

> I loathed cars, aeroplanes, wireless and television, in fact most of our civilisation's manifestations in the past fifty years, and was always happy, in Iraq or elsewhere, to share a smoke-filled hovel with a shepherd, his family and beasts. (59)

Having spent some eighteen years in the remotest regions of Africa and Arabia, Thesiger is searching for his next adventure in a place where there 'was no sign of that drab modernity which, in its uniform of second-hand European clothing, was spreading like a blight across the rest of Iraq' (60).

The Marsh Arabs is distinctly ethnographic in its style, depicting Madan society as much as Thesiger's activities. He acts as an amateur anthropologist, detailing a world for his Western readership. It is the prospect of travelling with an authentic tribal people that excites Thesiger. He journeys as a pseudo-physician, a medicine man for the Marsh Arabs. Though untrained, Thesiger, with his medicine chests, is not merely a passive tourist but a valuable asset to the wellbeing of the marsh people. His doctoring provides him with a *raison d'être* in the eyes of the Arabs (and perhaps the reader). In order to aid his acceptance, he pretends he can circumcise and soon has carved a niche for himself:

> In time few of these people were prepared to let the local specialists circumcise them; they preferred to wait until I visited their village or to come and find me somewhere else. On one exhausting occasion, a hundred and fifteen turned up, and I was hard at work from dawn until midnight. They believed that, after circumcision, the smell of baking bread, or of scent, would inflame the wound. Consequently their custom was to stuff their nostrils with pieces of cloth and hang onions around their necks, if they could find any in the local shop. (107)

The adjunct of Madan belief layers anthropological elements into the travelogue. As Thesiger merges deeper into the society of the marshes, so he adds detail as to the thoughts and practices of that world. Most of the time he is dealing with 'colds, headaches, constipation, or minor cuts and bruises' like a local GP. There are some patients he can do nothing for:

> I am still haunted by the face of a small boy, dying of dysentery. Often, too, it was very difficult to convince them that I could do nothing. They would bring me, perhaps from a great distance, an old man dying in agony of cancer, or a girl coughing up her lungs from tuberculosis, confident that I could cure them, and would go on begging pathetically, 'Just give us medicine, sahib, give us medicine.' (109)

Thesiger secures a gang of four teenage marsh boys: Yasin, Hassan, Sabaiti and Amara. It is Amara who becomes Thesiger's medical assistant, and of whom Thesiger is most fond: 'Slightly built and remarkably handsome, he was deft and self-possessed, a natural aristocrat' (136). The day after Thesiger meets him, Amara is circumcised, as is Sabaiti. The two stayed with Thesiger all the time that Thesiger visited Iraq. Rather than receiving regular payment, the relationship Thesiger held with his crew or gang was rather more flexible. Each was under the financial patronage of Thesiger: 'I clothed them and in fact gave them more money than they could have hoped to earn. Later, when they married, I helped them with their bride price' (138). Their duties included a nightly 'thorough massage' of their leader.[31]

With his band of young companions and his graceful *tarada* [war canoe], Thesiger now heads out to truly explore the marshes. So too, the main action of the text commences. Alongside his duties as a doctor, Thesiger finds a role as the leader of hunting expeditions to kill the notorious boar that roam the marshes. For Thesiger, brought up to African game shooting, it is a role he can happily take on. He is not only a highly skilled shot but has the weaponry in his .275 Rigby shooting rifle.

Chapter 16 is entitled 'Falih's Death'. On 'an early afternoon' in February 1953, Thesiger returns to his friend Falih bin Majid's *mudhif* [guest-house] only to find himself removed to the main home. He is now one of the family. Abbas, a cousin, is persuaded to stay and shoot with the Englishman. Thesiger drops in the line that, 'Unfortunately, Abbas allowed himself to be persuaded' (142). It is the second clue foreshadowing the death of Falih, after that of the title. After breakfast the following day, Thesiger notices that some of the cartridges in Abbas's belt contain larger shot: 'I said, "They are only for pig; for God's sake, don't use them to shoot at duck or you will kill somebody"' (143). The advice operates to ratchet the tension of the scene. By recounting the episode, Thesiger notes the ironic nature of his words. He may also be assuaging his personal guilt at having been unable to prevent the death of his friend.

The hunting party start to shoot coot. Before long a fatal blast has been fired:

> I shouted, 'For God's sake look out where you are shooting!'
> A little farther and we saw Falih's canoe stationary in the

middle of some open water, fifty yards from a reedbed. My
canoeman took one look, cried 'Falih is hurt,' and paddled
frantically towards him. (144)

Thesiger retells the events that follow, as Falih is carried from the
scene in his canoe, others wail and cry at the news that he has been
shot. The incident is the central action of the text. It comes mid-way
through the work, at a time when the reader has followed Thesiger
into the marshes and watched his reputation and standing amongst the
Madan rise. Like Thesiger, the reader has got to know Falih bin Majid
and come to understand his significance in Marsh society. He was the
first Marsh Arab to welcome Thesiger to his *mudhif* back in Chapter 2
when he was introduced as the son of one of the great sheikhs of the
Al bu Mohammed tribe. Now his slow death proves a moment of
poignancy.

The Etonian stiff upper lip prevents tears. Instead, Thesiger devotes
the next chapter to the process of mourning, making up in words for
the dryness of his eyes. When he does head off to the eastern marshes
with his adolescent gang, sadness and loss haunt the text like a
lingering leitmotif. Tales are told of a man killed by a hyena and
Thesiger, while continuing to shoot the animals of the marshes,
foresees a time 'when the last wild geese would be gone, and there
were no more lions in Africa' (163). He does not see or comment on
the incongruity of his position as a voracious hunter of both creatures.

Thesiger's paradoxical stands are soon evident again. He states his
distaste for the world of Western civilisation and his preference for
living with tribal peoples, yet Thesiger regularly takes time away from
the rigours of living in the marshes, escaping to Basra, 'every two
months to collect my mail, have a bath and buy some medicines. A
few days in a comfortable house was a pleasant change and my friends
at the Consulate were always good to me and my companions' (172).
Thesiger enjoys the luxury and protective embrace of the British
Consul just as naturally as he accepts the hospitality of a Marsh Arab
to rest in their *mudhif.*

Back in the marshes, Thesiger attends a wedding, where
consummation of the marriage is signalled by the firing of a shotgun.
The moment provides a brief and rare moment of levity before the
motif of mourning returns as wailing is heard across the waters. A
young boy has drowned that morning. Life in the marshes, it seems, is
ever precarious. Thesiger tells of the flood of 1954 and the following

drought of 1955. There is a seemingly inevitable slide back to the depressive vision of the marshes as a place of death. It may well be a reflection of the brooding Thesiger's apparition of the future state of the Madan. Certainly, it acts as a perpetual counterweight to those remembrances of the Marsh's wonder and beauty. In a section extolling the glorious construction of the *mudhifs* merely from the reeds of the Euphrates, Thesiger delights in their 'extraordinary architectural achievement' imagining himself 'inside a Romanesque or Gothic cathedral' (207-8). Yet he concludes the paragraph with the comment:

> Buildings similar to these *mudhifs* have been part of the scene in Southern Iraq for five thousand years and more. Probably within the next twenty years, certainly within the next fifty, they will have disappeared for ever. (208)

The lament is for a realm he has grown to love vanishing from the face of the world. Thesiger's mourning for the marshes is evinced in the sense of loss that seeps through his tale.

*

Gavin Maxwell's own travel in the marshes was initiated by just such a threnody from Thesiger. In 1954, Thesiger had published a stirring first account of his adventures in the marshes for the Royal Geographical Society. In concluding his article, he had foreseen the demise of the Madan, noting: 'Like many others, I regret the forces which are inexorably suburbanizing the untamed places and turning tribesmen into corner-boys.'[32] The phrase and the sentiment struck a chord with Gavin Maxwell. He met Thesiger in London in the winter of 1954, and two years later joined him for seven weeks in the marshes. Both men shared the trappings of the English upper classes. Both came from the aristocratic world of imperial British families and centred their enjoyment on shooting, wildlife and explorations. Maxwell had spent considerable money and effort on a basking shark enterprise after buying the island of Soay to the south of the Isle of Skye in 1945. The business had failed. When he met Thesiger in 1954, Maxwell was into another adventure, exploring the world of tuna fishing in Scopello, Sicily. The journey into the marshes was another escapade, though indirectly it was to provide the key to a change of fortune for Maxwell. He returned to London from the marshes with a young otter named Mijbil, the creature that was to star in his bestseller *Ring of Bright Water* (1962).

A Reed Shaken by the Wind (1957) tells of an inexperienced British traveller learning the ways and customs of the Madan. Maxwell is fortunate to have Thesiger to guide and lead him. He seems content to follow in the great explorer's footsteps as they head off in Thesiger's *tarada* ministering to the medical needs of the locals. Maxwell shoots coots, ducks and wild pigs, marvels at the size and deadliness of water snakes, and is gradually introduced to marsh life. He is initiated into Thesiger's gang but remains a novice throughout his time. Maxwell's text is a tale of a rather incompetent apprentice. He speaks very little Arabic and bumbles along haphazardly behind Thesiger.

When faced with a charging pig and duck shot in his rifle, all he can do is recall his leader's words: 'Wait till he's not quite touching you and shoot between his eyes and fall on your belly so he can't get his tusks in your guts. Never fall on your back.'[33] In the marsh clay, Maxwell stands 'sick with fright' as the boar's tusks charge ever closer. He holds his fire. At three yards, the pig veers away due to a ditch of deeper water. Maxwell fires anyway 'without realising that I was already out of danger, or that to fire could, logically, only lead me back into it' (177). Some distance apart, Thesiger stands up in his canoe to shoot at the fleeing animal, hitting it from 300 yards. Maxwell returns exhausted to the *tarada*:

> Thesiger was in the best of good humours, and the canoe boys were chattering like monkeys; each of them insisted on kissing me ardently. Sabeti's moustache tickled.
>
> 'What a man!' said Thesiger. 'Here he is, charged by a boar from an unprecedented distance, absolutely no right to be alive at all, saved by some extraordinary miracle that deflects the boar at the last possible second – and then, when he's safe, he has to go and *fire* at it with No. 5 shot! You really *are* a bloody fool!' (179)

Maxwell accepts the opprobrium. The two may come from the same high echelons of British society but inside they are distinctly separate creatures. While Maxwell confesses that he 'had rarely if ever been more afraid' he wonders if Thesiger 'has ever experienced physical fear, as I know it, in his life' (179).

Unlike Thesiger, Maxwell is particularly sensitive to the feelings of the animals of the marshes. Outside a *mudhif* he watches a sheep chewing on a pile of grass, noting that someone, possibly a child, 'had twined a blue ribbon in the wool of her neck' (195). When he believes the sheep is to be killed in their honour, he states, 'if I were required to swallow one mouthful of her I should be sick' (195). With sentimental overstatement, Maxwell imagines how the sheep would slowly die 'choked with her own blood, and the blue ribbon would be sodden with it' (195). In a nearby village, a captive eagle owl that Maxwell had intended to rescue does die. It provides a symbol of the inhumane world of the Madan:

> Poor humiliated eagle of the silent glittering night, wings clipped, tail pulled out, stuffed with bread and dates until it died squalidly on the ground, stained with its own excrement, in a dim corner of its captors' dwelling, one great orange eye still open and staring out to the stars. (200)

These incidents serve both to highlight the sentimentality of Maxwell and ensure a heightened emotional state to the narrative. Immediately following the death of the owl, Maxwell gets an offer of a young otter cub. He is delighted. Yet the impending death of the creature, named Chalala after the river where it was found, is soon relayed to the reader. It is the same narrative device which Thesiger operated when detailing the death of Fatih in the hunting accident. Maxwell foreshadows Chalala's death some twenty pages before the creature dies. Each moment of joy detailed in between is thus imbued with the knowledge of the forthcoming loss.

Chalala proves an exciting sight to villagers. Her reliance on Maxwell provides him, at last, with some sense of self-importance in the marshes. As a surrogate parent, he feeds her buffalo milk and weans her to bird flesh. She snoozes beside him, sharing his sleeping bag or tucked in his pullover. Now Maxwell can leave Thesiger to head off and hunt. He does not need to trudge after him, but has a role as protector of Chalala. The marshes are a brutal place to be. A man appears horrifically wounded to the face. A young boy catches two wagtails for Chalala but the birds stand 'eyes bright with terror', their 'tiny bodies shaken by the hammering of their hearts'. When they die it is with a 'little shivering flutter' (216). Maxwell watches as a black and white crow drops upon the slowest chick of a hen's brood: 'The crow killed him very slowly, allowing him to escape apparently unhurt several times and hurry cheeping pitifully after the hen.' The tiny chick is left one-eyed and 'still living' (218) as he is finally swept away by his killer. The narrator sees only cruelty and sadness. Soon, Chalala too is dying.

While *The Marsh Arabs* centred on the accidental death of Falih, it is the death of Chalala which provides the climax to Maxwell's text. The otter cub 'called faintly', uttering 'the little wild lonely cry that would come from her as she slept' before Maxwell 'felt the strange rigidity that comes in the instant following death; then she became limp under my touch' (221). Thesiger takes the pathetic body and throws it into the waters of the marshes. He rouses the canoe boys back from their sadness. But Maxwell is 'desolate' (222). In fact, Thesiger was later to state:

> Gavin had hysterics ... He was sobbing away and the tears were streaming down his face ... It seemed to me extraordinary. I could have understood it if it was to do with a human being he was very fond of, but it amazed me that it was over an otter we'd had with us for less than a week.[34]

Yet Maxwell does not leave his text on the same note of pessimism that Thesiger concludes with. In the epilogue, after departing from Thesiger, Maxwell receives a squirming sack and a note from Thesiger: 'Here is your otter, a male and weaned. I feel you may want to take it to London – it would be a handful in the *tarada*.' The otter is 'of a race quite unknown to science' (224) and named Mijbil, or *Lutrogale perspicillata maxwelli* to use the name science gave it. In this final twist to the text, there is not only hope in the form of a new creature for Maxwell and Western science, but a softer, kinder side to Thesiger is exposed.

*

The moment when Maxwell met Mijbil is captured by the third of the triad of British travel writers to have written on the world of the Marsh Arabs in the 1950s. Gavin Young opened this chapter dreaming of Baghdad aboard an airplane, so it is fitting that his vision of the marshes draws it to a close. Young recounts meeting Maxwell in 1956 in Basra. He has just spent 'two years wandering in south-western

Arabia'. To his surprise, he finds Ajram and Hasan, two of Thesiger's canoe boys, in the home of the British Consulate-General. With them is 'a slim Englishman with long blond hair, [who] wrestled intently with a struggling sack that seemed to have a life of its own'.[35]

Return to the Marshes (1977) is Gavin Young's enthusiastic eulogy to the Madan. His entry to their world is guided by Thesiger who takes him there in 1952. Young is a far more able lieutenant in Thesiger's gang than Maxwell will later prove to be. Not only does he speak Arabic, he is more emotionally stable. In his account of that first venture to the marshes, Young is quickly spellbound:

> Like Alice in Wonderland we had plunged into another world. However insignificant on a map, the Marsh is a world to get lost in: 6000 square miles, give or take a few. Shifting their paddles from one side to the other, the canoe-men threaded our needle-slim prow through a weaving half-tunnel of reed, rush and tangled sedge. I looked over the side and saw water as clear as glass and deep creepers, and flickering fish. 'You're there,' said Thesiger. 'This is the Marsh.' And the canoe-boy kneeling immediately behind me tapped me on the shoulder and excitedly echoed Thesiger, *'Hadha el Hor'*. (20)

Young is plunged into a surreal dreamland, just as he depicted in his in-flight dreams of Baghdad. The marshes provide a labyrinthine universe which fascinates the twenty-three-year-old novice. It is a place where nature abounds. Its beauty astounds Young. Travelling by canoe just across the level of the water, the environment of the marshes is mesmerising:

> The natural beauty of the place was hypnotic. Black and white pied kingfishers dived for their prey all around us, clusters of storks arced high above, snow-white flotillas of stately pelicans fished the lagoons; there was always at least one eagle in the sky. The reeds we passed through trembled or crashed with hidden wildlife: otters, herons, coot, warblers, gaudy purple gallinule, pygmy cormorants, huge and dangerous wild pigs. (21)

Once plunged into this Eden, the reader is then guided for the first half of the text through the history of the region and the various

British travellers who have been there. Young's tour ends with the revolution of 1958, a time that signalled not only the end of the monarchy but the declining power of the sheikhs. The text returns to the moment of Young's immersion into the marshes in 1952. Soon, he has acquired his own *tarada* and returns to voyage alone. His apprenticeship served, Young mimics his master and begins to take medicines with him such that he 'could return the tribesmen's hospitality by doctoring, and by shooting the terrible pigs' (110).

In 1973, Young finds himself on the same plot of earth 'on the water's edge more or less where I had found Thesiger beside the tarada twenty-one years before' (139). As dusk falls, he persuades a boatman to take him to Rufaiya and the house of Amara, Thesiger's favoured canoe boy, who Young has not seen since 1956. Amara greets the visitor with a welcome handshake but there is no sense of recognition:

> 'Amara,' I called in English, 'Amara, you bloody boy, damn and blast it!' It was the only English Amara had ever known. It had been Thesiger's shout of protest in the stress of doctoring if Amara dropped the syringe or handed him the wrong medicine-bottle. It had soon become a joke-phrase to all our Marsh friends. When Amara heard it now, he stood stock still with his back to me. Then he wheeled round, eyes wide, and [with] an expression of astonishment and gladness that I shall never forget.
> 'Sahib!' He came back to me in two strides, swiftly grabbing my hands. 'Oh, it's a long time, a long time,' he said.
> 'Twenty years, Amara. Bloody boy. You had forgotten.'
> (143)

The reunion is one full of emotion but it is one centred on the past relationship between Amara and Thesiger. The epithet of 'bloody boy' can be read as an affectionate nickname or a statement carrying the weight of the relationship between the imperial ethnographer and his native assistant. Once more, the overpowering figure of Thesiger appears. He is an invariable presence in both Maxwell's and Young's accounts of the marshes. They figure less securely in Thesiger's *The Marsh Arabs*: Maxwell gets one reference, Young none.

The following day, they head off in Sayyid Sarwat's *tarada*, meeting the marshes and old friends once more. Some things have changed. There is a vast sugar factory now, and acres of surrounding sugar cane.

Modernity has entered the Madan but their ways have held firm. Young has hope for their future: 'The Marshes are alive. They are not a variation on Disneyland. Real people live and work in them. They can be visited' (168). His declaration sounds rather like that of a proud tourist guide. Thesiger's apprentice envisions a far brighter prospect than that which concludes *The Marsh Arabs*.

When Young writes the postscript to his second edition in 1989, there is rather less to celebrate. He fears that many of his previous companions have vanished 'into the meat-grinder of the war between Iraq and Iran'. It is a war that 'has ripped, burned and laid waste increasingly large expanses of the Marshes for the best part of a decade' (171). When he managed to return to Basra in 1984, he found the city 'slit-trenched, bunkered and sandbagged like London during the Blitz'. Young is reluctantly allowed to visit the marshes under the guard of 'an Iraqi army major with a ginger moustache' (173) who is from Mosul and so knows little of the Marsh Arabs. His sergeant-major turns out to have been one of the boys circumcised by Thesiger thirty years before. In the marshes much has changed. The eminent figure of Sayyid Sarwat has died and the white *tarada* which he had given to Young 'lay in the stream like a pale echo of our friendship' (175). Artillery fire provides the background as he heads out for a final adventure, a last shooting competition.

'Is that the end of the Marsh Arabs? Are those thousands of years of exuberant life buried in this twentieth century shambles?' Young demands, as though throwing the questions up to the heavens. Yet he is an optimist at heart and he refuses to conclude his essay in such elegiac tone. In a final paragraph, he clings, as the Madan do, to a last hope: 'I take what comfort I can from the thought that only a fool would forecast the death of the world's oldest and perhaps wiliest people' (178). Though travellers' relations with the marshes have developed from Ethel Stevens's vision of 'hardy little savages', there remains something of this sentiment in Young's description of the world's 'wiliest people'. Thesiger had mourned the loss of the marshes with the rhetoric of imperial nostalgia, yearning for a more primitive, untouched land and people. It was such a lamenting which brought Gavin Maxwell to the marshes, though he left with the otter that would initiate his future literary success in *Ring of Bright Water* (1960). Gavin Young, staring at the wretched state of the region in 1989, struggles to see a bright future, yet he cannot bear to record the death of the marshes that he has known and loved for much of his life.

7

SOUTHERN ARABIA

There is not a breath of wind to stir the placid surface of the sea – not a breath to cause a draught upon the ship and cool us for a second. It is one of those terrible still tropical days, motionless, silent, oppressive. Nothing to hear but the hissing of the sea as the vessel's bows plough up the turquoise water, and the thud, thud of her never-ceasing screw. Even the Lascars [Indian seamen] in their white clothes and bare feet, children of the sun as they are, seem downcast.

We are passing Perim. It lies on the port side, a dirty blot upon a scene of opalesque transparence, of shimmering water and palpitating sky.

A youth travelling around the world stretches himself, jots a few lines in his diary, and commences to tell the old story of the taking of Perim. But he is soon cried down, and silence reigns again.

On both sides we can see the land, – burning rock seen through a burning atmosphere. A number of flying-fish buzz over the surface of the water, and with a series of little splashes disappear once again.

. . . .

A few hours later and Aden is in sight, with its broken and torn peaks and jagged outline. A little movement is noticeable amongst the passengers, but it is half-hearted at the best.

Then we enter the grand bay, surrounded by desolate rock and still more desolate desert, and drop anchor a mile or so off Steamer Point, as the shipping quarter of Aden is called.

The steamer is quickly surrounded. A few steam-launches, heavily awninged, screech their whistles; while a crowd of small boats manned by coal-black Somali boys, each striving to be the first upon the scene, crowd upon us. They are boatmen, divers, and sellers of curiosities – smart, bright little fellows, more than half nude, and as black as coal, many with their hair left long like the cords of a Russian poodle. Such a screaming and a yelling! Such a diving after small coins! Such a display of leopard-skins, antelope-horns, especially those of the lovely oryx, and ostrich-feathers, products of the opposite coast! A few dull austere Indians and Cingalese display embroideries and table-cloths, but the heat seems to depress them, just as it does the buyers.

It is a wonderful sight to watch the divers, balanced on the gunwales of the boats, their hands above their heads, watching eagerly for the tiny splash of a small coin, then breaking the water into a series of dancing circles as their dusky bodies disappear into the transparent blue. One can see them under water, turning like fishes in search of the slowly sinking money. When the excitement had worn off, and those passengers who cared to brave the sun's terrific rays by taking a short run ashore had left, I hailed a boy, who, with the aid of Abdurrahman, my ever-faithful Arab servant from Morocco, stowed my luggage into the boat. Then I said goodbye to the P. and O. steamer, and was rowed ashore.[1]

Walter Harris's travelogue, *A Journey Through the Yemen* (1893), steers the reader gently into Aden, the seat of British imperialism on the southern Arabian coast. At first all is still. Only the P & O steamer makes any noise. Then, the 'youth travelling round the world' recounts the story of Perim. By 1892, it is already 'the old story'. In 1799, during the Napoleonic wars, a British East India Company ship had taken the tiny island in the Red Sea for its strategic position and as a potential watering hole. It had been abandoned within six months. There was no fresh water to be had on Perim. Harris and his fellow passengers have heard it all before. It is a well worn imperial tale. The youth is 'soon cried down'. They proceed to Aden and anchor off Steamer Point. In the distance lies the heat of Arabia, but it is the sea that is the thing; mastered realm of the British. Aden looks not towards the 'desolate' deserts of Arabia, but to the Arabian Sea. Here is the place where Britain first stepped into Arabia back in 1839 and decided to stay. When Walter Harris stepped ashore, Aden had served as a coaling

station on the route to India for half a century and more. It was a piece
of Arabia that had been tinged British over time and it would remain
so for another seventy years. Long after many other imperial
possessions had been returned, Britain would truculently retain Aden
until 1967.

In the early nineteenth century, Aden was 'no more than a pirate
village, preying on the routine traffic of the Indian Ocean'. By the
1830s, when an Indian ship flying a British flag became the quarry, the
British navy reacted by sending two gunboats and 700 troops 'to teach
the presumptuous natives a lesson'.[2] Captain Haines commanded the
assault on Aden and in 1839 presented Queen Victoria with her first
imperial possession. While the colony developed as a coaling station, it
gained ascendancy with the opening of the Suez Canal in 1869. For a
century, Aden would flourish as its harbours expanded to hold a
growing flotilla of steamers, oil tankers and any number of cargo
boats, sailing vessels and rowing boats that filled its waters. By the
1930s, 'it was from Aden that the last imperial frontier was reached'.[3]
British influence extended out from Aden into an area defined as the
Aden Protectorate. A series of treaties had been initiated amongst the
local tribes by the combined efforts of a Colonial political officer and
his wife: Harold and Doreen Ingrams brought 'Ingrams' Peace' to the
Eastern Protectorate including the Hadhramaut region. In 1967,
Britain's withdrawal from Aden became a very public affair when
Lieutenant-Colonel Colin Mitchell (or 'Mad Mitch' as he became
known to the British public), triumphantly retook Crater from Yemeni
nationalists of the National Liberation Front. The recapture lasted
merely a few months before politicians pulled the plug on the escapade
and the remaining British forces were air-lifted from Aden. It was
finally time for Britain to leave southern Arabia.

For British travellers arriving in southern Arabia, Aden was
invariably the stepping-off point. Not that it always offered a
particularly welcoming sight. In 1893, Walter Harris noted:

> What a scene of desolation and dreariness Aden presents to
> the new-comer! ... A background of dreary blackish rock, a
> sandy road, half-a-dozen rickety *gharies* [horse-drawn carriages]
> under the shelter of a hideous iron-roofing, with sleepy little
> ponies and still more sleepy Somali drivers. (123)

In the heat of the sun, there is little to delight in, but as its fury fades, 'toward sunset the place wears a gay and flourishing appearance' (123). By the 1960s, the view 'from the roof of the Crescent Hotel' was of 'one of the widest, finest and busiest harbours between London and Bombay ... a great sweep of sheltered water, filled with ships'.[4] For those intrepid enough to continue their explorations of Arabia, there were two directions to head: east into the Aden Protectorate and the Hadhramaut in search of lost cities and the incense routes of old; or north, into Turkish Yemen.

In Yemen, once the Suez Canal opened in 1869, the Turks, who had held a presence on the Red Sea coast from 1849, made a push for the central Highlands, seizing San'a in 1872. Ottoman and British Empires now 'had lodgements with administrative centres 300km apart'.[5] The coffee trade had collapsed. Many Yemenis were poor and supported the Turks. In 1904, a new leader was installed. Imam Yahya immediately declared *jihad* on the Ottoman forces, taking San'a in 1905, until thousands of Turkish reinforcements retook the capital. The Ottoman Empire lost 30,000 men in one year and Yemen was dubbed 'the graveyard of the Turks'.[6] The turmoil continued with another uprising in 1911 until a treaty was finally agreed. When the Turks eventually withdrew between 1918 and 1919, it was Imam Yahya who gratefully filled the power vacuum. With these events taking place on Aden's doorstep, there was an urgent desire to gaze into this unstable world. Intrepid travellers could provide valuable information on this neighbouring imperial enemy.

In this chapter, I explore that band of British travellers who ventured beyond the confines of Aden, deeper into southern Arabia. Some travelled with the full support of British authorities while other travellers found that when they turned to their own government for help, their cases were summarily dismissed. Travellers would be tapped for the information they had gleaned once they had returned to Aden but rarely were they formally working for British secret services. Spying on the unknown regions of southern Arabia was commonly carried out by those undertaking personal exploration. Intelligence was often an additional souvenir from a far-flung corner of Arabia, eagerly collected by Aden and Indian Office officials. The machinations of British travellers and their government are often complex and a number of cases from the 1890s to the 1940s are detailed. From the 1940s to the early 1990s, there is a dearth of British travel commentary on southern Arabia. The drought is broken by two British travellers based in Yemen in the 1990s. Both Tim Mackintosh-Smith and Kevin Rushby provide a fresh perspective, their travelogues viewing the land and its peoples from a far more established position in Yemeni society than their travelling ancestors were able to offer.

*

When Walter Harris lands at Aden in 1892, he is on an extended sojourn from his position as Moroccan correspondent for *The Times*. He wanders around the town, as a tourist, but he is not there to see Aden: Yemen is his object. Harris speaks 'North-African Arabic' (153) and secures a Parsee to hire camels for his trek into Yemen. Preparations are made with Abdurrahman, his 'faithful Moor' (156), and Said, another servant. Harris heads happily along through the countryside towards the border of Turkish Yemen. He meets Turkish deserters and is kissed by a Bedouin lady who mistakes him for a woman. With a bluff, Harris is across the border pretending to be a Greek merchant:

> No Englishman crossed the frontier into Turkish Yemen in January of 1892. No; the only stranger was a penurious Greek shopkeeper of Port Said, who rode his baggage-camel. (210)

Now in Turkish Yemen, Harris is well aware of the perilous time he has chosen to travel. A rebellion by Yemeni insurgents which began in the summer of 1891 has just been put down by Turkish troops. The Ottoman Empire believes that Britain is guilty of actively arming the rebel forces. Yet Harris delights in the experience of the Yemen countryside. There is nothing of the blistering sun and empty desert which Arabia normally conjures:

> We had entered Arabia Felix! On all sides of us were tiny streams, splashing and tumbling through fern-covered banks over pebbles and stones ... Everywhere were green fields in which the young barley showed promise of rich crops, everywhere great shady trees and jungle covered the slopes. (228)

It is another world entirely. Harris is in the mountainous interior and wonders at the carefully tended terraces which striate the land.

As Harris and his party approach San'a, they bear witness to the current rebellion, 'listening to the sharp cracking of the rifles and the louder tones of the field-guns' (286). Once in the city, Harris arrives at the residence of Ahmed Feizi Pasha, who is Governor-General of Yemen. At first he is well received, but when Harris presents his British passport, the Pasha's mood changes. Fuming with rage, the Pasha has Harris arrested and imprisoned for five days.

He does not blame the Pasha as such, recognising that news of the rebellion was being kept hidden from the world and, 'to the jealous Turk the unexpected arrival of an Englishman was by no means a pleasant surprise' (297). The British government gets less favourable comment: 'Not so, however, with the actions of H.M. late Secretary of Foreign Affairs, who laid all the blame of my imprisonment upon myself' (297). There is little appetite to support one of its subjects who has travelled into Turkish Yemen in disguise and been caught in the process. Had Walter Harris returned unnoticed to Aden, he might well have received a far more favourable response.

When *A Journey Through the Yemen* was published in 1893, *The Times* review noted that Harris has 'unquenchable' spirit and good humour, describing his narrative as 'a lively record of an adventurous expedition'.[7] That good humour was severely tested in his dealings with various figures in British government over his imprisonment in San'a. A letter dated 16 May 1892 from Sir Francis Clare-Ford (British Ambassador at Constantinople) to Robert Cecil, the Marquis of Salisbury (then serving concurrently as Foreign Secretary and Prime Minister) shows little sympathy for Harris:

> It is much to be regretted that, in spite of the warning given him by the late Ambassador of the difficulties and dangers attending such a journey, Mr Harris should have, nevertheless, persisted in his expedition into the heart of a barbarous country, where, unfortunately, Englishmen are regarded with greater suspicion than other foreign travellers.[8]

In September 1892, a despatch from Clare-Ford to the Foreign Office concludes: 'The treatment which Mr Harris received was no doubt due to the conviction felt by the Turks that he had been sent from Aden as a spy to report on the country between that place and Sanaa.' While he may not have been operating as a spy, had he managed to return to Aden, his experiences of the country would, no doubt, have been gratefully received by government officials. Instead, having been discovered, Harris is nothing but a difficult embarrassment for the Foreign Office. Clare-Ford recommends that the newly appointed Foreign Secretary, the Earl of Rosebery, inform Harris that he cannot 'press on the Porte [Turkish government] Mr Harris's claim for pecuniary compensation'.[9] Though Harris has been falsely imprisoned as a spy, it is his own fault for travelling into Yemen. There will be no compensation claim. There is better news just over a week later in another letter from Clare-Ford to the Earl of Rosebery: 'the rifle which had been confiscated by the Turkish Authorities from Mr Harris was sent on June 30th last to Colonel E. V. Stace, First Assistant Political Resident at Aden, with the request that it should be forwarded to its owner'.[10] If Harris could expect no financial remuneration, he could at least await the return of his rifle.

*

When Arthur Wavell travelled into Yemen in 1910, he too was viewed as a British spy by Turkish authorities. Less than two years before, Wavell had successfully travelled to Mecca and Medina in disguise. He wrote up his two explorations into Arabia as *A Modern Pilgrim in Mecca: And a Siege in Sanaa* (1912). The account of his time in Yemen opens with a conversation Wavell had with a Turkish Pasha about his failure to travel within the country:

> 'Do not think,' [the Pasha] continued after a pause, 'that I blame you. On the contrary: I am a patriot myself, and I admire a man who works for his country. To be a spy requires courage and resource. I admire you, and think that you deserve the highest honours England can award you; but I daresay,' he continued with a grin, 'you are not doing so badly out of it, eh?'
>
> I tried to assume an expression indicative of my wounded feelings as I replied:
>
> 'I fear your Excellency has misunderstood me, or perhaps I have expressed myself badly. I was making or endeavouring to make, if you prefer it, a journey for purely scientific purposes. I wanted, as I have just told you, to explore certain parts of Arabia which are at present unknown, and my expedition had no connection whatever with the British Government or any

one else except myself, and, in a sort of way, the Geographical Society.'

'I see; and what was the Geographical Society going to pay you for it?'

'Part of the expenses, possibly, had I been successful – nothing more.'

'My dear boy,' said the Pasha, 'you can keep all that stuff for Mohammed Ali, and have the great kindness not to consider me a perfect fool. Have I lived more than half a century for nothing? Do you expect me to believe that you risk your life and spend your time in these beastly countries for nothing? You and your Geographical Society!'[11]

The notion that Wavell travelled as a British spy stems from the disbelief that he could be there conducting some amateur scientific survey. There follows a heated argument over whether the British government is, or is not, supporting the Yemeni rebels against the Turks. Less than twenty years since Walter Harris entered Yemen, travel there has not become any easier.[12]

Wavell explains how his plan was to leave under the cover of being a Muslim, and a hajji, though, 'not concealing the fact that I was an Englishman by birth' (204). In October 1910, Wavell departs Suez for a journey of eight days to Hodeidah. Getting out of town proves rather more difficult. The Turkish authorities are highly suspicious of Wavell's intentions in Yemen. Some days later, Wavell employs a servant named Ahmad and with him sneaks away by night to San'a by donkey and stays with the only European living in the city:

My first fortnight in Sanaa passed uneventfully. Signor Caprotti warned me that, while the Arabs were somewhat doubtful and suspicious concerning me, the Turks professed no two opinions: I was there as an agent of the British Government, and my purpose was espionage pure and simple. (239)

By early January 1911, the situation with the Yemeni rebels worsens. The Imam Yahya is believed to be 'advancing from the north at the head of a large army' (252). San'a soon becomes under siege and Wavell is stuck in the impasse. Wavell has two guards posted on his door, while two military policemen are assigned to watch over him under the pretext of uncovering a plot to assassinate Wavell. His Arab acquaintances and his tutor, Sheikh Ahmad, are all interned. Wavell passes the time by teaching his servant Ahmad cards. Unable to find anything alcoholic to ease the situation, Wavell experiments with 'hashish-smoking' (270), which sends him and Ahmad into paroxysms of laughter.

Against orders from the Turkish Pasha and the advice of the British Consul, Wavell and Ahmad prepare to escape San'a disguised as Turkish women. They are soon recaptured and the situation seems bleak: 'A sergeant who spoke Arabic and seemed to be in charge informed us that we were going to be hanged at the Bab-es-Sabah, where the gallows had been already erected' (306). Instead, Wavell is taken to Mohammed Ali Pasha who 'became on a sudden all kindness and courtesy. Dinner would soon be ready, he said, which no doubt I should be glad of' (307). After enjoying a cigar, Wavell is taken to prison where he is confined for two weeks and then escorted to the coast at Hodeidah where he is handed over to the British Consul. It is now June 1911.

Arthur Wavell emerges from the adventure as an extraordinarily intrepid traveller. According to Major Leonard Darwin, who wrote the Introduction to the second edition of *A Modern Pilgrim in Mecca* in 1918, Wavell showed not only 'a scholarly mastery of Arabic' but 'marvellous courage when faced by grave dangers'.[13] Both served him well in Yemen. Within days, the public was reading of his arrest as *The Times* published the story under the title: 'British Explorer Arrested in Arabia: Ill-Treatment by Turkish Officials'. The newspaper reported that Wavell, 'was paraded handcuffed for eight hours in the streets of Sanaa, and, after being subjected to gross indignities, was sent to Hodeidah, where he is still imprisoned'. This was immediately followed by an appending paragraph noting that 'a letter recently received in London from Mr. Wavell stated ... [he] was being treated in quite a friendly manner'.[14]

In the Foreign Office archives are a series of telegrams which illustrate just how the British government reacted to the incident. On 14 June 1911, Sir G. Lowther (Under Secretary of State, Foreign Office) noted he had:

addressed strong protest in writing to the Sublime Porte demanding immediate investigation with a view to reparation for Wavel (sic) and adequate punishment for those guilty of this unwarrantable proceeding against British subject.[15]

The Foreign Office stance altered as the circumstances of Wavell's arrival and behaviour in San'a became clear. By 21 August 1911, Lowther stated that:

It certainly looks as if Mr Wavell brought his troubles on his own shoulders and has no one to thank, but himself for the treatment he received at the hands of the Turks. He did everything to justify their suspicions that he was a spy.[16]

Initial sympathies had now quickly faded. But while the Foreign Office may have lost faith, Wavell did receive the support of the Royal Geographical Society. In a letter to Lowther in September 1911, the society commented it had:

promised to make him [Wavell] a Grant if the results of his expedition into Arabia were successful ... He passes as a Moslem physician from Zanzibar ... He is a man not in the least likely to do anything to irritate either natives or officials.[17]

From Hodeidah, Dr Richardson, the British Vice-Consul also continued to petition on Wavell's behalf.[18] In July 1911, he wrote to Major Jacob, Assistant Political Officer at Aden about the matter: 'I hope the Turks will show greater respect to the next scientific English traveller who may happen to visit SANA'A (sic). The Vali assumed a most unfriendly, if not a decidedly hostile attitude towards Wavell throughout, and practically regarded him as a British spy.'[19]

When Wavell returned to England late in 1911, he was advised to seek compensation and so wrote to the Foreign Office claiming £20,000 compensation for himself and £5,000 for his servant from the Turkish authorities. The claim was rebuffed. Wavell's reply stressed his concern for the safety of future British travellers to Turkish Yemen:

I would respectfully urge that the danger in adopting this attitude is that in consequence other British subjects will, with even less valid excuses, be arrested, beaten or knocked about with muskets and prevented from communicating with the British representative as was the case with me.[20]

His plea fell on deaf ears at the Foreign Office. Wavell had brought his situation upon himself. Just as had been the case with Harris, the British government found little sympathy for a traveller who had caused undue concern to Turkish authorities in Yemen. The political situation in Yemen had been unstable since before Walter Harris's exploits in 1892. When Wavell reached San'a in 1911 another rebellion was in full swing. Foreign Office eyes were again closely watching the reaction of Turkish authorities. The activities of Harris and Wavell were an annoyance. Acting beyond the government radar, they stirred up a rival imperial force in Arabia, and were a headache for the Foreign Office. They provided little information on Yemen and a great deal of unnecessary paperwork. However, had they successfully returned to Aden with valuable insight on the country and the state of the Yemeni insurgency no doubt they would have received a welcome reception.

*

While Harris and Wavell chose to explore the region west of Aden, Mabel and Theodore Bent's elected direction was east. In 1893, they were to head into the mysterious world of the Hadhramaut. Unlike Walter Harris, the Bents travelled without disguise. They also travelled with the best intentions of doing some good for the imperial cause, as Mabel Bent was to explain in *Southern Arabia* (1900):

> After our journeys in South Africa and Abyssinia, it was suggested to my husband that a survey of the Hadhramout by an independent traveller would be useful to the Government; so in the Winter of 1893-94 we determined to do our best to penetrate into this unknown district.[21]

The passive voice of 'it was suggested' conjures a sense of a whispered conversation in the back room of a London gentlemen's club. Whoever made the suggestion, the Bents were clearly closer to government voices than either Harris or Wavell. The Bents were not mere independent travellers; they travelled with the full support and authority of the British government. Yet in spite of their credentials and willingness to provide 'useful' information, there was considerable concern the expedition should avoid Yemen.

A letter from the Assistant Secretary to the Government of India, sent to the Acting Secretary of the Government of Bombay, Political Department, in November 1893, agrees to grant Theodore Bent the services of a native Indian surveyor, Imam Sherif, to accompany him on a 'tour of Makalla' though only on the understanding that 'his explorations will be strictly confined to Makalla territory and that he will not enter Turkish Arabia'.[22] The case of Walter Harris in 1892 was still firmly fixed in government minds. The unstable situation in Yemen did not need the meddling of wandering explorers. Government circles were looking to prevent any further incidents with British travellers.

When the Bents headed back to Arabia in 1894, the same concerns were raised. In September 1894, Sir Philip Currie (Ambassador for Constantinople) wrote to the then Foreign Secretary, John Wodehouse, the Earl of Kimberley, about the matter:

> It appears not to be certain whether Mr. Bent will enter Turkish Arabia, but if he does so, he will run the risk of being turned back and badly treated as was the case with Mr. W. B. Harris, who, although warned by H. M's Ambassador, entered the Yemen from the Aden side and was turned back at Sanaa ... if he [Bent] enters Turkish territory, he does so at his personal risk and H. M's Govt. cannot be held responsible for his safety.[23]

The Ambassador for Constantinople is aware of the fact that Yemen is currently beyond the pale. At the Political Department in Aden, intelligence is less secure on the matter. A pencil note in the margin states: 'We have nothing in our records about Mr. Harris' bad treatment by the Turks.' Clearly, knowledge of Harris's plight has not been evenly shared across the various government organs of the empire.

The expeditions which the Bents undertook from 1893 to 1894 are remarkable for many reasons. They were the first Europeans to enter the Hadhramaut region without any disguise and they did so, 'with a considerable train of followers' (72). In the preface to *Southern Arabia* (1900), Mabel Bent revealed another poignant aspect to their venture:

> If my fellow-traveller had lived, he intended to have put together in book form such information as we had gathered

about Southern Arabia. Now, as he died four days after our
return from our last journey there, I have had to undertake the
task myself. (v)

Theodore Bent had died of malaria almost immediately upon returning
to England. It was left to Mabel to write the record of their travels
from 'some lectures he had given before the Royal Geographical
Society and the British Association', the notes of her recently departed
husband and her own 'Chronicles' of their journeys (v). Her
endeavours produced a classic Victorian travel text.

In late 1893, the Bents left Aden heading some 230 miles by
steamer to the port of Mukalla. When they strike out for the interior,
their entourage consists of their 'faithful Greek servant', the Indian
surveyor, 'a young gardener from Kew' as botanist, and an Egyptian
naturalist alongside a number of servants, a caravan of twenty-two
camels and an interpreter who proved 'a constant source of difficulty
and danger' (73) the entire journey. Their venture was not merely to
travel through southern Arabia but to scientifically study the land and
its inhabitants.

With such a vast following, progress is slow, hampered by endless
rows and arguments with the local Bedouin. But soon, they are
climbing up on to the table-land, or 'Akaba', which divides the land of
the Hadhramaut.[24] There is much to record, from the geology of the
land to local cosmetics. If it is not always a welcoming population they
find, Mabel appears undaunted. The people at the village of Sief, she
finds 'a most unhealthy, diseased-looking lot. They are of the yellow
kind of Arab, with Jewish-looking faces' (95). Not that she is
intimidated:

> The people of Sief were so disagreeable that I told Saleh [the
> interpreter] to remind them that, if our Queen wanted their
> country, she would have had it long before we were born, and
> that they were very foolish to fear so small an unarmed party,
> who had only come to pass the winter in a country warmer
> than their own. (96)

Despite Mabel Bent's invocation of the imperial threat of Queen
Victoria glaring down on the minions of the world, as they climb the
Wadi Kasr, each village hurls a string of insults and abuse on the Bents

and their entourage. They find the notorious Hadhramis are living up to their reputation.

At Haura, Mabel Bent makes another kind of discovery:

> I felt something hard in one finger glove which I was putting on. I thought it was a dry leaf and hooked it down with my nail and shook it into my hand. Imagine my terror on lifting my glove at seeing a scorpion wriggling there. I dropped it quickly, shouting for Mahmoud and the collecting-bottle, and then caught it in a handkerchief. This was the way that *Buthia Bentii* introduced himself to the scientific world, for he was of a new species. (107)

The Bents secure a three-week stay at the castle of Al Koton, the home of the Sultan Salah of Shibam, the main town in the northern region of the Hadhramaut. Mabel Bent's narrative mood lifts now the land and its inhabitants have returned to a more traditional imagined vision of Arabia:

> Like a fairy palace of the Arabian Nights, white as a wedding cake, and with as many battlements and pinnacles, with its windows painted red, the colour being made from red sandstone, and its balustrades decorated with the inevitable chevron pattern, the castle at Al Koton rears its battlements towers above the neighbouring brown houses and expanse of palm groves; behind it rise the steep red rocks of the encircling mountains, the whole forming a scene of Oriental beauty difficult to describe in words. (111)

At last, an Arabia of *Arabian Nights* and the Bents re-secured in their own identity as the epitome of English landed gentry, visiting the upper-class of Arabia. All is as it should be. The masses are back in their 'brown houses' while the Bents are rightly ensconced in a picturesque castle. When they reach the city of Shibam, centre of the frankincense trade, they are put up in another impressive fortress. If the Sultan is welcoming, the people of Shibam are distinctly not. When Theodore ventures into town, 'the people crowded round him, yelled at him, and insulted him, trying their best to trip him up and impede his progress' (147). They stay for five days, then at the Friday prayer in the mosque a 'fanatical mollah' apparently decried 'O God! This is contrary to our religion; remove them away!' (154). They depart two days later.

As the Bents leave the protection of Sultan Salah, so the mood of the narrative shifts. They are refused permission to head to Tarim and suffer repeated harassment by their guides as they journey back from Shibam to the coast. Near the village of Bir bin Aboudan, they are shot at: 'The first shot threw up the earth nearly two yards from my horse's nose, and the next seemed to say 'tshish!' just at the back of my neck' (184). When they finally reach the relative safety of the coast, it is to intense heat and mosquitoes and fleas. Yet the Bents had managed somehow to drag their extended party into the hidden landscapes of the Hadhramaut; a high-ranking achievement in the order of Victorian imperial adventures. Rather an overt than a covert operation, the Bents were nevertheless carrying out an important mission of information gathering for British intelligence services. Travelling quite openly as a scientific expedition, not only were the flora and fauna of the Hadhramaut surveyed, but wider social, economic and political aspects of the region were being assessed. Yet the abrupt final lines of the text remind that only Mabel Bent was able to narrate their travels:

> We reached Aden at three next afternoon. This is all I can write about this journey. It would have been better told, but that I only am left to tell it. (429)

When *The Times* reported Theodore Bent's death, it lamented 'a real loss to archaeological research, as well as to geography'.[25] Some two and a half years later, Mabel Bent presented the British public with a further memorial in the publication of *Southern Arabia* (1900). She chose to stand in the shadow of her husband's achievements, but had created a work which 'was greeted with unanimous applause as a classic even of the great age of exploration'.[26]

If Mabel and Theodore Bent's travels can be seen as heroically prompted by a desire to provide the British government with a survey of southern Arabia, they were given greater pathos by Theodore's death on his return to England. The knowledge they retrieved from the rarely seen world of the Hadhramaut would be invaluable in coming decades. By the 1930s, that landscape so tentatively covered by the Bents would be under the direct control of British imperial administrators. Colonial officers operating in the field far from Aden would bring peace to the area. Those first steps by Theodore and

Mabel Bent into the Hadhramaut not only served their government with a 'useful' survey but set the foundations for future British exploration and ultimately for the region coming under British political rule.

*

Wyman Bury travelled in a very different manner. He explored southern Arabia from the late 1890s under the adopted guise of 'Abdullah Mansûr'. Bury spoke fluent colloquial Arabic, wore Arab dress and travelled alone, with nothing of the entourage the Bents dragged around. Though their style of travel may have varied, in the early twentieth century the names of Bent and Bury defined European exploration of southern Arabia. In the preface to Bury's *The Land Of Uz* (1911), Major-General Pelham Maitland drew the two figures together:

> Southern Arabia is still so little known, and contains so much of real interest, that such travels as those of Mr. Theodore Bent and Mr. Bury only serve to whet the appetite of the geographer and archaeologist. There is no one better qualified than 'Abdullah Mansûr' to undertake an extended exploration, and it is much to be regretted that circumstances have hitherto prevented him from carrying it out.[27]

Maitland had first appointed Bury to work for the Boundary Commission when Political Resident at Aden in 1902. Bury's enthusiasm for the role of Political Officer was matched by his ability to negotiate treaties between the tribes of the hinterland and the British government far from the security of Aden. By 1904, Bury was Extra Assistant Resident with a valued role in the British colonial service exploring unknown southern Arabia.[28] Yet Maitland hints at the 'circumstances' which prevented Bury from extending his travels. Rather than fêted by the establishment, as the Bents were, Wyman Bury sits more comfortably with Walter Harris and Arthur Wavell as travellers who British government and colonial hierarchies found a distinct nuisance.

In 1905, Wyman Bury was accused of taking bribes from a local sheikh and dismissed from service. In ill health, Bury eventually appealed later that year and by February 1906, received a letter from J. J. Heaton, Acting Chief Secretary to the Government of Bombay,

Wyman Bury as 'Abdullah Mansûr'.

which stated, 'you cannot be held to be guilty of having received a bribe'. Though the news was obviously welcome, it was tempered by the fact that while cleared of bribery, the letter pointed out, 'that Government do not feel that they can at present offer you further employment in the Aden Protectorate'.[29] Bury had been dropped by the British government.

Over the following years, Bury attempted both to gain reemployment at Aden and to undertake further exploration into the far reaches of the Aden Protectorate. His requests were continually turned down. Through 1908 there were a series of applications from Bury for permission to travel in south-west Arabia. He was repeatedly rebutted by the India Office and the Secretary of State, Arthur Godley. In early 1908, Bury wrote to O'Moore Creagh, Secretary of the India Office, from the Arundel Hotel in London. Requesting permission to work on behalf of the British Museum on 'zoological and archaeological research in the North eastern Districts of the Aden Hinterland', Bury drew on the fine line between traveller and government agent:

> I do not wish to allude to the services which I have been able to render Govt, while engaged on similar work in those very districts, but might mention that I hope – in the course of my journey, to amplify and bring up to date my confidential map and report on those regions (Bury's 'Tribes of the Western Hadramaut' W. O. Intelligence Dept 1901).[30]

But Bury's previous work to plot and gain knowledge of the region carried little weight now. The allegations of bribery refused to be dispelled, despite an official declaration that he was innocent. In 1908, the Resident of Aden, Major-General De Brath wrote to O'Moore Creagh in unequivocal terms of Bury:

> Although it was impossible legally to prove the acceptance of bribes, there is no doubt whatever that his financial transactions were intermixed with his political duties and were of an irregular and objectionable nature.

De Brath goes on to state he has 'consistently refused to have him over here at any price' and that 'his presence in the Hinterland would be objectionable and certain to give rise to trouble and intrigue'.[31] Though he had once been lauded and used as an intelligence gatherer operating far from the beaten track, Bury had been excommunicated from Britain's imperial fold in southern Arabia. The Resident of Aden had left him out in the cold.

By 1909, Bury had a proposed expedition into south-east Arabia supported with a £300 grant from the Royal Geographical Society which saw him as, 'in many ways exceptionally fitted for the task'.[32] In January 1909, the *Geographical Journal* and *The Times* carried articles on his proposed journey into southern Arabia. The government reacted swiftly, with the Under Secretary of State, Richmond Richie, noting privately in a letter to the Political Committee that, 'there are advantages in shutting our eyes: but the behaviour of the RGS is irritating'.[33]

Government machinery was soon actively working to disrupt any travel by Bury. In a drafted reply from the India Office, dated 4 February 1909, the Political Committee of the India Office placed the addendum that it has directed the Government of India, 'to inform the local rulers of the protected states on the coast that the British Govt. have not sanctioned and even disapprove of his tour'.[34] The bribery charges had been lifted, yet there was genuine hostility by the British government towards his return. Though the Royal Geographical Society recognised his skills as an explorer, imperial officialdom in both Bombay and Aden strove to deny him the chance to delve deeper into Arabia.

In May 1909, the India Office received the news that Bury's expedition had failed thanks to demands for £1,000 by the Sultan of Haura, a region thirty miles from the coast between Mukalla and Aden. In December 1909, Bury wrote to the newly appointed Secretary of State for India, Sir Richmond Richie, from Ceylon. After initially congratulating him on his promotion, he threw down a 'protest against the attitude adopted towards me by Aden officialdom'.[35] The reply showed little sympathy. Bury was reminded that he had been told repeatedly through 1908 that he should not travel into southern Arabia.

By April 1910, Bury was back in Aden 'with the object of penetrating to the Great Red Desert'.[36] The worry for the India Office was that Bury was writing a book on southern Arabia and 'will no doubt take the opportunity to make his grievances public'.[37] Bury had got up the nose of the British government in Aden and in Westminster. The Political Resident of Aden wrote to Richie noting:

> Mr. Bury's history is known to your Lordship and I was
> informed by an Arab friend that if Mr. Bury crossed the
> frontier [beyond the Aden protectorate], all further trouble
> would be avoided as the Tribes meant to shoot him.[38]

Though the comment may well be a flippant one, it illustrates the
extent to which Bury had wandered from the fold of British
intelligence. Now that he is operating as a lone traveller, his presence is
nothing but an irritation. When *The Land of Uz* was published in 1911,
Bury refrained from openly attacking the government. But he could
not resist a hefty dig. In the Introduction, Bury justified his work:

> based on the fact that the region dealt with, is still beyond the
> tide-mark of exploration, and since my researches there have
> been cut short by the precautions of a maternal Government,
> I choose this opportunity of making public some ten years'
> intimate experiences of a people whose country will ever
> exercise a great fascination for me as the gateway of an
> unknown land.[39]

The work consisted of a description of the tribes of the Aden
Protectorate and an 'account of certain districts beyond the limits of
the Aden Protectorate, which have not hitherto been visited by other
Europeans', based on Bury's experiences, 'of some Seven Years'
Travel, in the guise of a Down-Country Chief' (105). One chapter
recalled an intelligence gathering mission made in 1900, in the north-
east of the Aden hinterland. Bury travelled with a mixed tribal
gathering from the hills of Nisab out into the waterless deserts beyond,
towards Bayhan. The party are soon attacked by an unknown force as,
'lurid flashes stabbed through the fog across our front with a rattling
crash' and then 'the fog split before us with a flare and quavering roar,
revealing a brief shadowy vision of rampant horsemen and turbulent
manes' (237). It is a truly rip-roaring, imperial tale of desert adventure.
Before long Bury is staring towards a distant wonder:

> Face northwards and you will form a faint idea of the Empty
> Quarter – remember we are only on the fringe of its south-
> western corner. Away north as far as the eye can reach in the
> clear morning air, extends a vast sea of tawny rollers similar to

the one we're on. Far out – stretching east of north, rises a
pale spectral wall of lapis-lazuli and azure. (247)

The ghostly vision is of a desert landscape that no European will
cross for thirty years. Bury, travelling disguised as Abdullah Mansur,
steps across the edge of this imposing scene, into the periphery of this
unknown world. He gazes towards the '"Dwelling of the Void,"
merging imperceptibly into a violet haze – a veil of alluring mystery'
(248). Arabia is symbolised as a partially hidden feminine form. The
Empty Quarter becomes as tantalisingly oblique as an Oriental beauty
in a seraglio, shielded from view by gossamer. Had it not been for the
actions of the various elements of British imperial government
preventing his travels, it may well have been Wyman Bury who became
the first European to cross the Rub' al Khali some twenty years before
Bertram Thomas could claim the crown.

Bury was not done with exploring Arabia and, despite efforts to
prevent him, in 1912 travelled to Turkish Yemen, collecting birds for
the British Museum. The result was another acclaimed travelogue,
Arabia Infelix (1915). By then, Bury was actually working for British
intelligence services in Egypt: 'inevitably in disguise, among seditious
elements in the slums of old Cairo'.[40] Yet in other government
echelons the hatchet was far from buried. In November 1915, a
private telegram sent from Lord Hardinge, Viceroy of India, showed
that both Arthur Wavell and Wyman Bury were still ill-considered
figures:

> If you think it necessary to send a British Officer to him
> [Sayyid Muhammed al-Idrisi, known as the Idrisi, and then in
> rebellion against the Turks] would Leachman do? Wavell and
> Bury have also been suggested, but former is not
> recommended by F.O., and latter is notoriously untrust-
> worthy.[41]

It was eleven years after his alleged bribery charges. Though Bury
had recently travelled extensively throughout Yemen, he was still not
thought reliable enough to act as a government emissary to the Idrisi.
Though he was later employed across the Red Sea with British
intelligence services in Egypt, Bury's reputation in southern Arabia
never recovered from the allegations of bribery which surfaced in
1905. There appears to be no coordinated policy concerning Wyman

Bury. In Cairo, during the First World War, his talents for operating undercover are gladly employed to provide information on the native Egyptian population. In Aden, it is a quite different matter. A decade after the alleged bribery charges, Bury remained persona non grata.

*

Aubrey Herbert was a traveller who maintained a very different relationship with the British government. Born of the land-owning classes, Herbert travelled widely before becoming a Conservative Member of Parliament. Like Bury, Herbert served in the intelligence forces in Egypt during the First World War, reporting to the Arab Bureau alongside T. E. Lawrence. If something of a maverick like Bury, Herbert belonged to the British establishment and was highly respected within government. It was Aubrey Herbert who would become the model for John Buchan's eponymous Greenmantle – Sandy Arbuthnot, the epitome of the British secret agent: a disguised British upper-class traveller exploring enemy lands for the greater good of Britain.

In 1905, Aubrey Herbert had headed off on what was to be one of the first of his adventures in foreign climes. The circumstances of his travel plans are typically eccentric:

> One day, early in 1905, I met Leland Buxton in the Lobby of the House of Commons, and, in ten minutes' conversation, we decided that we would try to reach Sanaa, the capital of the ancient Arabia Felix and of the modern province of Yemen.[42]

In August, Herbert met up with Buxton in Cairo and they sailed down the Red Sea for Yemen. In San'a, 'a grey and tragic town, with the savage memories of famine written upon it' (65), they stay with Signor Caprotti, who Arthur Wavell will visit six years later. It is only two months since a blockade by Yemeni rebels had been relieved by Turkish troops. The population of San'a has fallen from 70,000 before the siege to an estimated 20,000:

> The Ghetto of Sanaa was like the dream of some haunted painter. Many of the men were still skin and bone, and the crowd of dark faces with cavernous cheeks, half-hidden by

twisted, black elf-locks that hung on either side, begging eyes and clutching hands, were horrible. (67-8)

When Aubrey Herbert looked on the scene, he saw the answer to the suffering in the possibility of imperial salvation:

> Those were the days when the majority of our countrymen were full of imperialist ambitions, and I confess I left the Yemen looking forward to the day when it should be controlled and its extraordinary resources should be developed by Great Britain, when a British railway should run from Hodeidah to Sanaa and from Sanaa to Aden. (75)

Herbert's dream of a British Yemen never materialised, but he was only one of a handful of travellers to witness the country at a time when Turkish control became less secure. Unlike both Walter Harris and Arthur Wavell, Herbert managed to avoid getting arrested and causing an upset for the Foreign Office. Herbert's method of travelling openly as an English gentleman may well have operated as a kind of double bluff to Turkish authorities, preventing him from being seen as a British spy. Whatever Turkish authorities felt, Aubrey Herbert managed to travel into Yemen at a very fragile political moment, observe the devastated state of San'a after the Yemeni insurgent siege and return safely to London where he could divest all he had learnt to his close colleagues in the highest echelons of the Foreign, Colonial and Political Offices of the British government. It was a useful glimpse into the closed world of Turkish Yemen, neighbour to Aden.

*

Some thirty years later, another British traveller travelled to Yemen, keen to explore the ecology of the Yemeni Highlands. In August 1937, Hugh Scott and his fellow entomologist at the British Museum, Everard Britton, headed to Aden. Their objective in exploring Yemen was primarily scientific: 'One of our principal motives was to investigate the insects, plants, and other forms of life at very high altitudes, say above 9,000 feet.'[43] The chief difficulty was gaining permission from the Imam of Yemen to enter his country. As Scott put the matter: 'Could he be convinced of the innocence of our purpose?' (4).

The 'innocence' of the expedition is a moot point, for Hugh Scott carried out work that was not only valued scientifically, but by British military intelligence. In 1942, *In the High Yemen*, Scott's record of his travels in Yemen was published. Four years later, in 1946, *Western Arabia and the Red Sea* appeared. It had been written largely by Scott and was published by British Naval Intelligence as part of a Geographical Handbook series providing up-to-date intelligence information on the Middle East. It was for a strictly restricted official audience of naval officers. When he had travelled in Yemen in 1937 and 1938, Scott did not travel as a British spy or secret agent but as a scientist. However, the knowledge he gained of the rarely seen world of Yemen was too valuable to ignore. For much of the Second World War, he was attached to the Admiralty.[44] It was a short step from there to turn information garnered during a journey around Yemen into vital naval intelligence.

From Aden, 'with the guidance of the British Political Officer' (4), Scott and Britton headed north to the Dhala Highlands of the Amiri mountains. They collected for two months. At the end of November 1937, 'the Aden Government at length got permission from the Imam for us to visit Ta'izz, in Southern Yemen' (4-5). They travelled on to San'a and spent two months in the central highlands before heading to Hodeidah. Together, Scott and Britton collected 'about 27,000 insects' and 'about 600 specimens of flowering plants and ferns' (10). Much of Scott's narrative is focussed on the nature of the lands and its people.

In San'a, Scott heads off to meet the only other British people in the city: Dr Petrie, his wife and a nurse, Miss Cowie of the Keith-Falconer (Church of Scotland) Mission. Petrie leads Scott on the required official visits and introductions, yet the Imam remains sceptical as to the nature of the expedition. Though Scott secures an interview, he is refused permission to leave for the coast by the old Manakha road with its 'magnificent scenery' (176). Instead, they must travel by the newly built motor-road. It is a sore disappointment. When they reach Hodeidah, Scott tries to arrange to travel on by road to Ta'izz but like Walter Harris in 1892, is refused. They are forced to take a *sambuq* out to the steamship anchored two miles out to sea which will transport them to Aden.

When it came to writing *Western Arabia and the Red Sea* (1946), Hugh Scott collated his knowledge of the region with material gleaned from such figures as St John Philby and Harold and Doreen Ingrams. There is an accompanying collection of photographs from such figures as

Philby, Bertram Thomas, Gerard Leachman, Douglas Carruthers, Gertrude Bell, Freya Stark and Norman Lewis. It is an impressive roll-call of British travellers in Arabia, and all had worked at some time for British intelligence. The fact serves to emphasise the strength of those connections between travellers and British secret services during the period from the First World War to the 1930s. It is a distinctly active period of consolidation for British imperial control over Arabia. Travellers and explorers provided vital information. As Turkey's empire collapsed and German influence in Arabia shrank, so British knowledge of the more distant quarters of Arabia enabled a stronger and wider imperial reach across the region. That link between travel and politics so implicit in much twentieth-century British travel in Arabia is often made explicit in *Western Arabia and the Red Sea*. In the history section, the account of 'The War of 1914-18' looks first at the Nejd region, noting: 'Thanks to the pre-war travels of Captains W. H. I. Shakespear and G. E. Leachman, the Government of India was aware of the situation in Nejd and the desert south of the Euphrates' (289).

The text is aimed at arming British Naval officers with everything they may need to know of the ways and worlds of western Arabia. They can learn the types of myrrh; the nature and position of the port of Qunfidha in south-western Saudi Arabia; that both whooping-cough and chicken-pox 'are very common' (463); and that the telephone service in Saudi Arabia is 'rudimentary' (525). While Hugh Scott protested his innocence at travelling Yemen for purely scientific reasons in 1937, the knowledge with which he left the country would prove invaluable as intelligence information on a sensitive and vital district of Arabia. The isolationist policies of the Imam of Yemen ensured that any traveller who ventured into the country might be usefully tapped for their knowledge by British intelligence, as was the case with Hugh Scott. The writing career of the travel writer Norman Lewis actually started when he was, 'asked by the British secret services to go and photograph Yemen in 1937'.[45] Though he was denied entry, he travelled the Red Sea region and had his experiences published as *Sand and Sea in Arabia* (1938).

The 1930s offered British travellers novel destinations. As British control extended further from Aden into the Protectorate, so it became relatively less dangerous for travellers to venture further into southern Arabia. In the Hadhramaut, while earlier European travellers had numbered merely a handful over centuries, suddenly British travellers were virtually stepping on each others' toes. There remained that distinctive divide among explorers of this new world: those who travelled in the service of British government, and those who did so independently. Then there is the odd exception like St John Philby who began exploring in the pay of the British only to transfer his allegiance to a rival power in Arabia.

Doreen and Harold Ingrams travelled widely throughout the Aden Protectorate in the 1930s in the role of political peacemakers on behalf of the British imperial administration. Their names are particularly remembered for the three years of harmony known as 'Ingrams' Peace' they forged from 1936 to 1939 in the Eastern Protectorate of Aden. A pioneering British colonial couple, the Ingrams were the first Europeans extensively to explore the Hadhramaut and in the process pacify a notoriously unsafe area for foreign travellers. In 1934, they journeyed across the Hadhramaut region from Shibam to Tarim, travelling in a car, 'a Graham Paige, in bad condition and without a driver'.[46] While Doreen was the first European woman to enter Tarim, the town had to wait no time before the next. In 1935, Freya Stark arrived. She had already made her way from the coast at Mukalla, heading into the Hadhramaut to become 'the third European woman to visit the interior, and the first to go there alone'.[47] In the 1890s, the Hadhramaut had seen its first female traveller in the shape of Mabel Bent. Thirty years later, two more arrived less than a year apart and over the next few years, both Doreen Ingrams and Freya Stark would return to the region.

Through the 1930s, a number of independent travellers took the opportunity to explore the mountainous lands of the Hadhramaut seeking Shabwa, a town no Western eyes had witnessed before. In 1936, Norman Pearn stepped from a P & O liner into Aden, on a quest for 'Sheba's lost city'. Following Freya Stark's footsteps, Pearn travelled down the coast to Mukalla before striking inland towards the Hadhramaut under the rather dubious guidance of Abdu, described as 'short, sturdy, and extremely ugly' and in his mid-fifties.[48] Pearn is anything but the intrepid traveller. He refuses most food offered him, even when there is 'an enormous bowl of rice from which protruded the legs of chickens and goats, spiced with a nut that gave them an appearance of mildew'. Instead he longs for 'tomato soup, corned beef and fruit' (56). Yet he is travelling for the honour of being the first European traveller to reach Shabwa.

At Shibam, in the middle of Wadi Hadhramaut, Pearn becomes more enthusiastic:

> Five hundred houses, each of them a skyscraper, standing on a slight eminence, cluster together to form one massive block of buildings. Shibam in the near distance is an unearthly citadel that might have been built by Aladdin out of mirage and magic; architecturally it belongs to the incredible imagination of the Arabian Nights, to the prodigality of an Haroun al Raschid, rather than to the sober daylight of the twentieth century. (133)

Here is the allusion to that mystical vision of Arabia so beloved by the West. It is not architecture and manpower that have created Shibam but 'mirage and magic'. The bubbling excitement at finding this ancient-looking world is only heightened when Pearn is offered the comfort of Sheikh Sa'id's hospitality. He can rest in the luxury of the villa put at his disposal. There is even the chance to meet a fellow Englishman as St John Philby is in town. Unfortunately, Pearn discovers that Philby has just spent five days in Shabwa.

Pearn decides to head for Shabwa anyway. He does not get far before Philby appears once more in his Ford. While he does shake off Philby, Pearn soon manages to lose his own party in the Wadi Hadhramaut. He is saved by a group of tribesmen. Disorientated, alone and with no water, Pearn had been travelling in the wrong direction. There is nothing for it, but to reassemble a caravan and trek back to the coast at Shisr, where he meets the doctor who attended to Freya Stark. References to Freya Stark are made throughout the text and are significant in that both travellers failed to reach their declared destination of Shabwa. But while Stark's *Southern Gates of Arabia* records this failure as a pathetic finale to the work, in *Quest for Sheba* the narrative rather drifts to an end. Pearn leaves Arabia downhearted, with Philby once more appearing to wave him off. There is a tangible sense of anticlimax.

Harry St John Philby had in fact been pipped at the post as the first European to reach Shabwa. The German Hans Helfritz had just beaten him. *Sheba's Daughters* (1939), Philby's account of his travels to Shabwa, references both Stark and Pearn. Though Philby had been in the service of the British government for some eighteen years, by the time he explored Shabwa, he did so as an independent traveller though with a powerful friend and employer in Ibn Saud. In the preface to *Sheba's Daughters*, Philby outlined his break with the British establishment in 1925 over its mandate policy in Palestine. His stance is forthright: 'British political penetration of Arabia has already gone farther than it should have done.'[49] With the imposition of 'Ingrams' Peace', from the mid-1930s the Hadhramaut had suddenly become a far more attractive destination for British travellers. Just as in other regions of Arabia at other times, when the Hadhramaut came under the umbrella of British imperial administration in Aden so a number of explorers ventured to expand British intelligence still further. By visiting and reporting on unseen towns such as Shabwa, the traveller could gain a great deal of personal acclaim and, in addition, add to the accumulated knowledge which Britain held on Arabia. This symbiotic aspect to the relationship between British imperial control and British travellers was well established. Of course, in the case of St John Philby, he had long been lost to British intelligence services.

*

Though the 1930s saw an explosion of British exploration in southern Arabia, it was not to last. Over the next half century there was a distinct lack of British travellers venturing into the region and little travel writing.[50] British influence peaked in the 1930s. Never again would British-run Aden exert such control over the surrounding lands and peoples. After the rush of British travellers into the Hadhramaut in the 1930s, there is a noticeable dearth of travel texts in the following decades. As British control fell away so did the British travellers. The drive for British intelligence on the region had run hand-in-hand with extending imperial control in the Aden Protectorate. Once that process halted in the 1940s, British explorers were deprived of a key ingredient: the desire within government to broaden British influence in Arabia. It would not be until the final decade of the twentieth century that a British travelogue would return readers' gazes to a post-imperial southern Arabia. By then, much had changed from the imperial heyday of the 1930s. British withdrawal from Aden in 1967 had led to the former colony and its protectorate becoming the People's Democratic Republic of Yemen or South Yemen. In May 1990, North and South Yemen united as the Republic of Yemen. The title 'Yemen' now encompassed all the area of southern Arabia once ruled by Britain and Turkey.

In *Yemen* (1997), Tim Mackintosh-Smith provides the first substantial travelogue on the region since Hugh Scott's *In the High Yemen* was published back in 1942.[51] While Scott travelled as an entomologist, Mackintosh-Smith ventures as an Arabic scholar and wordsmith. Yemen is, for Mackintosh-Smith, 'Dictionary Land'. The work not only provides an utterly delightful personal take on Yemen but serves to illustrate how things have changed from the days of Aden and the Protectorate. No longer does the British traveller need to fear imprisonment in San'a, nor does he find British imperial administration at Aden. It is thirty years since the debacle of Britain's final retreat from Aden; sixty since the golden days of the 1930s. The Ingrams are no longer working to pacify the indigenous tribes of the Hadhramaut, nor is there a scramble to be the first to view Shabwa.

After studying Arabic in the dusty confines of Oxford, Mackintosh-Smith leaves for Yemen. He compares his preconceived notions of San'a to the way in which Ingres created a version of the East from the comfort of his Paris studio as he, 'sanitized it, giving us the odalisques but not the odours, the eunuchs but not the screams of castration – so I had invented San'a in Oxford'.[52] The city is painted by a series of snap-shots of the author's existence there. Mackintosh-Smith is far more entrenched in Yemeni society than earlier British travellers, from Walter Harris to Hugh Scott, who merely visited the country. He lives there and has done so for years. His house forms a central point from which to view San'a, specifically from the belvedere or *ẓahrah*: 'My house is a few centuries old but the changeless style of San'ani architecture makes it hard to date' (10). He pops out for cigarettes down the 'seventy-seven (I think)' steps to the front door, and introduces the streets of San'a to the reader. Among the wares of the second-hand clothes sellers, Mackintosh-Smith recalls finding a young boy wearing a jacket of 'grey flannel with navy piping and a fleur-de-lis on the breast pocket: my prep-school blazer'. Inside, he discovers, 'Steer & Geary Gentlemen's Outfitters' and 'the ghost of an inkstain on the pocket, where my birthday Parker had sprung a leak in 1972' (12-13). Bowled over by nostalgia, Mackintosh-Smith experiences 'a strange, deep stillness of spirit ... the calm of completeness, of the wheel turning full circle, of being in the right place at the right time' (13).

It seems Mackintosh-Smith was destined to be in Yemen. He is keen to introduce his world. At Ali's Restaurant, he is a regular:

Ali himself stands in a cloud of smoke on a platform high above the ground, ladling beef broth, eggs, rice and peppers into a row of stone bowls. In front of him is a rank of cauldrons, each one big enough to boil a missionary. Below him minions tend gas cylinders that send great blasts of flame shooting up. Conversations are impossible in the roar; explosions are not unknown. The bowl of *saltah*, as they call the mixture, is brought to you red-hot, carried with a pair of pliers and topped with a seething yellowish-green dollop of *hulbah*. Lumps of meat are flambéed in a wok-like vessel, and ten feet above this the ceiling is black from years of fireballs. (15)

Mackintosh-Smith's narrative operates to detail and to amuse, but also to educate. Specific Yemeni words are thrown in to add authenticity while illustrating the linguistic complexity of travel in 'Dictionary Land'. A meal at Ali's is part of a Yemeni ritual: 'the first step on the way to *kayf*' (16). From Ali's, Mackintosh-Smith heads to buy his *qat* and then off up to another lofty room of a San'ani house to enjoy a session of *qat* chewing. This is a central tenet of the typical Yemeni male, and Mackintosh-Smith's, day. Enough quality *qat* chewing, in the right environment and the chewer will achieve that hard to define state of *kayf*:

Kayf stretches the attention span, so that you can watch the same view for hours, the only change being the movement of the sun. A journey ceases to be motion through changing scenery – it is you who are stationary while the world is moved past, like a travelling-flat in an old film. Even if briefly, the chewer who reaches this *kayf* feels he is in the right place at the right time – at the pivot of a revolving pre-Copernican universe, the still point of the turning world. (26)

While he sees *kayf* as 'a form of untravel' (26), it is travel to Yemen that has educated Mackintosh-Smith into the ways of *kayf*, something the formal Arabic teaching of Oxford could never do. It is *qat* which is the key to *kayf*. Another British traveller and friend of Mackintosh-Smith has taken his appreciation of *qat* even further. Mackintosh-Smith and Kevin Rushby share not only a love of Yemen, but a love of *qat.* For Rushby, it forms the subject of his travelogue *Eating the Flowers of Paradise* (1998):

> In San'a, *qat* governs. Each day at three, climbing the steps to a smoky room with a bundle under the arm; then closing the door to the outside world, choosing the leaves, gently crushing them with the teeth and waiting for the drug to take effect. No rush, just a silky transition, scarcely noticed, and then the room casts loose its moorings.[53]

Kevin Rushby's journey follows an ancient trade route from Addis Ababa across Ethiopia and Djibouti and over the Red Sea to Yemen where he winds his way around the country chewing *qat* with an assortment of characters. *Qat* proves the impetus for his travel. As he chews with a variety of Yemeni figures, so Rushby traces the history of *qat* and its place in Yemeni society.

In *Yemen*, too, *qat* is often a vital component to the text. With humour and candour, the author narrates a series of journeys scattering tales of the past and lexicographical wonders in the text. There are anecdotes, adjuncts from the main path, which lead the reader deeper into the strange and fascinating world of Yemen. While narrating a trek tracing the course of Wadi Surdud from close to San'a to the coast, the tale is splintered by a digression on the creatures of Yemen including a tale of *qat* and a scorpion:

> Once, a baby one walked out of my bundle and across my lap, and disappeared among the leavings in the middle of the room. I have never seen *qat*-chewers move faster. Another creature that sometimes pops up in *qat* is the *fukhakh*, the hisser – the Yemeni name for the chameleon. Its blood taken externally is a cure for baldness, but its breath makes your teeth fall out. The gecko too is often killed, as it eats the remains of food from around your mouth as you sleep, pisses and gives you spots. Despite this I have been attached to several that have grown up in my house as they are clever flycatchers and converse, like the Hottentots, in clicks. (55)

The passage is typical Mackintosh-Smith. The recounting of each humorous anecdote is layered with additional knowledge of Yemeni beliefs gathered over the years. Often, Mackintosh-Smith is to be found chewing *qat* and the meandering narrative is perhaps symptomatic of the stimulant effect of that pastime. There is a sense of the narrative mimicking a *qat*-fuelled mind as it shifts gently from one thought to another. In this sense, to read *Yemen* is to experience a form of second-hand *kayf.*

The past is always close to the surface in Mackintosh-Smith's text. From the mythological ancient, through the Islamic history of Yemen, the record of the country is retold. He details the reign of Imam Yahya and the 1905 siege of Turkish-controlled San'a in which 'people were reduced to grinding straw for bread and to eating cats, dogs and rats' (94). This is the siege Aubrey Herbert witnessed. Stepping amongst these Yemeni figures and events are other British travellers. Hugh Scott, the entomologist, is briefly spotted. So too, Freya Stark who was part of British attempts to counter Imam Yahya's isolationist stance. In 1940, she was 'sent to show Pathé newsreels to the ladies of the royal court' (95). Mackintosh-Smith knows that he is the latest incarnation of the British travel writer on southern Arabia, but his world is now one from which the imperial British have disappeared. He is a lone figure in the land. His presence in Yemen no longer causes the nuisance and embarrassment to Foreign Office officials which Harris or Wavell provoked. Neither does Mackintosh-Smith sweep the country for useful intelligence to report back to secret services in Aden, Bombay and Whitehall.

Having covered the modern history of Yemen, the narrative can take off once more, following Mackintosh-Smith on his travels around the country. In Chapter 5, he is heading for 'an unrest cure in the mountains of Raymah' (114). Again, the ubiquitous *qat* accompanies his travels and thoughts. He arrives in a packed taxi, hypnotically chewing *qat* to the rhythm of a *mizmar*, a double reedpipe, blasting from the stereo. At Kusmah, he fails to avoid the town's 'principal pedagogue', a 'fat, middle-aged Egyptian' who descends with his entire religious instruction class:

> Fifty pairs of eyes were on me.
> 'What is your name, sir?' the Egyptian asked in English.
> 'Tim.'
> 'No! "*My name is Tim.*"'
> 'Oh, yes. Sorry. My name is Tim.'
> 'And where are you from, Professor Tim?' He rolled his r's like a big cat purring. (123)

Once the Egyptian has established his subject's credentials, he brings
to the front the teacher's pet, a small boy called Ali, and continues his
interrogation in Arabic:

> 'Now. How many eyes has Professor Tim got?' he asked the
> class.
>   'Two!' they shouted.
>   'And how many eyes has Professor Ali got?
>   'Two!'
>   'How many ears has Professor Tim got?'
>   '*Two!*
>   'And Professor Ali?'
>   '*TWO!*
>   'How many ... noses has Professor Tim got?'
>   'One!' There were a few 'twos' from the back of the class.
>   The questioning went on until we had covered all
> mentionable parts of the body. Our respective religions were
> then re-established. 'So, although Professor Tim is a Christian
> and Professor Ali is a Muslim, God has created them the same
> in all respects.'
>   'But he's taller!'
>   'Silence! This!', said the Egyptian, finally releasing us, 'is
> proof of the oneness of His Creation.' (124)

Here, once again, is evidence of Mackintosh-Smith's often charmingly
light style in some innocent humour reminiscent of Joyce Grenfell.
There is a genuine sense of the author recounting happy moments
passed.

At Aden, or 'Dugong City', Mackintosh-Smith is initially found in a
disco listening to 'an Egyptian glam-rock number' when 'the floor
filled with young men dressed in Paisley pattern shirts and pleated
trousers' (137). They are the *mutamaykalin*; the 'Michaelesques' or
Michael Jackson fans. He slips from the scene when confronted with 'a
mountainous figure' with a chest which 'could be seen shuddering
beneath her *abayah*, like a couple of hippos trapped in a marquee'
(137). Aden is a surreal world. It has a strangely British feel. It is
'Coventry in the sun' (145). But Mackintosh-Smith proclaims it is time
to set Aden free; 'time to lay the imperial ghosts' (143). He trawls
Aden's history from the first arrival of the British in January 1839 and
points out the variety of imperial detritus that the British left behind in

1967. Alongside the, 'right-hand-drive Humbers, Rileys and Morris Minor 1,000s' is a Bedford van from which fish and chips are sold. There are still pillar boxes, 'but with the royal cipher chiselled off' (159). He chats to a local trader, eyeing the Baltic amber:

> 'How much are they?'
> 'Nothing. I like to give my best customers a little present.' It was my first visit and I hadn't bought anything. 'Where did you say you were from? Germany? France? Italy? Belgium?'
> *Belgium.* We were here for 128 years, for heaven's sake. We were the ones who *understood* the Arabs. We gave them pillar boxes, and Coventry. 'I'm British.' (159)

The internal outrage and mock use of the collective 'we' create the humour. For all those years in southern Arabia, the modern British tourist is just another foreign face. Mackintosh-Smith recognises the imperial baggage for what it is but cannot quite take it seriously. The notion that his people, the British, ran the region of modern Yemen is hard to swallow. The evidence lies scattered all around Aden yet still seems strangely incongruous. What *were* the British doing there? They may have only left thirty years before but it seems an utterly alien world that they produced in southern Arabia. Yemeni traders have short memories.

Matters have moved on from a time when Aden was British-controlled and travellers in southern Arabia could be divided into two camps: those whom the government supported on their expeditions, and those who found themselves without official backing. Those caught by Ottoman authorities received little sympathy. When Walter Harris and Arthur Wavell on separate occasions found themselves imprisoned in San'a, neither received government backing for their claims of compensation. On the other hand, Mabel and Theodore Bent's expeditions into southern Arabia in the 1890s were instigated by a desire within British intelligence circles for an independent survey of the area. Though Harris deliberately hid his nationality, travelling incognito around Turkish Yemen, the Bents found leading a scientific survey was the only disguise required to undertake extensive espionage. Similarly, half a century later, Hugh Scott's scientific exploration of Yemen would prove valuable to British Naval Intelligence. Travelling and intelligence gathering could be a dual process. For those close to government, like Aubrey Herbert, a venture beyond Aden would offer a useful survey of a neighbouring Ottoman-run land. Other figures, such as Wyman Bury and St John Philby had more complex and tempestuous relations with British authorities.

Things have turned full circle since Walter Harris arrived in Aden back in 1892. Then, the British imperial enterprise was embryonic. The Suez Canal offered a short cut to India and Aden grew as a distant British outpost, an overnight stop for tourists, and a base to explore southern Arabia for travellers. A century on, Tim Mackintosh-Smith discovers the British presence is fading fast. Post-1967, Aden is rapidly shedding the vestiges of Britain's extended adventure in Arabia.

8

AFTER EMPIRE

We squatted in the room by the glimmer of the lamp. Somebody had gone to connect electricity to the house. I could only make out a spinning-wheel and a paraffin stove in one corner of the room, and clay shelves piled with more blankets and jars.

I offered the woman some tea which I had bought in the village. At first she refused, but we had taken her unawares, and she had nothing in the house, so eventually a hand hovered out of the gloom and took the bundle. The stove flared up. People filtered into the room: robust men swathed in *keffiehs*, awkward and formal at first, but soon smiling. A joke that they were all fools was spreading among them in squibs of laughter. They hailed me, through the dimness, as 'Mr Colin', and each one asked me to pardon the behaviour of the rest.

Then the electric bulb lit up and we saw each other. They had mild, honest faces − except, perhaps, for the village intellectual, whose eyes were shining and close-set, like a pair of tempered daggers ...

As the hours ran by in talk, a tric-trac board was produced, fondled and put away. Then the men began to sing in the long, impassioned cries of Arabia, old songs which I could not understand, but which were 'very wonderful'. The joke about fools was revived. I was asked to sing too. *The Duke of Plaza Toro* evoked bewildered silence, but fierce applause greeted *Stranger in Paradise*. Again the wild Arabian songs filled the night. The phrases would begin 'Mr Colin ...' and would dance from mouth to mouth until they cascaded into assurances that the words were welcoming.

Soon the room was exploding with noise and I thought the village policeman would enter and demand my passport. Later I saw that he was sitting at my elbow, his head thrown back in song. Passers-by squatted in the doorway and chanted under the stars. Refaiyeh, sitting apart, tried to read stories aloud to herself, sometimes smiling at us remotely. After a long time she put the children to bed, but for almost an hour the little girl Majida fixed me with a hazel stare from between her blanket and her tangled curls.

The intellectual moved to my side and monopolised a silence.

'What are the British doing in Aden?' His demand fell on our friendliness like a policeman's hand on a criminal's shoulder. He must have been listening to a wireless. Even the others appeared to resent the intrusion, though every Syrian's mind is a honeycomb of political notions. Nobody else expressed interest in Aden, so I professed ignorance of it. What was Aden? Did you eat it, smoke it, blow bubbles with it? (Since the Arabs pronounce it Ah-den, I felt quaintly justified.)

Somebody began to sing, someone resurrected the joke about fools, and the moment passed.[1]

This passage comes from Colin Thubron's first book, *Mirror to Damascus* (1967). A young Englishman has cycled from Damascus to explore the route of the Barada river. As dusk rolls in, he seeks shelter in the village of Ashrafiyeh where he is warmly welcomed by the villagers. Thubron is joined in a barren room by a stream of locals. Laughter spreads. His choice to sing 'Stranger in Paradise' from the musical *Kismet* may seem both a rather sentimental evocation of an exotic vision of Arabia and an allegorical *cri de coeur*, but it finds a jubilant audience. The melodies of the locals are 'the long, impassioned cries of Arabia' and 'wild Arabian songs' conjuring further romantic impressions from the young Thubron. The English outsider finds himself ever more comfortably ensconced in the hold of his hosts. But all is not as it seems. The 'intellectual' steps into a hiatus in the chatter and destroys the happy scene with one question: 'What are the British doing in Aden?'

The moment occurred some time in 1965. Several hundred miles south, the British occupation of Aden, which had lasted for close to 130 years, was drawing to an ignoble end. Though Thubron may feign bewilderment, the spluttering final military actions of the British imperial presence in Yemen have echoed across the vast lands of Arabia. When asked recently of the incident, Thubron told how he thought: "'Oh dear, I'm going to get this" but it was sort of that feeling of it not being my fault and nothing to do with me. Typical of my sort of slightly apolitical British liberal: not wanting to be associated with my government in that way.'[2] Here is the modern British travel writer starting to emerge. Even though there may be painful questions to answer on the role of the British government in the region, the dialogue of the personal encounter with the people of the Arab lands is now a central element to the traveller's tale. Thubron may try to sidestep his association with that government, but he cannot avoid the interrogation of its foreign policy.

This chapter explores the nature of travel writing from that moment when the tide of British imperial presence in Arabia ebbed away, through to 2003 when British forces returned to invade Iraq.[3] How did the removal of the last vestiges of British imperial structures impact on travel writing about the region? What form did post-imperial travelogues take? The influence that earlier British imperial travelogues had on the post-imperial travellers is examined, as is the effect of the debate following the publication of Edward Said's *Orientalism* (1978). Four key writers of this period are discussed: Colin Thubron, Jonathan Raban, William Dalrymple and Tim Mackintosh-Smith. All four were interviewed about these matters during the research for this chapter, and their words provide essential material for the analysis.[4] The oral testimony of these authors was of considerable value here, the advantages of using their comments and insights outweighing any concerns over constructed memory. In drawing this study of British travel writing on Arabia to a close, some thoughts are offered as to the future direction of the genre.

*

Mirror to Damascus (1967) opens with a climb up to the relative peak of Mount Kassioun from which Thubron and his reader can gaze down on Damascus. To the west rise the Anti-Lebanon mountains and Mount Hermon (Jebel es Sheikh). A line of poplar trees marks the

course of the Barada river as it snakes its way to Damascus. Thubron
strives to understand the city. He visits the supposed cave of Abel
where Cain is said to have hidden his brother's body. Veins of red rock
are seen as Abel's blood. However, even tracing Old Testament
legends does not ensure the true place to start the tale of Damascus.
On Tel es Salihiye, Thubron 'blundered among the wreckage of sixty
centuries' (8). The site is an amalgam of all Damascene history: 'Every
stratum of brick or pottery marks the graves of an era' (8). He is finally
stepping amidst the first Damascenes. It is a scene that serves as a
metaphor for his book: in the coming pages of *Mirror to Damascus* the
reader will be guided through the layers of distant time and lovingly led
through the past lives of the most ancient city in the world.

Yet *Mirror to Damascus* evolves as far more than a historically based
travelogue of Damascus. As the opening quotation to this chapter
illustrates, the presence of the current population of Syrian folk plays
its role too in defining the city. The incident at the village of
Ashrafiyeh spotlights Thubron as a young Englishman immersing
himself in the lives of his hosts. His own experiences will form a part
of the narrative. When Thubron heads for the hills once more, it is for
the village of Maloula which has held its Christian traditions. He
reaches the convent at Seidnaya which Justinian founded in 547 AD.
Thubron stays in 'a small, tiled room with an iron bed and a view over
grey hills: Brother Colin's cell' (56). In the morning, he joins the
Mother Superior for morning Eucharist where he witnesses a miracle:

> In the shadows the nuns were crying and kissing the icons.
> Two of the paintings were streaming fluid. On one of them
> the water rose directly from the eyes of the Virgin, which
> looked away, abstracted and languorous, into the candlelight. I
> accepted these tears without surprise. Syria is the country of
> miracle.
>
> The Mother Superior smeared away some liquid from the
> ikon with a cloth and dabbed it against my forehead and
> eyelids murmuring 'Dieu vous garde', and on my wrists: 'Dieu
> vous donne la force, l'intelligence, la santé." (58)

Blessed with these words, Thubron takes off on his bicycle. At
Maloula, he meets the remaining Greek Catholic priest at the
monastery of Saint Sarkiss. He asks Father Theodor to speak the
Lord's Prayer in Aramaic, the language of Christ: "Obo*ch* tee bishmo

lyit kad dash issma*ch* theyla malakoo tha*ch* ...' I can transcribe no more of the Lord's Prayer as it was first spoken, for here the old man's voice, steeped in mortification, faltered and died. He had forgotten the rest' (61).

It is meetings with figures such as the Mother Superior and Father Theodor that personalise the historical trail through Damascus and the surrounding Syrian countryside. Thubron's enthusiasm to tell the tale of the past is clear. With swift ease he is able to depict vast, sweeping, eons of history. He gallops through the Damascene timeline with dashing allure. From early Christian eras, through the death of Mohammed and the various lives of the Ommayads, the narrative tears joyfully through time. The years from 750 brought little but Abbasid vengeance to Damascus. The Crusades brought sieges but the Damascenes held firm. In 1154, Nureddine brought new hope to the city: 'Damascus put on a new dress' (104).

The mid-thirteenth century brought the Mongols to Syria, severing the Abbasid caliphate: 'In a single week they gutted Baghdad, butchered a million people and destroyed Mesopotamia's timeless irrigation systems, turning her to marsh and desert' (118). The great figures of Syrian history all appear. The Mamelukes under Sultan Qutuz defeat the Mongols at Goliath Springs, then Baybars 'passed a dagger through the sultan's neck' (119) and proceeded to rule Egypt and Syria for seventeen years: 'He linked his two capitals by a road which enabled him to play polo in Cairo on a Saturday and lead prayers in the Ommayid Mosque the next Friday' (119). Two more centuries of Mameluke rule followed before the Damascenes expelled them in a bloody overthrow. It was not to last long:

> Nemesis came out of the east. Tamerlane only captured Damascus by treachery, for his warriors were repulsed at the walls. For three days and nights the city burned. Thirty thousand men, women and children were bolted into the Great Mosque, and convulsed in flames. Every surviving male over five years old was carried away to Samarkand, and Damascus lay among her orchards like the carcass of a mountain, peopled by tiny children. (124-5)

When Thubron recounts his own conversations with the Damascenes he has met, the narrative soars. He goes to seek the remaining Jews of the city at Djobar and quickly finds himself embroiled in politics. At a school for Palestinian refugees, built on land taken from the synagogue, he is given tea by the masters and told of their hatred for England:

> 'You see the children out there? You know who they are? England gave their homeland to the Jews. You have heard of Lord Balfour?'
> I said I had heard of no other Englishmen since entering Syria.
> 'Today is the anniversary of the Balfour Declaration. In a moment each of us will speak to the children about what has been done to them; how an Englishman gave Palestine to men who had never even been there. And how it will be taken back again.' (168)

The statement made in 1917 by Arthur Balfour, the then British Foreign Secretary, concerning a Jewish homeland would reappear persistently during Thubron's travels. He talks of it as 'the constant Balfour thing'. Though 'not being a political sort of animal', Thubron was consistently faced with the past policies of British imperial administration: 'Being somebody very naïve about Middle Eastern politics or any politics, I was surprised a little by the constancy with which that agreement came up like that.'⁵ As a young British traveller in the mid-1960s, Thubron was educated in imperial politics by the people of Damascus. When Jonathan Raban journeyed around Arabia just over a decade later, he found himself presented with similar considerations:

> It was impossible when I was travelling there to even take a ride with a taxi driver without one being questioned on two phrases: 'What do you think of the Sykes-Picot agreement?' and, 'What do you think of the Balfour Declaration?' Arabia is a memorious culture and the slight of both those documents were as keenly felt, or seemed to be as keenly felt, in the late 1970s as they would have been forty years before. To that extent they were part of the contemporary landscape and I found myself having to prepare: 'What am I going to say when I am next asked about the Sykes-Picot agreement, the Balfour Declaration?' That became a matter not of history, but of immediately contemporary relevance, like dealing with an

outraged taxi driver telling me how evil the Balfour Declaration was.[6]

The past takes on a pressing significance for both these British travellers. Neither one is allowed to forget the enormity of previous British foreign policies. Knowledge of the political past is held by a significant proportion of the Arab population, who keenly question modern British travellers on such matters. Education of the next generation, as Thubron witnessed in the school at Djobar, ensures those policies are not forgotten.

In the busy home of the Bahena family of Elias and Umm-Toni and their six children on the Street Called Straight in the Christian quarter, Thubron is safe from the ire induced by Balfour. Instead, as he draws his portrait of Damascus to its close, he has other fears and concerns. Thubron finds it hard not to lament the loss of the ancient city as it adapts to new ways:

> Industry spreads into the orchards. Where growth used to create beauty, it now destroys. Paradise is trampled under stone, and man has dealt with the Barada as he does with most of his great rivers: begins by worshipping, and ends by polluting them. (208)

Into this Garden of Eden stomps the devil of modernity. But if Thubron decries the change, his humanity finds it 'difficult to grudge men the extra wealth it will one day bring' (208). Yet his grief is for the inevitable loss of the city's soul:

> In time, a distressing logic will creep into the streets. The summers will be purged of fever. Each of Rahda's [a girl of the Bahena family] children may have a room of his own. And the traveller will not wake again in a jasmine-scented night, to hear the sherbet-seller calling for him to refresh his heart. (211)

So it is on a distinctly melancholic note that *Mirror to Damascus* ends. The modern world sits on the edge of the city like the latest invading force to sweep through its gates. This grieving epilogue to the text can be compared to the manner with which Wilfred Thesiger bemoaned the modernisation of Arabia. Thesiger's overt nostalgia was apparent throughout *Arabian Sands* (1959) and has been explored in earlier chapters. It is perhaps not surprising to find a young British traveller to Damascus in the mid-1960s expressing similar emotions. Thesiger sat as a monolithic figure of British travel. His work had been published merely six years before Colin Thubron commenced his portrayal of the Syrian capital. Asked about the ending to *Mirror to Damascus* some forty years after its publication, Thubron describes the finale as 'sentimental, of course ... unashamedly romantic, really'. He is 'pretty sure' he had read *Arabian Sands* 'and admired it' before writing his own first travel text:

> I couldn't write such a thing now, and that's the benefit in a way of accepting that you were rather ignorant and a bit less cynical than now. I don't know about Thesiger. I must have had a feeling that this was on the way out and one was certainly very conscious even at the time of Salihiye and Kassioun [two historic quarters of Damascus]; that the suburbs were backing up there and this was a doomed world probably. I didn't think that world would remain, the things that I loved. This is flagrant Orientalism by the standards of today but there we are. That's what one felt.[7]

If aspects of his text may tie him to the sentiments of Thesiger, Thubron is distinctly post-Thesiger and modern in his portrayal of personal encounters, lifting the narrative with conversational dialogue on matters political, on British imperial policy, or simply the everyday. Yet he did not set out deliberately to include such passages as some form of light antidote to the factual nature of much of the text: 'The important things to me were the history, the architecture', whereas of the moments of conversation, Thubron notes: 'I remember thinking, "It's nice when these things happen", and they give an idea, well some idea, of the people seen through rather naïve Anglo eyes. But they weren't as important to me as they later became.'[8] In subsequent travel texts, on Russia and China, the texts 'almost pivot on the individual encounters'. In *Mirror to Damascus*, 'the conversations [were not] things which I sought as particularly valuable for the book. They were pleasantly innocent in a way, compared to my later encounters.'[9]

In Thubron's second travel text, *The Hills of Adonis* (1968), he traces a journey through Lebanon in 1967. Some years earlier, Ralph and Molly Izzard had written *Smelling the Breezes* (1959) detailing their

adventures exploring Lebanon with four young children in the summer
of 1957. In an authors' note, they commented that 'much of the
territory we walked through then has now slipped back into the
lawlessness common to the country in the last century, and it will be
some time before a foreigner can venture with any confidence into the
wild mountain regions of the northern Lebanon'.[10] Less than a decade
after this warning, Thubron was trekking those hills alone.

Thubron decides to walk from 'the fishing towns of the south'
across Lebanon on the trail of 'many-faceted divinities' such as Astarte
and Adonis.[11] He starts in Sidon which 'is secretive and seems to have
grown from the waves' (17). In a tale of ancient gods, Thubron traces
Adonis back to his Sumerian antecedent Tammuz, and Astarte back to
Ishtar. 'Every summer he died and Ishtar searched for him in "the land
from which there is no returning"' (19). All life faded, until Ishtar
brought Tammuz back to earth. It is springtime and Thubron's
narrative reflects the joyful steps of his journey. All is fecund and
bursting with the glory of rejuvenated life. There is an innocence in the
air to accompany other gentle aromas:

> The first day of spring, and the hills are flushed with
> anemones. Simply to walk through the orchards of Sidon is an
> intoxication, for it is the month of the orange and lemon
> harvest. Behind their walls the groves are bent and graceful
> with fruit. (26)

As he travels, he finds himself 'empathizing with the ancient view of
nature', such that he is 'trying to re-sanctify' (97) the lands, to
understand the Phoenician mind. Thubron heads into the mountains,
staying with crowded families in isolated villages, gazing at their ways
and still wondering at the Phoenician elements. When he falls asleep,
he expects 'to wake to the cymbals of Astarte' yet instead it is to 'a
mouse pulling my empty sardine tin into the rocks' (112). A passing
goatherd plays a 'three-holed flute' leaving a trail of sound that is
'haunting and Phrygian' (112). The hills of Adonis are alive with the
sounds of the ancient past. Yet there is also a distant rumble. It seems
this genial world is under fire.

On the road to Yammouneh, the threat of violence resurfaces: 'I
saw a fortress-village, the hashish crop young in its fields, and men
with guns walking on the crags' (143). He sees the signs paralleled in

nature: 'anemones had wilted and dropped their petals one by one,
Adonis already dying' (144). The narrative now crackles with tension:

> I approached the Christian hamlet of Ainata and knew from a
> distance that something had happened. The street was filled
> with men and boys, who stared at me so bemused that I
> almost passed before a burly man stopped me. 'You realize
> there's a war on? Egypt, Syria and Jordan attacked Israel an
> hour ago. Lebanon is in it too.'
> They crowded round me without smiling or enmity, but
> with a kind of stifled pity which frightened me. (148)

The moment brings a decisive shift in the text. An innocent wander
over ancient hillsides while Adonis is reborn in the springtime
anemones has been brutally halted. The flowers of the countryside are
fading. They are emblems of change and a prelude to war. The violent
present destroys the ancient wonder. As Thubron creeps over the
High Lebanon mountains, there exists 'a light, vague fear, only
articulate in my body' (149) and when he reaches a village it is to locals
enthusiastically repeating reports from Radio Cairo on the state of the
war:

> I asked them to switch to the BBC and they did; for a moment
> there was only crackling.
> 'They are machine-gunning the BBC,' someone said.
> Then from the circle of swarthy faces the notes of Big Ben
> rose one by one with an exotic majesty. The Overseas Service.
> I interpreted: 'Israel claims to have pressed back Egypt in the
> Gaza strip ...' Faces fell. (150)

In a preface written in 1986, Thubron notes that, 'this four-month
walk through the mountains and coasts of Lebanon describes a world
irrecoverably gone ... So this journey belongs to a time of innocence –
both Lebanon's and mine' (13). If there exists that same sentiment as
expressed at the end of *Mirror to Damascus*, here the lament is for a
defined loss:

> I realised, it wasn't difficult to realise, that something was
> disappearing as indeed it has from the Lebanon. It wouldn't
> be possible probably to make a walk like that again, if at all. It

seemed then to me, and I'm not normally particularly clear-sighted or politically driven as I say, but in this instant it seemed to be a tinkering with the make-up of something which was already very fragile in terms of government, the French legacy, so delicately poised and I felt that was all gone.[12]

With these sighs of lament for a lost world, perhaps Thubron should be seen alongside Thesiger? When asked this question, Thubron stated: 'I don't see myself with Thesiger. I feel very divorced from that, although I know you've suggested even a sort of romantic link. I don't think I was ever ennobling about the Arabs. I never felt that there was this glamorous race that Thesiger eulogised or supposed that they exist. That was all foreign to me.'[13] Perhaps instead, it would be fairer to state that Thubron's work steps from the romantic, imperial vision of Thesiger to that of a more modern, post-imperial traveller:

> I think I'm probably modern in the sense that I'm entertaining of ordinary people in my books in a demotic kind of way, a way that is non-imperial. If you stage yourself in a particular way, in my case, it's pretty much unconscious. My feeling about the people I meet is that it's not as though I'm an inheritor of an imperial tradition or anything. One's just fascinated in making these friendships with these young guys on the whole. I mean, I was very young. In that sense, it is the modern tradition of attempted sympathy, empathy with the people you're travelling around which you don't really get much with travel books before my time.[14]

*

When Jonathan Raban came to write *Arabia* (1979), he made sure that the break from a Thesiger-esque vision of Arabia was absolute. The depictions of Arabs by British travellers of imperial times were far removed from the figures which Raban saw on the streets of 1970s' London. But Doughty, Lawrence and Thesiger were significant, none the less:

> They were figures to rebel against. I remember I'd just got back from travelling in the Middle East and found myself at

dinner one evening in London seated next to an ineffably silly, somewhat upper-class woman who asked me what I was doing and I said I was writing a book about Arabia. She said 'Oh Arabia – I so love the desert; so romantic.' And I thought, 'Fuck it! I'm going to write a kind of 'anti-you' book. No camels; no little brown boys.' What I was identifying in the introduction was I think that kind of homoerotic tradition of finding a simpler world of simpler people. I always remember reading Thesiger with particular ire when he laments the new riches befalling Arabia. He fears that the people are going to be totally spoiled and cease to be these essentially simple people; tough, hardy, the public school dream. Now that money has fallen on their heads, they're all going to be softened and wet and what a tragedy that will be. I thought, 'Well, fuck that.' My sense of Arabia was shaped by going there but also to some extent formed before I went, as this land of passionate city builders: Alexandria, Jerusalem, Damascus, Aleppo, San'a. These were cities in place when London was just a sort of muddy ford across a rather nasty looking estuary. The way in which the British have been inclined to think of Arabia as an unpopulated land of sand dunes, camels and people living in tents is so far from the actual history of Arabia which is a place of spectacular cities. I wanted to get into that second world, to a large extent the truer one.[15]

The desire to break with the past is central to Raban being able to portray this 'truer' Arabia. Instead of plodding along in the ancestral footsteps of earlier British travellers, Raban flew around the modern world of Arabia in an effort to redefine their vision. There were to be 'No camels; no little brown boys'. In *Arabia* there exists an irreverence to Thesiger not seen before. When Raban finally came to meet Wilfred Thesiger at the BBC some years before his death, Raban's fear was that 'he might have at me with a knobkerry for what I'd written about *Arabian Sands*'.[16] In fact, Thesiger 'turned out to be the perfect gent. He told me how much he liked *Arabia*, which took the wind out of my sails and also made me metaphorically take off my cap to him for being able to be so generous under the circumstances. But then I wondered, 'Well, perhaps he hasn't read it''.[17] If Thubron is to be considered as modern due to his use of dialogue and a step away from

Thesiger, Raban's *Arabia* is distinctly post-modern in style, taking British travel writing a giant stride into a post-imperial world beyond the desert romance envisaged by Thesiger, Lawrence and many earlier travellers. His Arabia is a world of cities.

In the 1970s when Raban travelled in Arabia, the Oil Crisis of 1973 coupled with the Yom Kippur War ensured the region remained a focus for Western eyes. Yet what is worth noting is the lack of travel texts written on Arabia in the period following British imperial withdrawal from the region. After Aden in 1967, there are three texts by Colin Thubron: *Mirror to Damascus* (1967), *The Hills of Adonis* (1968), and *Jerusalem* (1969); then merely a handful of travelogues covering the period through to the mid-1990s.[18] The 1980s see little British travel writing on Arabia. What reasons are there to account for such a scarcity of texts during the late twentieth century, when so many travelogues were published in earlier decades? Jonathan Raban puts the matter down to the nature of travel writing: 'the presupposition of the genre of travel writing is the places you must go to should be romantic and exotic and a place full of oil wells and cities and rich people rather defies the conventions of the genre'. The paucity of travel texts from the 1970s had resulted from the Arab countries' new found wealth. As Raban expresses it, 'Arabia perhaps had been taken off the map by the very fact of its riches'.[19]

Another matter to consider is the enormous impact which Edward Said's *Orientalism* (1978), and the subsequent rise of postcolonial studies, had on travel writing. After Said's thesis, the notion of an 'Orientalist' vision of Arabia took on new meaning. It may well be true to say that British travel writers were now wary of being labelled as 'Orientalist' in their outlook, even avoiding Arabia as subject matter. Perhaps this explains the lack of travel texts in the 1980s. Jonathan Raban's *Arabia* (1979) offered a novel perspective on the Arab world. Raban, although, 'prickly about anyone taking it as an 'Orientalist' work', has stated that 'Edward Said, when he read it on publication, congratulated me on steering clear of all the Orientalist pitfalls'.[20] Raban is fervent in his support for the Saidean thesis: 'I know the world is full of attacks on *Orientalism* and how Said got it wrong but it seems to me an immensely powerful and important book and in broad outline absolutely right. He caught perfectly the way in which the West has infantilised, trivialised, feminised the East for its own purpose.'[21]

What is apparent is that the output of British travelogues on Arabia decreases as the British imperial presence in the region diminishes. It may be simply that the loss of imperial administrative structures disabled potential travellers from heading into that world. In the apogee of British imperial rule in Arabia in the 1920s and 1930s, travellers such as Doreen and Harold Ingrams, Bertram Thomas or Gertrude Bell were actively working for the colonial services. Alternatively, perhaps the lack of travelogues should be viewed as a post-end-of-empire breathing space; a period of reflection. When presented with this summation, Tim Mackintosh-Smith agreed and noted that, 'travel seems to give way to memoirs - like that clutch of Aden and Protectorate memoirs in the 1960s'. On an individual scale, he points to the example of Jan Morris: 'a sort of "national memoir" ... who wrote that book on knocking about with the Sultan of Muscat in the 1950s [*Sultan in Oman*, 1957] (which she, or he then, could do because of late imperial connections), then her big imperial history; and then she went on to pretty empire-free travel. Perhaps an interesting case of a writer who straddles that time of change?' [22]

*

In the 1990s, the drought in British travel writing on Arabia lasted until the second half of the decade, when it decisively broke. The breathing space from imperial times was over. In 1997, two important travel texts appeared. Tim Mackintosh-Smith's *Yemen* has already been appraised in the previous chapter. [23]

The other work to be published that year was William Dalrymple's *From the Holy Mountain*. Dalrymple's text opens with a vision of his cell 'bare and austere' in the Monastery of Iviron, Mount Athos, Greece. [24] The opening pages, in the form of a diary, note that it is 29 June 1994. He has just seen the manuscript of the book which has apparently brought him to this place. It is the work of the sixth-century monk and traveller John Moschos - *The Spiritual Meadow*. For Dalrymple, it is 'the great masterpiece of Byzantine travel writing' (13). He sits in the cell and prepares to write up the first stage of his journey and his hopes for the remainder. As Dalrymple retraces the footsteps of John Moschos so his own exploration will detail the precarious present state of the Christian population in the Middle East.

Near Antioch, at the remains of the pillar of St Symeon Stylites the Younger, Dalrymple is the only visitor. A church had been buil around the pillar while Symeon stood and looked on. It was : remarkable chapter in the history of orthodox Christianity: 'The stylit had become like the Christian version of the Delphic oracle: raised up on his pillar at the top of the highest mountain, a literal expression of his closeness to the heavens, he spoke what all assumed to be the words of God' (59). Coming to view these holy men was, in Moschos's time, a popular afternoon activity for the good people of Antioch. The crowds of Christians witnessed by Moschos on his Byzantine travels have vanished. Dalrymple sits alone in the ruins, re-reading *The Spiritual Meadow* and imagining the past.

Dalrymple's path leads him through the war zone of south-eastern Turkey to the monastery of Mar Gabriel. He must avoid both the Turkish army and PKK Peshmerga guerrilla raids. It is a perilous and tense time in Dalrymple's journey which serves to highlight the precarious existence of the remaining Christians in the region. Commenting on the hazardous nature of much of his trail, Dalrymple stated:

> I don't think I was aware when I set off quite how dangerous it was going to be, quite how much sort of serious gun stuff there was going on, en route. When you're on a journey for a travel book, you have a doppelganger travelling with you and one of you is scared shitless that you're going to get shot or blown up by a land mine and the other is rubbing his hands and saying, 'Copy'. Like, 'Thank God, something's happened. It's going to make a great chapter ... I nearly got kidnapped, I nearly got blown up.' And the closer you can get to complete disaster without the disaster actually taking place is the perfect journey for the travel writer because you have a story in itself.[25]

The split nature of the traveller's mind when faced with danger is closely paralleled in an observation by Colin Thubron:

> In a way, there's a sort of excitement to the writer because in a crude way you're thinking, 'This is good copy' just like any journalist. There's this one part of you thinking you're in slight danger ... But there's the other one [part of you], the one who's writing about it as it were, sitting on your shoulder, the one who's travelling, saying, 'I can use this.'[26]

In Syria, conditions are improved both for Dalrymple and the
Christian communities. Though there are concerns over the rising
fundamentalism amongst the Muslim population, when Dalrymple
meets the Metropolitan of the Syrian Orthodox Church in Aleppo he
has been granted permission to rebuild Tel Ada, the monastery of the
young St Symeon Stylites. The conversation takes a surprising turn:

> 'The church is to be based on St Symeon's church at Qala'at
> Semaan: it will be an open octagon and in the middle will be
> our stylite's pillar.'
> 'As a Symbol?'
> 'No, no. It will be the real thing. It will have a stylite on top
> of it.'
> 'Are you being serious?'
> 'Perfectly serious.'
> 'But how are you going to find a stylite?'
> 'We have one already. Fr. Ephrem Kerim has volunteered to
> be our first pillar-dweller. He is in Ireland presently, at
> Maynooth, finishing his thesis. When he has his doctorate he
> wishes to mount a pillar.' (148-9)

Once more in the modern travelogue, it is dialogue which works so
effectively to bring wonder and surprise to the reader. Dalrymple
reaches the convent of Seidnaya, where Colin Thubron apparently
witnessed the miracle of a crying icon. The miracle Dalrymple
witnesses is that the congregation appears to consist 'almost entirely of
heavily beaded Muslim men' (187) and their wives. This religious
syncretism was once a common place thing in the East, but in the
twentieth century has become 'a precious rarity' (188). A nun explains
how the Muslims Dalrymple watches have come for the blessing of
Our Lady the Virgin of Seidnaya, who grants babies to those desirous,
regardless of their religion. The women sleep on blankets before the
holy icon and even eat the wick of the lamp burning there:

> 'Then in the morning they drink from the spring in the
> courtyard. Nine months later they have babies.'
> 'And it works?'
> 'I have seen it with my own eyes,' said Sister Tecla. 'One
> Muslim woman from Jordan had been waiting for a baby for
> twenty-five years. She was beyond the normal age of

childbearing, but some-one told her about the Virgin of Seidnaya. She came here and spent two nights in front of the icon. She was so desperate she ate the wicks of nearly twenty lamps.'

'What happened?'

'She came back the following year,' said Sister Tecla, 'with triplets.' (189)

The narrative skips along at a jaunty pace, the story enhanced in its retelling by Sister Tecla. Yet *From the Holy Mountain* is essentially a travel text with a sober agenda. In Syria, it seems the Christian communities have a far easier time than in Turkey. As Dalrymple notes, it 'is a very political book and the fate of the Christians is entirely determined on the politics of the individual regimes'.[27] As the narrative proceeds, so the importance of tracing Moschos's footsteps diminishes in relation to the exposition of the current state of Christianity in the Middle East.

When he reaches Beirut, Dalrymple hands over his commentary to Robert Fisk who takes him on 'a nostalgic tour through the scenes of Fisk's civil war glory days' (218). As a bizarre guide, Fisk notes the places where friends were blown up, where Terry Anderson was kidnapped, and where the American Embassy once stood. His voice is strangely nostalgic for the days of war. In a 'great wide square, desolate and empty', Fisk explains it was once the Place des Martyrs:

It was like Dresden until they pulled it all down. Shame, really. In the old days there was almost total silence in this area. No traffic. No people. Just the gentle *crack, crack* of snipers. Wonderful. (219)

In Jerusalem, Dalrymple lets the voices of the local Christian community speak directly. Bishop Hagop is an Armenian who tells of his fears: 'the settlers were now stepping up their efforts to buy Armenian land in the Old City' (313). When Dalrymple meets Palestinian Christians, they echo the same sentiments: 'Rightly or wrongly, the Palestinians all seemed to believe that there was a concerted campaign to drive them out, or at any rate to make their life so difficult that the majority would opt to leave of their own volition' (316). Statistics serve to strengthen the voices of the Jerusalem

Christians: from the 52 per cent Christian population of the Old City in 1922, Dalrymple reports, the figure is now just 2.5 per cent.

Back in Moschos's footprints, Dalrymple heads to the monastery of Ein Fara where Moschos had spent ten years contemplation. It is now only accessible through the Israeli settlement of Pharan. Mere fragments of the Byzantine monastery remain. Even less is visible of the 385 Palestinian villages erased from Galilee during the war of 1948:

> It was the cactus plants that always gave the old villages away: however efficiently the Israelis had bulldozed the buildings and erased the Palestinian communities from the map, the old villages' cactus hedges had deep roots, and kept sprouting again and again to mark the sites of the former garden boundaries and the shadows of former fields. (363)

Both Muslims and Christians were 'cleansed' (364) from the land to make way for Israeli settlements and kibbutzim.

In Upper Egypt, it is the Coptic Christian community which is under attack. Dalrymple decides to head to the heart of the recent troubles: Asyut. He has a transcript of a recent interview he had conducted with President Mubarak stating travel to Asyut was 'no problem' (435). To the Byzantine mind, Asyut was Lycopolis, close but 'not quite the end of the known world' (446). That title went to the Great Oasis of Kharga where heretics such as Nestorius were banished to 'the very last outpost of Christendom' (447). As John Moschos and his companion Sophronius followed this dangerous trail to the far reaches of the Egyptian desert, so too must Dalrymple. It is the last leg of his voyage of discovery. At the monastery ruins, Dalrymple draws the continuum from Moschos's days to his own travels:

> Christianity is an Eastern religion which grew firmly rooted in the intellectual ferment of the Middle East. John Moschos saw that plant begin to wither in the hot winds of change that scoured the Levant of his day. On my journey in his footsteps I have seen the very last stalks in the process of being uprooted. It has been a continuous process lasting nearly one and a half millennia. Moschos saw its beginnings. I have seen the beginning of its end. (453-4)

There is an echo of Churchillian rhetoric in the final words of this passage and a hint of Thesiger-esque lament. Dalrymple has explained the value of following John Moschos's path as a way of illuminating the current plight of the Christian population. Moschos's trail and text appeared 'a very useful literary method ... you had the mirror with the Christian high tide of the fifth-century reflecting back to the low tide of the present, so every place you went you could measure what was left with what had been before'.[28] The best form in which to tell that tale only emerged gradually: 'It would have been equally possible to have done the study of the whole story of Christians in the Middle East by doing a more formal book which had a chapter on each country, in a sense an extended essay on each, the problem in Turkey, the problem in Syria ... but at the time I was very, very keen on the English travel writing tradition.'[29]

*

In *Travels with a Tangerine* (2001), Tim Mackintosh-Smith is also on the trail of a distant figure. Rather than a sixth-century Christian monk, he is keen to follow the path of Ibn Battutah (or 'IB', as he calls him), a fourteenth-century Arab traveller who covered some 75,000 miles. *Travels with a Tangerine* traces Battutah from his birthplace in Tangier to Constantinople. Just as Dalrymple employed the trope of following Moschos's footsteps to spotlight the predicament of modern Christians, so Battutah's *Travels* operate as 'a vehicle for explaining the Islamic world in one of its great periods - and at the same time for giving some insights into that world today'.[30] The parallel in text construction between Dalrymple and Mackintosh-Smith's books is striking.

In *Travels with a Tangerine*, Battutah's winding route and Mackintosh-Smith's stylistic approach ensure there are many elliptical pathways and etymological wonders to the journey. From Morocco, Mackintosh-Smith heads for Alexandria, noting that in both eras 'the wastes of Barbary were not a place in which to linger'.[31] So begins a process of 'inverse archaeology' (54), whereby he traces the mediaeval world which Battutah witnessed from the remnants still extant. There is the Pharos lighthouse 'reduced to a magnificent pile of rubble after his visit' and Pompey's Pillar where he examines the 'centuries of graffiti ... hoping against hope to find "IB, AH 726"' (54). Mackintosh-Smith seems to be getting nowhere until a taxi driver's talk of Alexandrian saints sends him straight back to Battutah's *Travels* where various *karamah* or saintly miracles are detailed. It was a time of saints and spiritual wonders, many of whom came, like him, from the Maghrib: 'IB was born not just in a medieval Age of Aquarius, but in its California' (64). When Mackintosh-Smith ventures into the countryside on the trail of another saint, Al-Murshidi, he is taken to the tomb by a local schoolmaster who asks, 'Did you know that the traveller IB came to see him in – when was it? – 1326, I think'. Mackintosh-Smith is astounded: 'In a secluded spot surrounded by rice fields, someone was talking about his visit as if it had happened within living memory' (68). His guide commences to recite passages from the *Travels*. Battutah is anything but forgotten in Egypt.

Culinary matters are an important ingredient to the process of 'inverse archaeology'. In Damietta, Mackintosh-Smith delves into the gastronomic delights that may have filled Battutah's stomach. He goes on the hunt for quail, for Battutah praised the quail of Damietta as 'exceedingly fat' (75). A single brace are found in the market and soon 'roasted with their heads on and stuffed *à la mode de Damiette* with onion, garlic, hazelnuts, sultanas and cumin' (76). Then it is off for buffalo milk, *batarikh* (grey mullet roe) and *fissikh*: 'fish which are left in the sun until they begin to blow up. Next the gills are stuffed with salt, and after eight days the fish are put in a barrel of brine' (77). In Cairo, there is the chance to sample *mulukhiyyah*: a 'mucilaginous and delicious dish made from Jew's mallow' (85).

As in his earlier work, *Yemen* (1997), one of the wonders of Mackintosh-Smith's text is the sprinkling of both Arabic and English linguistic intrigues from the author's stream of consciousness. For the journey south to Upper Egypt, Mackintosh-Smith elects to take the train:

As we left Giza station I thought of the Pyramids and the Sphinx, invisible from the railway line. The thought set off an old ditty, '*The sexual life of the camel is stranger than anyone thinks* ...' I tried to make mental notes on the landscape, but the rhyme kept intruding, to the rhythm of the train. '*For during the mating season, it tries to bugger the Sphinx* ...' What was that stuff in the fields like giant rhubarb? '*But the Sphinx's anal orifice is blocked by the sands of the Nile* ...' I must do something about my abysmal knowledge of botany ... '*which accounts for the lump on the camel ...*' Note: palm trees '*... and the Sphinx's inscrutable smile.*'

It was no good. I gave up on the landscape and opened the *Travels*. (108)

The passage is illustrative of the text's irreverent comic style. The splicing of Mackintosh-Smith's thoughts, juddering with the motion of the train, weaves a mischievous narrative, another lighter moment in his mapping of mediaeval travel.

Battutah reached Damascus in August in time for the vast fruit harvest. Mackintosh-Smith lands in November, also seeking the local fare: 'In Damascus you can while away a whole day grazing on grilled offal, pastries and crystallized fruit' (140). For breakfast, he has a 'brainburger – a whole lamb's cerebrum poached, peppered and squashed into a bun' (140). At the Umayyid Mosque, Mackintosh-Smith is bedazzled by the 'perfect architectural soufflé' which forms the mosque and its mosaics.

He is soon searching for the Sharabishiyyah, the Hatter's College where Battutah lodged during his stay in Damascus. He finds a reference in an obscure Arab text which explains the college was on the street of the Hair-Sellers, 'adjoining the Bath of Salih, north of the Bird Market' (152). Mackintosh-Smith leads his hunt in the mode of the 'diligent inverse archaeologist' (152). An exhaustive search leads him to Hajj Yusuf, an old and rather deaf man on the Street Called Straight. Mackintosh-Smith explains his quest as a crowd gathers:

'Who? Baddudah? Can't say I know the fellow.'

'He was here a long time ago. Nearly seven hundred years.'

'I know I'm a *shaybah*, a greybeard, but I'm not that old.'

The audience laughed.

'What about the Bath of Salih?' I shouted. 'And the Bird Market?'

Hajj Yusuf was silent for a long time. He seemed to have gone into a trance. Then his face began to twitch. A dreadful thought crossed my mind: he's having a stroke. 'Really, don't worry if ...'

'That's it! Elizabeth will know!'

The name rang a bell ... perhaps someone at the Institut Français.

'Who's Elizabeth?'

'Elizabeth the Second, Queen of Great Britain. Who else?'
He grinned, grabbed me by the beard and gave me a
smacking, slobbery kiss on the cheek.

The audience laughed; and after the initial surprise I, the
fall-guy, joined in. As I watched Hajj Yusuf shaking and
wheezing, a vision came to me: of an earnest Syrian walking
into a shop in the City of London in the late 1990s and asking
for directions to something that sounded suspiciously like the
Wild Goose Market, at the Sign of Ye Olde Cock and Bull.
(152-3)

The lot of the twentieth-century travel writing sleuth is not always a
happy one. But Mackintosh-Smith generally keeps his humour on an
even par with his historical foraging.

Mackintosh-Smith traces Battutah to Oman. At al-Haffah market,
close to the mediaeval city of Dhofar, Battutah had noted 'most of the
sellers in the bazaar are female slaves, who are dressed in black'. In the
modern *suq*, Mackintosh-Smith is delighted to find women still
running the stalls. He meets Radiyyah, 'a bulky African-looking lady
swathed in jazzy prints' (226), who sells frankincense and describes
herself and the other stall-holders as *khuddam*, or slaves. He even finds
a linguistic fillip as she trails her sentences with a distinctive rising
interrogative: 'Perhaps our men are stupid, no?' (227). The form is
something Battutah had commented on: 'Every sentence they speak
they follow up with "no?" So for example they say "You eat, no? You
walk, no? You do so-and-so, no?"' (227). This 'dialectic quirk – the
equivalent of the "innit" of Estuarine English' (228) has survived the
670 years to the modern day.

Earlier British travellers to the region are not forgotten. Theodore
and Mabel Bent are remembered alongside Bertram Thomas, and the
name of Mubarak bin London, or Wilfred Thesiger, enters the
conversation when Mackintosh-Smith meets members of the Khawar
clan of the Bayt Kathir:

In *Arabian Sands*, Thesiger grumbled at the Khawar for
banning him from their territory in the late 1940s. Recently,
the book had been translated into Arabic. 'He called us
avaricious,' Shaykh Musallam said. 'Nothing but praise for our
neighbours; but we Khawar are avaricious!' (234)

Here is a peculiar situation where Mackintosh-Smith encounters native Arabs who have read, and wish to contest, their depiction by an earlier imperial travel writer. When he returns to the hospitality of the Khawar tribe once more, it is time to rewrite the words of the previous generation:

> Back in Salalah, Qahtan, his *shaykh*, a goat and I went for a picnic on a mountainside from which only three of us returned. (I shall put it in writing: contrary to Sir Wilfred Thesiger's statement in *Arabian Sands*, the Khawar are a noble clan and generous to strangers.) (264)

*

Both Mackintosh-Smith and Dalrymple employed far earlier travelogues to structure their own journeys. Yet it is not merely the employment of a historical figure and following in their footsteps that links *From the Holy Mountain* and *Travels with a Tangerine*. Both Dalrymple and Mackintosh-Smith readily turn to wit and comic moments in order to lighten the tone. Both, too, are far removed from the 'Orientalist' vision of the Arab world. Their narratives are more interested in presenting the voices of individuals met and in investigating the layers of history which make up landscape. Gone is the British traveller operating from a centre of British imperial foundation, whether it be Cairo, Aden or Baghdad. The texts of Dalrymple and Mackintosh-Smith explore a post-imperial environment. There are glimpses of the ancestors of these modern British travellers but there is a distinction between then and now. In the episode above, Mackintosh-Smith's narrative serves to clarify a disparaging comment from Thesiger in *Arabian Sands* (1959) on the Khawar. When asked how he saw himself in relation to past travel writers, Mackintosh-Smith offered the remark that he saw them, 'rather in the terms good Muslims address the dead when they pass a graveyard: "You are those who have gone before, and we are those who will follow you." I mean I see us all as a series, in which travel becomes Travels and reading the Travels generates more travel, and so on ad infinitum. It probably goes all the way back to Gilgamesh. We're all part of a sort of literary Fibonacci sequence, each new member taking in those who have gone before.'[32]

After the remaining British imperial structures in Arabia collapsed in the 1950s and 1960s, far fewer British individuals wrote about their travel experiences in the region. Those travellers who did were no longer directly affiliated with empire. They came not from the armed services or military intelligence, but were independent writers and journalists. However, the travelogues that had emerged from the imperial era and their depictions of Arabia provided the impetus for Jonathan Raban to write his own, updated vision of modern Arabia. Just as earlier writers' itineraries sometimes coincided with their contemporaries, so Raban writes of meeting Jan Morris in Cairo in 1978, and Dalrymple hands the narrative voice to Robert Fisk in Beirut. Such moments are paralleled in previous eras: Lawrence meeting Leachman at Wejh in 1917; Norman Pearn's encounter with Philby at Shibam in 1936. This aspect of travel writing appears unaffected by imperial factors.

If there is a clear form to the nature of post-imperial travel narratives on Arabia, it is in the depiction of personal encounters with local Arabs. Dialogue has emerged as a central feature of the modern travelogue. Conversations with the native inhabitants provide the backbone of what Thubron calls the 'modern tradition of attempted sympathy' found in post-imperial travel texts.[33] In the work of each writer discussed in this chapter, there is this concern with allowing the ordinary people they meet on their travels to have their own voice in the text. Whether they are a dispossessed Palestinian in *From the Holy Mountain*, or the intellectual who haunts Thubron's joyful evening in the opening passage to this chapter, their words are recorded for a distant readership. While their ancestors could sometimes be clearly heard in earlier travelogues, the post-imperial form of the text gives those local voices a more fundamental role in the narrative. It seems that the removal of imperial rule has ensured that those British writers who venture into the lands of Arabia, are now keen to portray not only their own impressions of that world, but the thoughts, fears and hopes of those who call that place 'home'.

*

At this point, it is perhaps intriguing to speculate on the nature of the next era of British travel writing on Arabia to emerge following the invasion of Iraq in 2003. Of the four writers explored in this chapter, none offer concrete plans to return to Arabia in the immediate future.

Tim Mackintosh-Smith is still following the trail of Ibn Battutah to India and beyond. William Dalrymple has stated he has 'got no plans to write any other travel book ever again'.[34] Colin Thubron offers more hope, noting: 'If I were to return to the Middle East to travel, it would fascinate me to go back to Syria. I've always loved Syria.' It has been forty years and more since he first visited. 'That, I think is partly why I want to go back. It's that feeling that mystery accumulates again when you've left the country. Immediately you've left the country, you can imagine that you've delved into it, had some understanding of it and transmitted that in some way to your reader. Actually, within a few years it's starting to accumulate mystique again in your head. You think, "I've never really understood it."'[35] For Jonathan Raban it is a language matter: 'It was possible when I went in the 1970s to travel with minimal, absolutely minimal, Arabic. In the world as it is at present constituted, it would be useless to go as a non-Arabic speaker. I just feel that I'd be a supernumerary there; just one more damn journalist.'[36]

When it comes to the matter of Iraq itself the voices are understandably reticent. Thubron declares that 'Iraq never appealed to me in the way that Syria did.' Rather than the splendour of Damascus, Baghdad by contrast is 'a sort of mud shambles and I'm sure it's even more so now, poor place'. As for travelling there, 'it will be a long time before anybody dares to travel in Iraq in the way that I like to travel. You can imagine making specific destinations but that loose-footed way of travelling is going to be very hard to do.'[37] For Mackintosh-Smith, there is the possibility of heading there 'if the dust - of history, never mind the explosions - ever begins to settle. At the moment there's too much of it about, and I'm too much of a coward.'[38] Jonathan Raban had similar thoughts: 'I thought recently about trying to go to Baghdad shortly after the invasion and then ditched that as being too old and frightened to go to Baghdad.'[39]

It seems that the British travel writers of the late twentieth century will not be those to venture into the chaos of post-invasion Iraq. Yet there is another figure that has already attracted their attention. In *Occupational Hazards* (2006), Rory Stewart provides a retake on the British imperial travel text with his depiction of life as a colonial administrator in Maysan province, home to the marshes of southern Iraq.[40] The words of Bertram Thomas and Wilfred Thesiger haunt the text, as Stewart strives to manage the new occupation while witnessing the moribund state of the Marsh Arabs. Jonathan Raban sees the parallel to the past: 'In a way, he's a throwback to the age of Bell and Lawrence and those people. He seems to have stepped out of the pages of *Boy's Own Paper* in 1920 and yet at the same time is somebody who has been educated in a sort of very bruising way by actual experience of colonial occupation and is consequently able to give a more vivid picture of that.'[41] It is a remarkable retelling of a long departed tale. For Colin Thubron, '[Stewart's] position was so unusual and anomalous ... that nobody's going to emulate that'.[42] It is with an eerie symmetry that the first British travel text to emerge from the post-Saddam era, is one that reflects the spotlight on the present occupation of Iraq to illuminate figures from an earlier imperial enterprise.

NOTES

Introduction

1 Robert Fisk, 'The march of folly, that has led to a bloodbath', *Independent*, 20 March 2006, pp. 1-2.

2 David Fromkin, *A Peace to End All Peace: Creating the Modern Middle East 1914-1922* [1989] (London: Penguin, 1991), p. 497.

3 In the body of travel writing explored here, Arabic places and names are variously spelled. Where necessary, I have employed the most commonly used current transliteration in the general narrative of my work, while leaving variant spellings alone when they are quoted from a specific source text. For example in Chapter 6, there are numerous spellings of 'Baghdad' by different authors including 'Bagdad', 'Baghdad' and 'Baghdâd' which appear in references, though the term 'Baghdad' is used throughout the chapter as the version most familiar to the modern reader.

4 The Maghreb states of North Africa, though linked by the Arabic language, are geographically, politically and culturally distant from Arabia.

5 See appendix for author's interview with Jonathan Raban, 12 June 2007.

6 Elizabeth Monroe, *Britain's Moment in the Middle East: 1914-1971* [1963] rev. edn (London: Chatto & Windus, 1981), p. 11.

7 The term is taken from Mary Louise Pratt, *Imperial Eyes: Travel Writing and Transculturation* (New York: Routledge, 1992).

Chapter 1 – Missionaries and Pilgrims

1 Marmaduke Pickthall, *Oriental Encounters* (London: Collins, 1918), pp. 90-4. Further page references are to this edition and given after quotations in the text. The textual inconsistencies are Pickthall's.

2 Peter Clark, *Marmaduke Pickthall: British Muslim* (London: Quartet, 1986), p. 36.

3 J. E. Hanauer, *Folk-lore of the Holy Land: Moslem, Christian and Jewish* (London: Duckworth, 1907).

4 Geoffrey Nash, *From Empire to Orient: Travellers to the Middle East 1830-1926* (London: I.B.Tauris, 2005), p. 179.

5 Anne Fremantle, *Loyal Enemy* (London: Hutchinson, 1938), p. 127.

6   Stephen E. Tabachnick, 'Art and Science in *Travels in Arabia Deserta*', in *Explorations in Doughty's Arabia Deserta*, ed. by Stephen E. Tabachnick (Athens, Georgia: University of Georgia Press, 1987), p. 5.

7   D. G. Hogarth, *The Life of Charles M. Doughty* (London: Humphrey Milford, 1928), p. 129.

8   Charles M. Doughty, *Travels in Arabia Deserta* [1888] (London: Jonathan Cape, 1926), p. 31. Further page references are to this edition and given after quotations in the text.

9   Hogarth, *The Life of Charles M. Doughty*, p. 35.

10   Barker Fairley, *Charles M. Doughty* (London: Jonathan Cape, 1927), p. 31.

11   Andrew Taylor, *God's Fugitive* (London: HarperCollins, 1999), p. 217.

12   Augustus Ralli, *Christians at Mecca* (London: Heinemann, 1909), p. 267.

13   Further page references are to the second volume of this text.

14   Alexei Vassiliev, *The History of Saudi Arabia* [1998] (London: Saqi, 2000), p. 184.

15   Taylor, *God's Fugitive*, p. 213.

16   Stephen Neill, *A History of Christian Missions* (London: Penguin, 1964), p. 366.

17   Andrew Porter, *Religion versus Empire? British Protestant Missionaries and Overseas Expansion, 1700-1914* (Manchester: Manchester University Press, 2004), p. 222.

18   Neill, *A History of Christian Missions*, p. 368.

19   James Morris, *Farewell the Trumpets: An Imperial Retreat* (London: Faber, 1978), p. 249.

20   Rev. W. H. T. Gairdner, *The Reproach of Islam* (London: Church Missionary Society, 1909), pp. ix and vii.

21   Constance E. Padwick, *Temple Gairdner of Cairo* (London: Society for Promoting Christian Knowledge, 1929), pp. 182-3.

22   S. H. Leeder, *Veiled Mysteries of Egypt and the Religion of Islam* (London: Eveleigh Nash, 1912), p. x.

23   Rev. Charles Biggs, *Six Months in Jerusalem: Impressions of The Work of England in and for the Holy City* (Oxford: Mowbray, 1898).

24   Rev. Haskett Smith, *Patrollers of Palestine* (London: Edward Arnold, 1906), pp. 1-2.

25   H. V. Morton, *In the Steps of the Master* [1934] (London: Methuen, 1984), p. v.

26   Michael Bartholomew, *In Search of H. V. Morton* (London: Methuen, 2004), p. 150.

27   Bartholomew, *In Search of H. V. Morton*, p. 151.

28   Bartholomew, *In Search of H. V. Morton*, p. 166.

29   Bartholomew, *In Search of H. V. Morton*, pp. 162-3.

30   Hadji Khan and Wilfrid Sparroy, *With the Pilgrims to Mecca* (London: John Lane, 1905), p. 257.

31   Khan and Sparroy, *With the Pilgrims to Mecca*, p. 299.

32   Ralli, *Christians at Mecca*, p. 2.

33   A. J. B. Wavell, *A Modern Pilgrim in Mecca: And a Siege in Sanaa* (London: Constable, 1912), p. 28. Further page references are to this edition and given after quotations in the text.

34   Peter Brent, *Far Arabia: Explorers of the Myth* (London: Weidenfeld & Nicolson, 1977), p. 164.

35 Peter Mansfield, *The Arabs* [1976] 3rd edn (London: Penguin, 1992), p. 188.

36 Eldon Rutter, *The Holy Cities of Arabia*, 2 vols (London: Putnam, 1928), pp. 13-14. Further page references are to this edition and given after quotations in the text.

37 Further page references are to the second volume of this text.

Chapter 2 – The Empty Quarter

1   Bertram Thomas, *Arabia Felix: Across the Empty Quarter of Arabia* [1932] (London: Jonathan Cape, 1938), pp. xii-xiii. Further page references are to this edition and given after quotations in the text.

2   Rana Kabbani, *Imperial Fictions* [1986] (London: Pandora, 1994), p. 17.

3   Mark Cocker, *Loneliness and Time* (New York: Pantheon Books, 1992), p. 39 and R. H. Kiernan, *The Unveiling of Arabia* (London: Harrap, 1937), p. 312.

4   [Anon], 'Across Arabia', *The Times*, 23 February 1931, p. 13.

5   Brian Marshall, 'Bertram Thomas and the Crossing of Al Rub' Al-Khālī', *Arabian Studies*, VII (1985), 139-50 (pp. 142-3).

6   Joan Pau Rubiés, 'Travel Writing and Ethnography', in *The Cambridge Companion to Travel Writing*, ed. by Peter Hulme and Tim Youngs (Cambridge: Cambridge University Press, 2002), pp. 242-60 (p. 250).

7   Felix Driver, *Geography Militant* (Oxford: Blackwell, 2001), p. 2.

8   See Peter Raby, *Bright Paradise* (London: Pimlico, 1997).

9   Elizabeth Monroe, *Philby of Arabia* [1973] 2nd edn (Reading: Garnet, 1998), pp. 164 and 151.

10 J. B. Kelly, 'Jeux sans frontières: Philby's Travels in Southern Arabia', in *The Islamic World from Classical to Modern Times: Essays in Honor of Bernard Lewis*, ed. by C. E. Bosworth and others (Princeton, New Jersey: Darwin, 1989), pp. 701-32 (p. 715).

11 Harry St John Philby, *The Empty Quarter* [1933] (London: Century, 1986), p. xvi. Further page references are to this edition and given after quotations in the text.

12 Michael Asher, *Thesiger: A Biography* (London: Viking, 1994), p. 247.

13 Leslie McLoughlin, 'Abdullah Philby's Crossing of the Empty Quarter', *Asian Affairs*, 22 (1991), 142-51 (p. 148).

14 Cocker, *Loneliness and Time*, p. 49.

15 Bertram Thomas, '"The Empty Quarter" by H. J. B. Philby', *Royal Central Asian Society Journal*, 20 (1933), 438-44 (p. 442).

16 Helen Carr, 'Modernism and Travel (1880-1940)', in *The Cambridge Companion to Travel Writing*, ed. by Peter Hulme and Tim Youngs (Cambridge: Cambridge University Press, 2002), pp. 70-101 (p. 74).

17 Wilfred Thesiger, *Crossing the Sands* (London: Motivate, 1999), p. 7.

18 Cocker, *Loneliness and Time*, p. 68.

19 Wilfred Thesiger, *Arabian Sands* [1959] (London: Penguin, 1964), p. 15. Further page references are to this edition and given after quotations in the text.

20 Renato Rosaldo, 'Imperial Nostalgia', *Representations*, 26 (1989), 107-22 (p. 107). Patrick Holland and Graham Huggan recognise this sentimentalising process

in a number of post-war travel writers. See *Tourists with Typewriters: Critical Reflections of Contemporary Travel Writing* (Ann Arbor, Michigan: University of Michigan Press, 1998), p. 29.

21 Kabbani, *Imperial Fictions*, p. 121.
22 Peter Brent, *Far Arabia* (London: Weidenfeld and Nicolson, 1977), p. 219.

Chapter 3 – Imperial Wars

1 J. E. Tennant, *In the Clouds Above Baghdad: Being the Records of an Air Commander* (London: Cecil Palmer, 1920), pp. 27-8.
2 H. V. F. Winstone, *Leachman: 'OC Desert': The Life of Lieutenant-Colonel Gerard Leachman D.S.O.* (London: Quartet Books, 1982), p. 173.
3 Telegram from Civil Commissioner Baghdad Sir Arnold Wilson to Secretary of State for India, sent 18 August 1920, Oriental, India and Commonwealth Office (O.I.C.O.) records, L/P&S/11/175 P7339/1920 (filed with P5890/1920).
4 Sir John Glubb, Letter to Mr C. H. Imray, 30 June 1976; quoted from Winstone, *Leachman*, p. 224. Glubb had no such reluctance to writing, and produced a number of military memoirs/travelogues including *A Soldier with the Arabs* (London: Hodder & Stoughton, 1957) and *War in the Desert: An R.A.F. Frontier Campaign* (London: Hodder & Stoughton, 1960).
5 Secret telegram dated 20 December 1913, O.I.C.O. records L/P&S/10/259 'Arabian travellers 1909-1920' P5125/1913.
6 O.I.C.O. records, L/P&S/10/259 'Arabian travellers 1909-1920', P2260/1914.
7 H. V. F. Winstone, *Captain Shakespear: A Portrait* (London: Jonathan Cape, 1976), p. 207.
8 Douglas Carruthers, 'Captain Shakespear's Last Journey', *Geographical Journal*, 59 (1922), 321-34 and 401-18 (p. 324).
9 Douglas Carruthers, 'Captain Shakespear's Last Journey', p. 321.
10 Telegram from Sir L. Mallet to Sir Edward Grey, dated 5 Jan 1914, O.I.C.O. records L/PS/10/259, 'Arabian travellers 1909-1920', P95/1914.
11 Gertrude Bell, 'A Tribe of the Tigris', O.I.C.O. records L/PS/10/617, 'Mesopotamia', P1110/1917.
12 Gertrude Bell, *The Arab of Mesopotamia* (Basrah: Government Press, 1918).
13 O.I.C.O. records L/PS/10/617, 'Mesopotamia', P5407/1916.
14 T. E. Lawrence, *Secret Despatches from Arabia* (London: Golden Cockerel Press, 1939), p. 33.
15 T. E. Lawrence, letter dated 15 August 1918; quoted in *Secret Despatches from Arabia and other writings*, ed. by Malcolm Brown (London: Bellew, 1991), p. 11.
16 Captain G. Leachman, 'A Journey Through Central Arabia', *Geographical Journal*, 43 (1914), 500-520 (p. 500).
17 Leachman, 'A Journey Through Central Arabia', p. 503.
18 T. E. Lawrence, *Seven Pillars of Wisdom* [1926] Book Club edn (London: Jonathan Cape, 1976), p. 3. Further page references are to this edition and given after quotations in the text.
19 N. N. E. Bray, *A Paladin of Arabia* (London: Unicorn Press, 1936), pp. 297-8.

20 *The Letters of T. E. Lawrence*, ed. by David Garnett (London: Jonathan Cape, 1938), p. 490; quoted in H. V. F. Winstone, *Leachman*, p. 180.

21 T. E. Lawrence, Reader's report (1929) for the publisher George Allen & Unwin on the manuscript *The Legend of Lijman* by Harry St John Philby (George Allen & Unwin archive, Reading University library MS 3282) www.library.rdg.ac.uk/colls/special/featureditem/lawrence/index.html (last accessed July 2006).

22 Jeremy Meyers, *The Wounded Spirit: A Study of Seven Pillars of Wisdom* [1973] (London: Macmillan, 1989), pp. 51 and 65.

23 Personal correspondence with G. M. C. Bott, archivist for Jonathan Cape, 6 Feb 2004.

24 Douglas Carruthers, *Arabian Adventure: To the Great Nafud in Quest of the Oryx* (London: Witherby, 1935), p. 32.

25 S. C. Rolls, *Steel Chariots in the Desert: The Story of an Armoured-Car Driver with the Duke of Westminster in Libya and in Arabia with T. E. Lawrence* (London: Jonathan Cape, 1937), p. 13.

26 Douglas Glen, *In the Steps of Lawrence of Arabia* (London: Rich & Cowan, 1941), p. 46.

27 Some fifty years later, a very similar homage is made by a group of four British soldiers who do travel by camel following 700 miles in Lawrence's footsteps. See Charles Blackmore, *In the Footsteps of Lawrence of Arabia* (London: Harrap, 1986).

28 Print run figures of *Seven Pillars of Wisdom* are reproduced with permission of Seven Pillars of Wisdom Trust and held in Random House archives.

29 Robin Maugham, *Nomad* (London: Chapman & Hall, 1947), p. 12. Further page references are to this edition and given after quotations in the text.

30 Desmond Graham, *Keith Douglas 1920 – 1944: A Biography* (London: Oxford University Press, 1974), p. 66.

31 Keith Douglas, *Alamein to Zem Zem* [1946] (London: Faber, 1966), p. 25. Further page references are to this edition and given after quotations in the text.

32 Keith Douglas, *Alamein to Zem Zem* (British Library Add. Ms. 53774).

33 T. E. Lawrence, *The Mint: A day-book of the R.A.F. Depot between August and December 1922 with later notes by 352087 A/c Ross* (London: Jonathan Cape, 1955).

34 Desmond Graham, Introduction to *Alamein to Zem Zem* by Keith Douglas [1946] (Oxford: Oxford University Press, 1979), p. 5.

35 George Rodger, *Desert Journey* (London: Cresset Press, 1944), acknowledgements. Further page references are to this edition and given after quotations in the text.

36 W. Scott Lucas, *Divided We Stand: Britain, the US and the Suez Crisis* (London: Hodder and Stoughton, 1996), p. 16.

37 James Morris, *The Market of Seleukia* (London: Faber, 1957), pp. 17-18. Further page references are to this edition and given after quotations in the text.

38 Keith Kyle, *Suez* (London: Weidenfeld & Nicolson, 1991), p. 560.

Chapter 4 – Modernising Arabia

1   Mark Sykes, *Dar-Ul-Islam: A Record of a Journey Through Ten of the Asiatic Provinces of Turkey* (London: Bickers, 1904), pp. 2-3. The textual inconsistencies are Sykes's.

2   Elizabeth Monroe, *Britain's Moment in the Middle East 1914-1956* (London: Chatto & Windus, 1963), p. 41.

3   Kathryn Tidrick, *Heart-beguiling Araby* (Cambridge: Cambridge University Press, 1981), p. 166.

4   Mark Sykes, *Through Five Turkish Provinces* (London: Bickers, 1900).

5   Hugh Hughes, *Middle Eastern Railways* (Harrow, Middlesex: The Continental Railways Circle, 1981), p. 7.

6   Hughes, *Middle Eastern Railways*, p. 61.

7   William L. Cleveland, *A History of the Modern Middle East* (Boulder, Colorado: Westview, 2000), p. 118.

8   Donald Maxwell, *A Dweller in Mesopotamia: Being the Adventures of an Official Artist in the Garden of Eden* (London: John Lane, 1921), pp. 69-71.

9   Maxwell, *A Dweller in Mesopotamia*, p. 72.

10 Hughes, *Middle Eastern Railways*, p. 89.

11 S. C. Rolls, *Steel Chariots in the Desert: The Story of an Armoured-Car Driver with the Duke of Westminster in Libya and in Arabia with T. E. Lawrence* (London: Jonathan Cape, 1937). Further page references are to this edition and given after quotations in the text.

12 T. E. Lawrence, *Seven Pillars of Wisdom* [1926] Book Club edn (London: Jonathan Cape, 1976), p. 362. Further page references are to this edition and given after quotations in the text.

13 Rosita Forbes, *The Secret of the Sahara: Kufara* (London: Cassell, 1921).

14 H. H. McWilliams, *The Diabolical: An Account of the Adventures of Five People who set out in a Converted Ford Lorry to make a Journey from Palestine to England across Asia Minor and the Balkans* (London: Duckworth, 1934), p. 25.

15 Robert Hutchison, *Juggernaut: Trucking to Saudi Arabia* (London: Heinemann, 1987).

16 C. S. Jarvis, *Three Deserts* (London: John Murray, 1936), p. 84.

17 C. S. Jarvis, *Yesterday and To-day in Sinai* (London: Blackwood, 1931), p. 291.

18 Harold Ingrams, *Arabia and the Isles* (London: John Murray, 1942), p. 155.

19 Ingrams, *Arabia and the Isles*, pp. 204-5.

20 *The Letters of Gertrude Bell*, ed. by Lady Bell [1927] (London: Penguin, 1987), p. 540.

21 J. J. Malone, 'Involvement and Change: the Coming of the Oil Age to Saudi Arabia', in *Social and Economic Development in the Arab Gulf*, ed. by Tim Niblock (London: Croom Helm, 1980), pp. 22-48 (p. 25).

22 Tidrick, *Heart-beguiling Araby*, p. 197.

23 J. B. Kelly, 'Jeux sans frontières: Philby's Travels in Southern Arabia', in *The Islamic World from Classical to Modern Times: Essays in Honor of Bernard Lewis*, ed. by C. E. Bosworth and others (Princeton, New Jersey: Darwin Press, 1989), pp. 701-32 (p. 718).

24 Kelly, 'Jeux sans frontières: Philby's Travels in Southern Arabia', p. 721.
25 Robert Barr, *The Unchanging East* (London: Chatto & Windus, 1900), p. 79.
26 H. Rider Haggard, *A Winter Pilgrimage: Being an Account of Travels through Palestine, Italy and the Island of Cyprus, accomplished in the Year 1900* (London: Longmans, 1901).
27 Norman Lewis, *Sand and Sea in Arabia* (London: Routledge, 1938), p. x.
28 James Morris, *Farewell the Trumpets: An Imperial Retreat* (London: Faber, 1978), p. 357.
29 Kenneth Hudson and Julian Pettifer, *Diamonds in the Sky: A Social History of Air Travel* (London: Bodley Head, 1979), pp. 45 and 70.
30 Lawrence, *Seven Pillars of Wisdom*, pp. 267-8.
31 Lewis, *Sand and Sea in Arabia*, p. 25.
32 Freya Stark, *The Southern Gates of Arabia: A Journey in the Hadhramaut* [1936] (London: Century, 1982), pp. 265 and 287.
33 *Over the Rim of the World: Selected Letters of Freya Stark*, ed. by Caroline Moorehead (London: John Murray, 1988), p. 216.
34 Charles Marvin, *Our Unappreciated Petroleum Empire: Oil Discoveries in the Colonies* (London: Anderson, 1889), p. 23.
35 Captain F. R. Maunsell, 'The Mesopotamian Petroleum Field', *Geographical Journal*, 9 (1897) 528-32 (pp. 530-31).
36 M. E. Yapp, *The Near East since the First World War: A History to 1995* [1991] 2nd edn (London: Longman, 1996), p. 31.
37 Maxwell, *A Dweller in Mesopotamia*, p. 14.
38 Marian Kent, *Oil and Empire: British policy and Mesopotamian Oil 1900-1920* (London: Macmillan, 1976), p. 5.
39 Fiona Venn, *Oil Diplomacy in the Twentieth Century* (London: Macmillan, 1986), p. 40.
40 Elizabeth Monroe, *Philby of Arabia* [1973] 2nd edn (Reading: Garnet, 1998), p. 192.
41 David Holden and Richard Johns, *The House of Saud* [1981] 2nd edn (London: Pan, 1982), p. 119.
42 Wilfred Thesiger, *Arabian Sands* [1959] (London: Penguin, 1965), pp. 11-12.
43 Wilfred Thesiger, *Arabian Sands* [1959] (London: HarperCollins, 2000), pp. xiv-xv.
44 James Morris, *Sultan in Oman* [1957] (London: Sickle Moon, 2000), p. 11. Further page references are to this edition and given after quotations in the text.
45 Thesiger, *Arabian Sands* [1959] (London: HarperCollins, 2000), p. xv.
46 Jonathan Raban, *Arabia: Through the Looking Glass* [1979] (London: Picador, 1987), p. 15. Further page references are to this edition and given after quotations in the text.

Chapter 5 – Women in Arabia

1 Louisa Jebb, *By Desert Ways to Baghdad* [1908] (London: Nelson, 1912), pp. 210-12. Further page references are to this edition and given after quotations in the text.

2   Sara Mills, *Discourses of Difference: An Analysis of Women's Travel Writing and Colonialism* (London: Routledge, 1991), p. 29.

3   Cheryl McEwan, *Gender, Geography and Empire: Victorian Women Travellers in West Africa* (Aldershot, Hampshire: Ashgate, 2000), p. 8.

4   [Anon], 'Mrs Roland Wilkins: Work for Women on the Land', *The Times*, 25 January 1929, p. 21.

5   See, for example, *Spinsters Abroad: Victorian Lady Explorers*, ed. by Dea Birkett (London: Gollancz, 1991), and, *Maiden Voyages: Writings of Women Travellers*, ed. by Mary Morris (New York: Vintage, 1993).

6   Margaret Fountaine, *Love Among the Butterflies: The Travels and Adventures of a Victorian Lady*, ed. by W. F. Cater [1980] (London: Penguin, 1982), p. 122. Further page references are to this edition and given after quotations in the text.

7   Penelope Tuson, *Playing the Game: The Story of Western Women in Arabia* (London: I.B.Tauris, 2003), p. 184.

8   Rosita Forbes, *The Secret of the Sahara: Kufara* (London: Cassell, 1921), p. 310.

9   Rosita Forbes, 'A Visit to the Idrisi Territory in 'Asir and Yemen', *Geographical Journal*, 62 (1923), 271-8 (p. 275).

10 Tuson, *Playing the Game*, p. 185.

11 Letter to Philby, 30 July 1925; quoted from Tuson, *Playing the Game*, p. 192.

12 Barbara Hodgson, *Dreaming of East: Western Women and the Exotic Allure of the Orient* (Vancouver: Greystone, 2005), p. 61.

13 Tuson, *Playing the Game*, p. 191.

14 Gertrude Bell, *The Desert and the Sown* [1907] (London: Virago, 1985), p. 3.

15 *The Times Literary Supplement*, 25 January 1907, p. 28.

16 Hodgson, *Dreaming of East*, p. 99.

17 H. V. F. Winstone, *Gertrude Bell* (London: Jonathan Cape, 1978), p. 96.

18 Gertrude Bell, *Amurath to Amurath* [1911] (London: Macmillan, 1924), p. ix.

19 Sudan Archives Durham, University of Durham, File F R Wingate's papers, 135/6/12 (November 1915); quoted in Maria-Dolors Garcia-Ramon, 'Gender and the colonial encounter in the Arab world: examining women's experiences and narratives', *Environment and Planning D: Society and Space*, 21 (2003), 653-72 (p. 664).

20 Letter to Florence Bell, 5 September 1918, in *The Letters of Gertrude Bell*, selected by Lady Richmond (London: Penguin, 1953), pp. 237-8.

21 Garcia-Ramon, 'Gender and the colonial encounter in the Arab world', p. 668.

22 Gertrude Bell, 'An Englishwoman's Desert Journey: Arab Intrigues', *The Times*, 13 June 1914, p. 7.

23 Janet Wallach, *Desert Queen: The Extraordinary Life of Gertrude Bell Adventurer, Advisor to Kings, Ally of Lawrence of Arabia* (London: Weidenfeld & Nicolson, 1996), p. 372.

24 D. G. Hogarth, 'Gertrude Bell's Journey to Hayil', *Geographical Journal*, 70 (1927), 1-16 (p. 6).

25 [Anon], 'Across Arabian Deserts: Miss Bell's Journey to Hail, An Untold Story', *The Times*, 5 April 1927, p. 17.

26 Jane Fletcher Geniesse, *Freya Stark: Passionate Nomad* (London: Chatto & Windus, 1999), pp. 81-2.

27 Molly Izzard, *Freya Stark: A Biography* (London: Hodder & Stoughton, 1993), p. 55.

28 Freya Stark ('Tharaya'), 'France in the Jebel Druse: A Fortnight's Travel Notes', *Cornhill Magazine*, 65 (1928), 534-56.

29 Freya Stark, *Beyond Euphrates: Autobiography 1928-1933* [1951] (London: Century, 1983), p. 84.

30 *Over the Rim of the World: Freya Stark Selected Letters*, ed. by Caroline Moorehead (London: John Murray, 1988), p. 41.

31 Geniesse, *Freya Stark*, p. 81.

32 Freya Stark, *The Southern Gates of Arabia: A Journey in the Hadhramaut* [1936] (London: Century, 1982), p. 8. Further page references are to this edition and given after quotations in the text.

33 Tuson, *Playing the Game*, pp. 230 and 224.

34 Eileen Bigland, *Journey to Egypt* (London: Jarrolds, 1948), p. 154.

35 Barbara Toy, *A Fool Strikes Oil: Across Saudi Arabia* (London: John Murray, 1957).

36 Ethel Mannin, *A Lance for the Arabs: A Middle East Journey* (London: Hutchinson, 1963), p. 43. Further page references are to this edition and given after quotations in the text.

37 Violet Dickson, *Forty Years in Kuwait* (London: Allen & Unwin, 1971), pp. 23-4.

38 Doreen Ingrams, *A Time in Arabia* (London: John Murray, 1970), p. 125. Further page references are to this edition and given after quotations in the text.

39 Theodore Bent and Mrs Theodore Bent, *Southern Arabia* (London: Smith, Elder and Co., 1900), p. v.

40 Tuson, *Playing the Game*, p. 31.

41 Robin Bidwell, Introduction to *Southern Arabia*, by Theodore and Mabel Bent (Reading: Garnet, 1994), p. vii.

42 Lady Evelyn Cobbold, *Pilgrimage to Mecca* (London: John Murray, 1934), p. 185.

43 Ingrams, *A Time in Arabia*, p. 49.

44 Ingrams, *A Time in Arabia*, p. 27.

45 Rosita Forbes, *Women Called Wild* (London: Grayson, 1935), pp. 31-2.

46 Susan Bassnett, 'Travel writing and gender', in *The Cambridge Companion to Travel Writing*, ed. by Peter Hulme and Tim Youngs (Cambridge: Cambridge University Press, 2002), pp. 225-41 (p. 238).

47 Jan Morris, *A Writer's World: Travels 1950-2000* (London: Faber, 2003), p. xiii.

48 Jan Morris, *Destinations: Essays from Rolling Stone* (Oxford: Oxford University Press, 1980), p. 172.

49 Jonathan Raban, *Arabia: Through the Looking Glass* [1979] (London: Picador, 1987), pp. 282-3.

Chapter 6 – Baghdad and Beyond

1   Gavin Young, *Iraq: Land of Two Rivers* (London: Collins, 1980), pp. 27-8. Further page references are to this edition and given after quotations in the text.

2   David Fromkin, *A Peace to End All Peace: Creating the Modern Middle East, 1914-1922* (London: Deutsch, 1989), p. 508.

3   Zaki Saleh, *Britain and Iraq: A Study in British Foreign Affairs* [1966] (London: Books & Books, 1995), p. ix.

4   Alfred Vowles, *Wanderings with a Camera in Mesopotamia (Babylonia)* (London: Simpkin, Marshall, Hamilton, Kent, 1920), p. viii.

5   Donald Maxwell, *A Dweller in Mesopotamia: Being the Adventures of an Official Artist in the Garden of Eden* (London: John Lane, 1921), p. 122.

6   Edmund Candler, *On the Edge of the World* (London: Cassell, 1919), pp. 190-1.

7   Gertrude Bell, *Amurath to Amurath* [1911] (London: MacMillan, 1924), p. 167.

8   T. E. Lawrence, *An Essay on Flecker* (London: Corvinus Press, 1937), no page number.

9   Arnold Wilson, 'E. B. Soane – A Memoir', in *To Mesopotamia and Kurdistan in Disguise: With Historical Notices of the Kurdish Tribes and the Chaldeans of Kurdistan* by E. B. Soane [1912] (London: John Murray, 1926), p. x.

10 John Fisher, *Gentleman Spies: Intelligence Agents in the British Empire and Beyond* (Stroud: Sutton, 2002), p. 28.

11 E. B. Soane, *To Mesopotamia and Kurdistan in Disguise: With Historical Notices of the Kurdish Tribes and the Chaldeans of Kurdistan* (London: John Murray, 1912), p. 18. Further page references are to this edition and given after quotations in the text.

12 Jonathan S. McMurray, *Distant Ties: Germany, the Ottoman Empire, and the Construction of the Baghdad Railway* (Westport, Connecticut: Praeger, 2001), p. 1.

13 David Fraser, *The Short Cut to India: The Record of a Journey along the Route of the Baghdad Railway* (London: Blackwood, 1909), p. 31. Further page references are to this edition and given after quotations in the text.

14 Young, *Iraq*, p. 43.

15 G. E. Hubbard, *From the Gulf to Ararat: An Expedition through Mesopotamia and Kurdistan* (London: Blackwood, 1916), p. 119.

16 Hubbard, *From the Gulf to Ararat*, p. 124.

17 E. A. Wallis Budge, *By Nile and Tigris: A Narrative of Journeys in Egypt and Mesopotamia on Behalf of The British Museum between the years 1886 and 1913* [1920] 2 vols (New York: AMS, 1975), pp. 216-7. Further page references are to the first volume of this edition and given after quotations in the text.

18 Wilson, 'E. B. Soane – A Memoir', in *To Mesopotamia and Kurdistan in Disguise* (1926), p. xiii.

19 Peter Sluggett, *Britain in Iraq 1914-1932* (London: Ithaca Press, 1976), p. 32.

20 Bertram Thomas, *Alarms and Excursions in Arabia* (London: George Allen, 1931), p. 71.

21 Freya Stark, *Baghdad Sketches* [1937] (London: Guild Books, 1947), p. 18.

22 E. S. Stevens, *By Tigris and Euphrates* (London: Hurst & Blackett, 1923), pp. 250-1.
23 Charles Tripp, *A History of Iraq* [2000] 2nd edn (Cambridge: Cambridge University Press, 2002), p. 270.
24 Fraser, *The Short Cut to India*, p. 254.
25 Hubbard, *From the Gulf to Ararat*, pp. 30-31 and 34.
26 Vowles, *Wanderings with a Camera in Mesopotamia*, p. 9.
27 Thomas, *Alarms and Excursions in Arabia*, p. 23.
28 Thomas, *Alarms and Excursions in Arabia*, p. 41.
29 S. E. Hedgcock ('Fulanain'), *Haji Rikkan: Marsh Arab* (London: Chatto & Windus, 1927), p. 248. Further page references are to this edition and given after quotations in the text.
30 Wilfred Thesiger, *The Marsh Arabs* [1964] (London: Penguin Books, 1978), p. 58. Further page references are to this edition and given after quotations in the text.
31 Michael Asher, *Thesiger: A Biography* [1994] (London: Penguin, 1995), p. 404.
32 Wilfred Thesiger, 'The Marshmen of Southern Iraq', *Geographical Journal*, 120 (1954), 272-81 (p. 281).
33 Gavin Maxwell, *A Reed Shaken by the Wind* [1957] (London: Penguin, 1983), p. 176. Further page references are to this edition and given after quotations in the text.
34 Douglas Botting, *Gavin Maxwell: A Life* (London: HarperCollins, 1993), pp. 185-6.
35 Gavin Young, *Return to the Marshes* [1977] (London: Penguin, 1989), p. 123. Further page references are to this edition and given after quotations in the text.

Chapter 7 – Southern Arabia

1 Walter B. Harris, *A Journey Through the Yemen: And Some General Remarks Upon that Country* (London: Blackwood, 1893), pp. 121-2. Further page references are to this edition and given after quotations in the text.
2 David Holden, *Farewell to Arabia* (London: Faber, 1966), p. 18.
3 James Morris, *Farewell the Trumpets* [1978] (London: Penguin, 1979), p. 317.
4 Holden, *Farewell to Arabia*, p. 17.
5 Paul Dresch, *A History of Modern Yemen* (Cambridge: Cambridge University Press, 2000), p. 3.
6 Dresch, *A History of Modern Yemen*, p. 6.
7 [Anon], 'Books of the Week', *The Times*, 3 November 1893, p. 14.
8 National Archives, Foreign Office, FO 78/4414 – 16 May 1892.
9 NA, FO 78/4416 – 30 Sept 1892.
10 NA, FO 78/4416 – 8 Oct 1892.
11 A. J. B. Wavell, *A Modern Pilgrim in Mecca: And a Siege in Sanaa* (London: Constable, 1912), pp. 180-1. Further page references are to this edition and given after quotations in the text.
12 The tale of another British traveller to Yemen in 1910 has been recently told by Jennifer Potter in *The Long Lost Journey* (London: Bloomsbury, 1989). Potter

researched the expedition of archaeologist Elinor Grace to Mareb and recounts her story in a series of fictionalised diary entries. Like Arthur Wavell, Grace was seen as a British spy.

13 A. J. B. Wavell, *A Modern Pilgrim in Mecca: And a Siege in Sanaa* [1912] 2nd edn (London: Constable, 1918), p. vi.

14 [Anon], 'British Explorer Arrested in Arabia: Ill-Treatment by Turkish Officials', *The Times*, 16 June 1911, p. 8.

15 NA, FO 371/1249 44 23232.

16 NA, FO 371/1249 44 32811.

17 NA, FO 371/ 1249 44 35295.

18 See NA, FO 371/1245 and FO 371/1249.

19 British Library, Oriental and India Office Collection (O.I.O.C.), R/20/A/1456.

20 NA, FO 371/1249 44 50846.

21 Theodore and Mrs Theodore Bent, *Southern Arabia* (London: Smith, Elder and Co., 1900), p. 71. Further page references are to this edition and given after quotations in the text.

22 British Library, O.I.C.O., R/20/E/184, p. 215.

23 O.I.C.O., R/20/E/187, p. 45.

24 Mabel Bent describes the region as the 'Akaba' though Tim Mackintosh-Smith has pointed out that '"Akaba" (or aqaba) is usually a pass, while the table-land between the coast and Wadi Hadramawt is called the jawl/jol'. Personal correspondence, email, 17 June 2007.

25 [Anon], 'Obituary: Mr. J. Theodore Bent', *The Times*, 7 May 1897, p. 11.

26 Robin Bidwell, Introduction to *Southern Arabia*, p. x.

27 G. Wyman Bury (Abdullah Mansûr), *The Land of Uz* (London: Macmillan, 1911), p. xv.

28 Clive Smith, Introduction to *The Land of Uz* [1911] (Reading: Garnet, 1998), pp. xv-xvi.

29 Letter dated 10 Feb 1906; O.I.C.O., L/PS/10/135, p. 170.

30 O.I.C.O., R/20/E/1363, p. 199.

31 O.I.C.O., R/20/E/1363, p. 200.

32 Letter from Leonard Darwin, President of Royal Geographical Society, to Sir Arthur Godley, Permanent Under-Secretary of State for India, dated 21 January 1909; O.I.C.O., L/PS/10/135, p. 112.

33 O.I.C.O., L/PS/10/135, p. 116.

34 O.I.C.O., L/PS/10/135, p. 110.

35 O.I.C.O., L/PS/10/135, p. 77.

36 Letter to Sir Richmond Richie, dated 7 June 1910; O.I.C.O., L/PS/10/135, p. 63.

37 Note from the Legal Adviser, 16 June 1910; O.I.C.O., L/PS/10/135, p. 62.

38 Letter from J. A. Bell, Political Resident of Aden, to Secretary of State for India, 7 July 1910; O.I.C.O., L/PS/10/135, p. 42.

39 Bury, *The Land of Uz* (1911), p. xxi. Further page references are to this edition and given after quotations in the text.

40 Clive Smith, Introduction to *The Land of Uz* (1998), p. xxiv.

41 O.I.C.O., L/PS/10/135, p. 4.

42 Aubrey Herbert, *Ben Kendim: A Record of Eastern Travel* (London: Hutchinson, 1924), p. 51. Further page references are to this edition and given after quotations in the text.

43 Hugh Scott, *In the High Yemen* (London: Murray, 1942), pp. 3-4. Further page references are to this edition and given after quotations in the text.

44 E. Hindle, 'Obituary: Dr. Hugh Scott', *Geographical Journal*, 127 (1961), p. 142.

45 Nicholas Wroe, 'The Great Escapist' in *The Guardian*, 11 November 2000. http://books.guardian.co.uk/departments/artsandentertainment/story/0,600 0,395859,00.html (last accessed 27 March 2007).

46 Harold Ingrams, *Arabia and the Isles* (London: Murray, 1942), p. 190.

47 Freya Stark, *The Southern Gates of Arabia: A Journey in the Hadhramaut* [1936] (London: Century, 1982), p. 56.

48 Norman Stone Pearn and Vincent Barlow, *Quest for Sheba* (London: Ivor Nicholson and Watson, 1937), p. 21. Further page references are to this edition and given after quotations in the text.

49 Harry St John Philby, *Sheba's Daughters: Being a Record of Travel in Southern Arabia* (London: Methuen, 1939), p. xi.

50 There are two notable political travel memoirs: Governor and High Commissioner for Aden 1960-63, Charles Johnston's *The View from Steamer Point: Being an Account of Three Years in Aden* (London: Collins, 1964); and *Landscape with Arabs: Travels in Aden and South Arabia* (Brighton: Clifton, 1969) by Donald Foster, Permanent Secretary to the High Commissioner of Aden in the 1960s. There is also the military memoir of David Smiley, *Arabian Assignment* (London: Cooper, 1975).

51 Jonathan Raban offered a chapter on Yemen entitled 'Arabia Demens' in his *Arabia: Through the Looking Glass* [1979] (London: Picador, 1987), pp. 198-257.

52 Tim Mackintosh-Smith, *Yemen: Travels in Dictionary Land* [1997] (London: Picador, 1999), p. 9. Further page references are to this edition and given after quotations in the text.

53 Kevin Rushby, *Eating the Flowers of Paradise: A Journey through the Drug Fields of Ethiopia and Yemen* [1998] (London: Robinson, 2003), p. 2.

Chapter 8 – After Empire

1 Colin Thubron, *Mirror to Damascus* [1967] (London: Penguin, 1996), pp. 18-19. Further page references are to this edition and given after quotations in the text.

2 See appendix for author's interview with Colin Thubron, 19 June 2007.

3 It should be remembered that British withdrawal from Aden in 1967 still left a presence in Arabia only ended with the termination of protectorate relations with the Gulf States in 1971. See Glen Balfour-Paul, *The End of Empire in the Middle East: Britain's Relinquishment of Power in Her Last Three Arab Dependencies* (Cambridge: Cambridge University Press, 1991), pp. 96-136.

4 William Dalrymple and Colin Thubron were both interviewed face-to-face, in May and June 2007, while Jonathan Raban's interview was conducted on the telephone in June 2007. All of the conversations were recorded and

transcribed. Tim Mackintosh-Smith provided two email replies to questions in June and July 2007. The four transcripts have been collated into an appendix.

5 Author's interview with Colin Thubron, 19 June 2007.

6 Author's interview with Jonathan Raban, 12 June 2007.

7 Authors' interview with Colin Thubron, 19 June 2007.

8 Author's interview with Colin Thubron, 19 June 2007.

9 Author's interview with Colin Thubron, 19 June 2007.

10 Ralph and Molly Izzard, *Smelling the Breezes: A Journey through the High Lebanon* (London: Hodder and Stoughton, 1959), p. v.

11 Colin Thubron, *The Hills of Adonis: A Journey in Lebanon* [1968] (London: Penguin, 1987), p. 16. Further page references are to this edition and given after quotations in the text.

12 Author's interview with Colin Thubron, 19 June 2007.

13 Author's interview with Colin Thubron, 19 June 2007.

14 Author's interview with Colin Thubron, 19 June 2007.

15 Author's interview with Jonathan Raban, 12 June 2007.

16 Personal correspondence, email sent 5 June 2007.

17 Author's interview with Jonathan Raban, 12 June 2007.

18 Notable works are Linda Blandford's *Oil Sheikhs* (1976), then Gavin Young's *Return to the Marshes* (1977) and *Iraq* (1980) which sandwich Jonathan Raban's *Arabia* (1979).

19 Author's interview with Jonathan Raban, 12 June 2007.

20 Personal correspondence, email, sent 30 May 2007.

21 Author's interview with Jonathan Raban, 12 June 2007.

22 Author's interview with Tim Mackintosh-Smith, 2 July 2007.

23 That year also saw the publication of Michael Wood's *In the Footsteps of Alexander the Great* which passed through Arabia and drew popular success with an accompanying BBC television series. The previous year had seen Michael Asher's Thesiger-esque lament, *The Last of the Bedu* (1996).

24 William Dalrymple, *From the Holy Mountain: A Journey in the Shadow of Byzantium* [1997] (London: Flamingo, 1998), p. 3. Further page references are to this edition and given after quotations in the text.

25 Author's interview with William Dalrymple, 22 May 2007.

26 Author's interview with Colin Thubron, 19 June 2007.

27 Author's interview with William Dalrymple, 22 May 2007.

28 Tim Youngs, 'Interview with William Dalrymple', *Studies in Travel Writing*, 9 (2005) 37-63 (p. 55).

29 Author's interview with William Dalrymple, 22 May 2007.

30 Author's interview with Tim Mackintosh-Smith, 2 July 2007.

31 Tim Mackintosh-Smith, *Travels with a Tangerine* [2001] (London: Picador, 2002), p. 53. Further page references are to this edition and given after quotations in the text.

32 Author's interview with Tim Mackintosh-Smith, 17 June 2007.

33 Author's interview with Colin Thubron, 19 June 2007.

34 Author's interview with William Dalrymple, 22 May 2007.

35 Author's interview with Colin Thubron, 19 June 2007.

36 Author's interview with Jonathan Raban, 12 June 2007.
37 Author's interview with Colin Thubron, 19 June 2007.
38 Author's interview with Tim Mackintosh-Smith, 2 July 2007.
39 Author's interview with Jonathan Raban, 12 June 2007.
40 Rory Stewart, *Occupational Hazards: My Time Governing in Iraq* (London: Picador, 2006).
41 Author's interview with Jonathan Raban, 12 June 2007.
42 Author's interview with Colin Thubron, 19 June 2007.

APPENDIX

Author's interview with William Dalrymple, 22 May 2007

JC You talk about going backpacking ten years before the journey with Moschos. How did that affect *From the Holy Mountain*?

WD I had backpacked in 1984 round India, and in 1985 it was my first time ever round your part of the world and I made all the mistakes I could possibly make on that journey. So it meant I knew the region and it's there that I got my interest and after that was the *In Xanadu* trip. I mean, in between I'd been on little trips and journalistic trips around the region to Israel, Palestine, Turkey.

JC If we talk about *From the Holy Mountain*, when you travelled earlier Turkey seemed the quiet, peaceful place. Ten years later, it's the other way round and crossing into Syria is lovely. There are political aspects to this book.

WD Of course, it is a very political book and the fate of the Christians is entirely determined on the politics of the individual regimes. As we see in Iraq in dramatic effect, there were 750,000 Christians there and half of them have gone in three years, a community that has been there since the first century.

JC And a lot have gone to Syria.

WD A lot have gone to Syria, huge numbers have gone to Syria and also to Jordan.

JC I know that you've talked about wanting to make this book about studying the Christians in the region and you used this sixth-century monk as a kind of device, if you like. Can you say more about that because it's interesting in the way the book is structured because you don't get that sense from reading the book but rather the other way round, that you'd always loved his text?

WD   There are many ways to skin a rabbit. It would have been equally possible to have done the study of the whole story of Christians in the Middle East by doing a more formal book which had a chapter on each country, in a sense an extended essay on each, the problem in Turkey, the problem in Syria ... but at the time I was very, very keen on the English travel writing tradition and some of my favourite books had been *In Patagonia* and *The Road to Oxiana* and the way I was thinking about travel, which is not necessarily the way I do at the moment or how I write at the moment, it seemed the obvious way to tackle the subject. And also I went to university at the time of a travel writing boom so a lot of people of my generation were reading a lot of British travel. I think that not only has it gone out of fashion in a wider sense, I personally don't read so much travel writing myself now and if I was doing the same subject now I might well approach it in a completely different way and certainly I've got no plans to write any other travel book ever again. In a sense, I feel I did all I could with the genre in that book. Colin Thubron has written a wonderful book on the Silk Road but hearing him describe journeys with taxi drivers, the crazy hotelier ... it did bring back to me that even in the hands of a writer as amazingly capable and beautiful prose stylist as Colin Thubron, that there are a limited number of tricks that you can play, particularly with that one part of the world and you are in serious danger of repeating yourself. And I felt that even as I was writing *From the Holy Mountain* in that I was self-consciously trying not to write *In Xanadu* stuff; it's a very different tone; it's a much more serious book.

JC   You talk about it as the book you're proudest of as a piece of work.

WD   Certainly of my travel books. I mean *In Xanadu* is a real book of juvenility. It's written by a kid at university. A hugely embarrassing book in all sorts of ways.

[Interview interrupted by a chance meeting with Colin Thubron who appears strolling past in the courtyard of the British Library

WD　How embarrassing. And here was I being rude about poor Colin. He's a brilliant writer ... but it does bring back to me the fact that everyone says there are only seven great plots to the novel. There are only two to travel: one is the journey, and one is sitting still in a place, whether it's *A Year in Provence* or *Venice*, as a genre it's a sitting still book. I'm loving writing history books. I don't know what I'll do next, but I very much doubt it'll be a straightforward English narrative of travel.

JC　But you still have produced one of the great travel books of the twentieth century.

WD　Thank you. I certainly don't think I could do better, so the point is perhaps not to try, to go backwards in a sense.

JC　You make very good prose about travel writing. You say that 'dialogue is *the* aspect of travel writing in the twenty-first century as place was perhaps in the nineteenth century' and I go along with that in that there are an enormous amount of writers from the 1920s and earlier, and the ones that 'pop out' as being readable now are the ones that use dialogue.

WD　Sure and there's a sense in which, early on, travel writing is about empirical information and that ceases to be the case usefully by about 1920 when already by that stage you can read more usefully about a place in terms of facts and figures in other genres in a way you couldn't in the nineteenth century; Stanley's/Livingstone's goings about Africa was all there was.

JC　And in Arabia, the Empty Quarter, once it's been crossed ...

WD　Indeed, so it becomes a new job. And in a sense it's the same job as now, to describe people, to try to understand a place, to describe a different route. And if you want it to be, it can be a comedy, it can be part-biography, part-nature book, part-history book. There's a huge variety of different games, genres, but using this one structure of the journey.

JC　In *From the Holy Mountain* it seems to become more political as you go in the text. Was there a deliberate policy of trying to create that sense?

WD　I don't think I was aware when I set off quite how dangerous it was going to be, quite how much sort of serious gun stuff there was going on, en route. When you're on a journey for a travel book, you have a doppelganger travelling with you and one of you is scared shitless that you're going to get shot or blown up by a land mine, and the other is rubbing his hands and saying,

'Copy'. Like, 'Thank God, something's happened. It's going to make a great chapter ... I nearly got kidnapped, I nearly got blown up.' And the closer you can get to complete disaster without the disaster actually taking place is the perfect journey for the travel writer because you have a story in itself. And on that you can hang successfully the other stuff you want to show up, the dialogue ...

JC   And you manage to get some comic dialogue coming out of these seemingly ultimately dangerous situations.

WD   And again this is an example of trying to lighten the tone.

JC   In terms of seeing yourself in a history of British travel writing on the Near East, let's say, were you conscious of that? I mean, you reference Colin Thubron with his miracle at Seidnaya and then you went back there and saw your own 'miracle' of the bearded Muslims. You reference T. E. Lawrence in Aleppo ...

WD   Was I aware of being part of a tradition? Yes, in the sense that at that period I was reading a great deal of material and loved that stuff. I mean if you read about novelists, they are often inspired by some other novelists. If you read biography of Beethoven, he's inspired by Mozart and starts off by writing pseudo-Mozart. And *In Xanadu* is pastiche Robert Byron to a very large extent.

JC   I still think that's being harsh on yourself.

WD   Thank you. There's a lot of Robert Byron in there, and there's even more in the note books.

JC   And I'm sure your editor probably had a word.

WD   No, that's not true actually.

JC   There's a lot of imperial writers that are travel writers within the twentieth century, particularly in the 1920s/30s. I see yourself in a more sympathetic line, a more independent line perhaps, not following a particularly imperial perspective on what they're seeing.

WD   Travellers are individuals. You do have the imperial travellers and someone like Curzon obviously goes out as a British MP, very deliberately with a mind to carve India up into bits. There are many other characters, early Gertrude Bell is independently spirited whatever her subsequent work, through to the Robert Byrons the Waughs and everyone else ... so these are individuals doing their own thing and though there is some crossover and we do find there are travel writers from that period who are to different degrees tied up with imperial projects, the better ones aren't. They are the ones who've survived and are read. Like Kinglake.

JC   There are those that were tied up [who] weren't necessarily tied to the beliefs of that system. Perhaps Lawrence would be a good example.

WD   Yes, and was a rebel. And within the system there are fissures. Curzon was arguing for a particular approach and in a sense a more successful approach than many others.

[Interruption by Sophie Hoult from David Godwin Associates]

JC   We get this sense, as the reader, of a single journey which I believe *From the Holy Mountain* was and yet you say that your wife came over at one time.

WD   She's edited out of the text.

JC   I wondered why that was.

WD   Because I thought that would break the narrative to have someone coming and going. I did a journey in May [1994] which was Mount Athos, a long journey to Palestine and a middle length period in Egypt, and experiences from that got subsumed into the longer journey which began in September.

JC   So there are two journeys at least

WD   There are two journeys. There was one journey which is overriding but there are episodes from the earlier journey which is acknowledged in the acknowledgments.

JC   I like that process as well which you use where you take two weeks off and go and visit diplomatic friends in Damascus. It reminded me of Thesiger who goes off to Basra, has a couple of weeks at the British Consul and then goes back into the Marsh Arabs.

WD   It wasn't the formal break it might seem as I was travelling around from that base and had initially thought I'd probably write the Damascus part up, but for various reasons the Damascus material didn't get in.

Author's interview with Tim Mackintosh-Smith, June-July 2007

Part 1 – Emailed by Tim Mackintosh-Smith, 17 June 2007

Questions by JC:
1) In Yemen, *you reference Thesiger, Hugh Scott and Freya Stark all of whom had strong connections to Britain's imperial role in Arabia. You clearly have an in-depth knowledge of these previous British travellers, but how do you see yourself in relation to them? How have they shaped your thoughts on Arabia and your writing?*

Answers by TM-S
I think of past travel writers (not a term I always like, but it serves as shorthand) in general rather in the terms good Muslims address the dead when they pass a graveyard: 'You are those who have gone before, and we are those who will follow you.' I mean I see us all as a series, in which travel becomes Travels and reading the Travels generates more travel, and so on ad infinitum. It probably goes all the way back to Gilgamesh. We're all part of a sort of literary Fibonacci sequence, each new member taking in those who have gone before. Perhaps I've realized this more since I started working on Ibn Battutah, being inspired by him and seeing how he in turn had been inspired by his predecessors like Ibn Jubayr. But even before my Yemen book had a publisher, I remember saying to my agent, 'Tell John Murray that if he doesn't say Yes, then I'll send a load of tribesmen to Albemarle Street and *make* him say Yes.' And all because they'd published Freya and Ingrams and so on. It was my first book, and I suppose I wanted to appease the ancestral spirits in the shrine of Arabian Travel.

That said, while Thesiger and Freya (I only came to Scott when I was already here) were a huge influence on my coming to Arabia and then writing about it, and while we're probably all romantics of different hues, I don't think they've shaped my thoughts or writing in a direct way; or at least I'm not aware at a conscious level that they have. The place we've written about has changed, since the thirties and forties, in social, political and other ways; but much has stayed the same, and it's that continuity that fascinates me. It's more the case that where I come from has changed – that I bring with me a different cultural kit-bag to the ones my predecessors brought, that I see through a different lens. Even more important, while Thesiger could find companionship in his fellow-travellers, he was always painfully, almost indulgently aware that the companionship was transient. Arabia was a place where he collected beautiful memories to take away and sigh over. Freya delighted in the strangeness of it all – and I think in her own strangeness in Hadhrami eyes. In contrast to them both, I'm at home here, not a transient, and the 'strange' is familiar; in fact I rather resent it when I'm seen as a stranger – even if, I suppose, it gives me a certain perspective to write from.

In terms of approach and style, by the way, my biggest influence is probably a non-'Arabian', Patrick Leigh Fermor; in those of content, the old Arab authors of works on travel, geography, anecdotal history and wonders have something to answer for.

2) My thesis is essentially that British travel writing on Arabia through the twentieth century is intimately tied to the British imperial presence in the region. Do you see yourself as a 'post-imperial' British traveller? In what ways does this distinguish your work from 'imperial' British travel writers? (The scene in Yemen *springs to mind where you talk of 'laying the imperial ghosts' and then use a mock imperial 'we' to a stall-holder who asks if you were from Belgium.)*

Obviously I'm post-imperial in the sense that the Empire's dead and gone, but I think that as a British traveller I'm more precisely paulo-post-post-imperial. 'Post-imperial' in an Arabian context smacks of Edward Said, and while I have tremendous respect for much of what he wrote, I do think – and of course a growing number of other people do too – that when it came to *Orientalism* he airbrushed out a lot of stuff that didn't suit his theory. To put it another way, I'm not post-imperial in the sense that I think we Brits should continually flagellate ourselves over what went wrong. We should admit that a lot did go dreadfully wrong, and that much was absurd, that a lot of travellers were also furthering imperial aims – but also that *some* things went right. Perhaps the only good thing to come out of the last few years of history is that we can now look at the total fuck-up the Americans have made of their own imperial adventures and say, maybe ours wasn't quite as bad as it used to look. But then in *Yemen* we do have memories of the Ingramses, who are rare and shining examples of Britannia's best.

But really I don't think I've ever thought of myself in terms of labels – post-imperial, post-modern, British or anything else. I've just tried to observe and write well, and the ability to do that is what I admire in my predecessors – however closely they've been tied to the imperial presence. At the same time, I suppose I was slightly … well, taken aback by some of your revelations about people I'd always viewed (perhaps ingenuously) as people propelled by sheer love of finding out – as curiosi. E.g. the Bents: to read of the extent of their collusion perhaps even *diminished* them in my eyes, initially; but, on reflection, they and the others were all products of their age. In the end, for me it's what they wrote that matters more than why they travelled.

My petulance over being thought to be Belgian wasn't entirely feigned, by the way: there's only one thing that's worse than being hated (as an ex-occupier), and that's being forgotten.

Two additional notes, vaguely connected: a) I was rather chuffed to have provided the ironic opening epigraph in Robert Irwin's *For Lust of Knowing*; b) I believe my last, book, on India, has a rare distinction for one written about the country by a Brit – that it is almost, if not totally, Raj-nostalgia-free.

3) Humour has been a strong element to your writing, interwoven into the text with vast layers of historical information and Arabic etymological wonders. Is this a deliberate policy to lighten the tone, perhaps allowing you to feel you can pursue the more highbrow aspects of the text?

Certainly if all the fun was surgically removed from my books they might be rather heavy – as far as the 'general' readership I write for goes – on information and tricky names. Pace, or rhetoric, is tremendously important in what I write: I always try to picture the reader, and if I see him being lulled, or overloaded, I'll give him a verbal slap or tickle him (or make him groan) with a pun. But it's not just that I think, Oh, we've had too much History I ought to stick in something silly here. It's also a nod to the omnipresence of bathos – to the banana skin that lurks at the end of the red carpet; or, as the poet Abu Tammam put it (and I alluded to this in the preface to *Yemen*), to the fact that the line between seriousness and frivolity is as thin as the edge of a sword.

4) And, I have to ask … did you really find your prep school blazer being worn by a young Yemeni lad in a serendipitous moment in San'a? It does create such wonderful sense of meant-to-be-ness.

I can't state in all certainty that it was my *very own* prep-school blazer. It was the blazer as worn at my prep-school and supplied by the school's outfitters; it had the trace of an inkstain in the right place; it was the right size. It might well have been mine. But I couldn't have proved it – which is why I used (deliberately) woolly syntax: 'my prep-school blazer' should properly have been 'my prep-school's blazer' or some such. I then finessed further in the bit about the stain, which would more accurately have read something like, 'an inkstain on the pocket, where (at least in a blazer of the same design and size, if not this actual one) my birthday Parker had sprung a leak'. If I've hoodwinked my readers at all I feel only very slightly naughty: I *believed* the blazer was mine, and still do, but it's a matter of faith and faith is rarely perfect. Perhaps the fact that you have your doubts and I have mine means that the passage works. Or is that arrant sophistry?

Part 2 – Emailed by Tim Mackintosh-Smith, 2 July 2007

1) There was a vast amount written on Arabia/Middle East through the first half of the twentieth century by British individuals who travelled there in a variety of capacities. The output seems to decrease, understandably, as the British imperial presence in the region decreases. Is this a valid summary of British travel writing on the region across the twentieth century?
2) In the 1970s and 1980s there is a paucity of British travelogues on Arabia/Middle East (with the notable exception of Jonathan Raban's Arabia *and two texts by Gavin Young), even though the region was very much in the news with oil/Six Day War etc. Have you any explanations for this fact? Is this perhaps due to some kind of post end of empire breathing space?*

I think your summary in 1) is valid. Travel seems to give way to memoirs – like that clutch of Aden and Protectorate memoirs in the 1960s. And, in one notable case that comes to mind, to a sort of 'national memoir' (?): I'm thinking of Jan Morris, who wrote that book on knocking about with the Sultan of Muscat in the 1950s (which she, or he then, could do because of late imperial connections), then her big imperial history; and then she went on to pretty empire-free travel. Perhaps an interesting case of a writer who straddles that time of change? I think your idea of a breathing space sounds right as well: a period of self-assessment in the aftermath of Suez. I wonder if there's a parallel in the way many orientalists began to question what they were doing, and whether they should be doing it at all, in the aftermath of Edward Said's book.

3) In Yemen your text reflects back on occasions to British imperial times and earlier British travellers rather as Raban did in Arabia *in 1979. Do you see a continuity in your work to Raban's?*

I wouldn't say continuity. Raban's book, as I remember it, was a sort of anthropological expedition – in, out, and very sharply observed in snapshots. I suppose I was trying with the Yemen book to unfold, slowly, a scene of which I'd become a part – if an anomalous one. At the same time, I found Raban's an inspiring book: it proved that Arabian travel wasn't dead. A memorable book too. In the diary I kept recently in Sri Lanka, I noted that the walls of my bathroom in a provincial rest-house were 'gecko-shitty' – and suddenly the 'chicken-shitty eggs' came back to me from Raban's Yemen chapter, which I haven't read for years.

4) Do you see a division of modern British travel writers from say Raban in the late 1970s or even Colin Thubron's texts of the late 1960s? Can a divide be drawn to define a post Thesiger age of British travel writing on Arabia/Middle East?

Whatever was happening in political terms, and to the opportunities people had for travelling in the region, I wouldn't personally think in terms of a neat chronology with a divide – at least in a literary sense. I mean, Thesiger is obviously much older-fashioned than his predecessors in many ways (and positively archaic in some respects – I wrote a foreword to his two first books for the Folio Society a couple of years ago, and pointed out that some of his own brand of Arabian romanticism is in fact closer to pre- and early Islamic literature than it is to that of the more recent West). In contrast, Kinglake, e.g., can be surprisingly 'modern'. Travel books, even if they're not overtly in-the-footsteps, are particularly liable to be haunted by the ghostly tread of their predecessors. But, yes, if there wasn't exactly a divide there was a dip; or, as you say, a breather.

I wonder, by the way, whether the Hippie Trail – which did give impetus to a kind of new-wave, post-imperial orientalism – might have inspired a renewed interest in writing about the nearer East?

5) In Travels with a Tangerine, *Ibn Battutah, or IB as he's affectionately known, acts as a narrative spine to the text but there are other related ribs to the book such as the parts on the Assassins or Alawis and times when the present day takes over. Did you set out to write a 'footsteps of IB type of book' or envisage that IB would act as a good device for creating a travel text of wandering Africa and Arabia exploring mediaeval history?*

I saw from the start that a pure 'footsteps' approach would end up as a stunt, and a tiresome one as well – relentless travel can be as exhausting to read as it is to do. You've got to have the breaks. (Didn't Robert Byron suggest a prize for the first person to follow Marco Polo's route, *reading a fresh book and drinking a bottle of wine every day?*) Besides, IB himself isn't that interested in the actual business of travelling, in the sense of motion: he's interested in being in places and meeting people. So I realized early on that I should be doing what he did – stopping the narrative and digressing into mini-chapters ('Account of the coconut/of the Indians who burn themselves to death' etc.). Later on, I realized that, just as I'd tried to 'explain' Yemen, I had a vehicle for explaining the Islamic world in one of its great periods – and at the same time for giving some insights into that world today. But then, IB is pretty unique. When my TV series on him got the thumbs-up from the critics, the production company asked if I could think of anyone similarly 'iconic' who could act as another vehicle for exploring the Islamic world, past and present. I'm still thinking.

6) In the Baron Hotel bar, in Aleppo, you exchange 'nods and semi-smiles' with an Englishman who 'looked suspiciously like a travel writer.' Who was this? William Dalrymple had been there some two years previously as recounted in From the Holy Mountain. *Could it have been some vision of him?*

It didn't *look* anything like WD. I suppose I was gently poking fun at myself (or at readers' expectations of what I might be like) by intimating that the Baron is just the sort of place where young fogeys writing books would head for. I had similar thoughts staying recently at the Galle Face Hotel in Colombo – not that I am especially fogeyish (or especially young, any more). I confess though that the sentence beginning, 'There have been murmurings about the Baron's standards of hygiene ... ' was a gentle dig in WD's ribs, as he claimed he'd been bitten by descendants of the bedbugs that had bitten (I think)

Lawrence. Never my experience of the Baron; although of course William may have stayed in some lower grade of room.

7) You said in answer to an earlier question that you don't think of yourself in terms of labels, including being British. Many British travellers often include moments in their texts when they've been questioned on past British imperial policy in the Middle East. For example, Thubron and Raban have said they were continually asked their opinion on the Sykes-Picot agreement and the Balfour declaration and included such moments in their writing. Have you ever been questioned on these matters, perhaps when travelling for Travels with a Tangerine*?*

I haven't been grilled on those particular matters that I remember. Perhaps I haven't been in the right places. Then again, Sykes-Picot and Balfour were still living memories when Thubron and Raban were travelling. Obviously their consequences are still lived through by millions, but Albion has been sufficiently perfidious in more recent times to provide new topics of conversation.

8) You have written two brilliant travel texts on the Middle East/Arabia which both have a wonderful balance between serious learned matters (historical, linguistic, culinary and etymological) and humorous levity, often hilarious. Thubron talks of writing to 'humanise the map.' Now that Iraq has exploded into world affairs, do you see yourself turning to that part of the region to provide your own unique voice to matters? Perhaps as Rory Stewart did?

Perhaps, if the dust – of history, never mind the explosions – ever begins to settle. At the moment there's too much of it about, and I'm too much of a coward. On the subject, a while ago I wrote a foreword for a book (Shane Brennan's *In the Tracks of the Ten Thousand*, London, 2005) that works up to the author wandering through Iraq in the build-up to the invasion. A strange book, but an honest one – and one that for me succeeded in humanizing the map.

Author's interview with Jonathan Raban, 12 June 2007

JC   You've said that you dislike the term travel writing and that it 'sets your teeth on edge'. Is that still true?

JR   Oh yes, entirely. I think that *Arabia* is as near as I've ever come to writing, as it were, a straight travel book.

JC   You've talked about it as being more of a travel memoir ... what you write.

JR   I loathe the term travel writer. I know who travel writers are; travel writers are people who write for newspapers sampling other people's holidays for them. I'm not that kind of writer. I do see a book which has a journey as its narrative spine as being a tremendously open-ended form and the moment you call it a travel book you narrow the form to a kind of formula, and one knows all too well the formulaic books in that genre. I've always seen it as an interesting form because it is part-fiction, part-non-fiction ... I mean the word 'fiction' does not come from an imaginary Latin verb 'fictio' meaning I make it up as I go along, it comes from the actual Latin verb 'fingere' which means to shape, as in to shape the narrative. 'Fingere' has the same route as finger. There's some Roman potter at his wheel, shaping the pot. All my books that get labelled as travel books, well I would say that they are more deliberately shaped than *Arabia* is. *Arabia* is a book that is much more shaped by the succession of experience that went into it. The other ones are much more complicated narrative braids, to the point where the narrative gets increasingly internal and personal and less and less concerned with reporting on the outside world, whereas *Arabia* stands out from the rest as being less that way. It has distinct tendencies. It is the one book of mine that I think might fairly be called a travel book.

JC   In my thesis I'm looking at a large number of texts that I'm collectively calling travel texts, so they include everything from Bell and Doughty and Thesiger etc.

JR   T. E. Lawrence?

JC   T. E. Lawrence, certainly.

JR   I was just thinking this morning as I sat down to look at the *New York Times* over coffee that I think *Seven Pillars of Wisdom* should be classified under the genre adventure travel. I mean when you go off somewhere to fight a war, I think that's adventure travel.

JC   Certainly. And I don't know if you've read Keith Douglas's work which came out of Alamein. I don't know what you'd describe it as; as a war memoir or poetry in some senses but I've included it within my thesis. I think it's one of the finest pieces to come out of Arabia, certainly during the British rule times there. I've been re-reading *Arabia* today and one of the things which is really noticeable is that right from the start you make a deliberate recognition of past British travellers to Arabia. Lawrence, Doughty, Thesiger all come into your introduction. Were they key figures for you as a kind of reading history?

JR   They were figures to rebel against. I remember I'd just got back from travelling in the Middle East and found myself at dinner one evening in London seated next to an ineffably silly, somewhat upper-class woman who asked me what I was doing and I said I was writing a book about Arabia. She said 'Oh Arabia – I so love the desert; so romantic.' And I thought, 'Fuck it! I'm going to write a kind of 'anti-you' book. No camels; no little brown boys.' What I was identifying in the introduction was, I think, that kind of homoerotic tradition of finding a simpler world of simpler people. I always remember reading Thesiger with particular ire when he laments the new riches befalling Arabia. He fears that the people are going to be totally spoiled and cease to be these essentially simple people; tough, hardy, the public school dream. Now that money has fallen on their heads, they're all going to be softened and wet and what a tragedy that will be. I thought, 'Well, fuck that.' My sense of Arabia was shaped by going there but also to some extent formed before I went, as this land of passionate city builders: Alexandria, Jerusalem, Damascus, Aleppo, San'a. These were cities in place when London was just a sort of muddy ford across a rather nasty looking estuary. The way in which the British have been inclined to think of Arabia as an unpopulated land of sand dunes, camels and people living in tents is so far from the actual history of Arabia which is a place of spectacular cities. I wanted to get into that second world, to a large extent the truer one.

JC   To an extent you miss out the whole desert experience of Arabia entirely?

JR   Well, I was going to write something about that but that was until this silly woman, and I thought 'No fucking sand dunes!'

JC   That's lovely. You said in an email, which did tickle me, about when you met Thesiger, and obviously he comes across in a complex way in your text *Arabia*. Can you say more about that meeting because I found that fascinating; the idea of you being terrified of Thesiger coming at you with some large South African club?

JR   Well, I walked into Broadcasting House with some apprehension and feeling considerable trepidation knowing that I had not been all that polite about him in print, but he turned out to be the perfect gent. He told me how much he liked *Arabia*, which took the wind out of my sails and also made me metaphorically take off my cap to him for being able to be so generous under the circumstances. But then I wondered, 'Well, perhaps he hasn't read it.'

JC   I think you get Thesiger absolutely spot on, I mean he's obviously one of the great travellers but his depiction isn't what we'd like to see Arabia as. I love the way you talk about 'one of the privileges of the rich is to idolise poverty from a safe distance'. That sort of sums him up. In Qatar, you talk about this play 'Umm Ziin' which could have been written by Thesiger if he'd been a playwright.

JR   Yes, I'd forgotten that.

JC   Another thing that came out of your email. Initially, I know you were concerned as to whether I was going to start on an 'Orientalist perspective' kind of line. You said that Edward Said had read your work and enjoyed it and really rated it.

JR   He congratulated me on avoiding Orientalism. But I know that every so often those tiresome people just writing in jargon about the literature of imperialism have sometimes picked up *Arabia* and said 'This dreadful Orientalist bloke.'

JC   I can't understand that. They clearly haven't read it, would be my reaction, or they haven't considered it. There's a number of things I like about your book. I love the way you use the word 'Arabia'. You tend to use it rather than the term 'Middle East'. Was that a deliberate policy?

JR   Yes, it was. But it started with, well, the word was just there and I didn't think about it. But the more I thought about it, the more it seemed appropriate. Better at least than 'the Peninsula', which is the other difficult one. Then I had trouble when I arrived in Cairo. I went up to my hotel room and there were a few brochures which said 'Welcome to Cairo: the First City of Africa'. I thought, 'Fuck! I'm on the wrong continent.' But broadly speaking, where Arabic is spoken along the length of North Africa (Is Libya a country in Africa or a country in Arabia?), I think one could argue it either way. I think of Arabia as a cultural entity extant, as the community of Arabic speakers encircling or half-encircling the Mediterranean.

JC   I use the same term in my thesis and I only really noticed the connection today with your work. Obviously, if you use the term 'Middle East' or 'Near East' you're defining a perspective positioning, if you like.

JR   Yes, yes, yes. A perfect example of this is, where I am sitting right now, the place that everybody calls the Far East is actually my Near West.

JC   Exactly. It's purely perspective. I think the term 'Middle East' is slightly pejorative, in some ways. I prefer the term 'Arabia' but then we get into definitional issues. So I will be using you to back me up on that. You write a lot about imperial history, particularly more recently, since *Arabia*. Did your knowledge of imperial history affect the writing of *Arabia* or did it come out of your interest in Arabia as a region?

JR   Refresh my memory. I can't ever remember writing about imperial history. I mean, Gertrude Bell tracing a line in the sand, defining Iraq verses Saudi Arabia. Yes, I suppose that's imperial history. But I don't really know much about imperial history.

JC   In *Arabia*, your text, you reference a number of British travellers who happen to be very much connected with the British imperial project in Arabia.

JR   Yes.

JC   Whether they were sympathetic or not, Bell was certainly key and even Thesiger, though he was an independent traveller, he certainly had connections to the imperial world. And, obviously, Lawrence. So to that extent, they are in there, even if you're not directly referencing their history.

JR   Well, they're unavoidably in there. It was impossible when I was travelling there to even take a ride with a taxi driver without one being questioned on two phrases: 'What do you think of the Sykes-Picot agreement?' and, 'What do you think of the Balfour

Declaration?' Arabia is a memorious culture and the slight of both those documents were as keenly felt, or seemed to be as keenly felt, in the late 1970s as they would have been forty years before. To that extent they were part of the contemporary landscape and I found myself having to prepare: 'What am I going to say when I am next asked about the Sykes-Picot agreement, the Balfour Declaration?' That became a matter not of history, but of immediate contemporary relevance, like dealing with an outraged taxi driver telling me how evil the Balfour Declaration was.

JC   It was exactly the same in the 1990s, I can promise you that, when I was travelling in the region. People writing the date of the Balfour Declaration in the dust on their car, I seem to remember at one point. I believe it's still remembered. Balfour Day is certainly still celebrated in parts of Lebanon, Jordan and Palestine.

JR   Celebrated?

JC   Remembered, let's say.

JR   I would imagine it as something like Guy Fawkes Night.

JC   Absolutely, that's probably a very good comparison. But I see you as a traveller who is clearly aware of that history, and that comes out in your text. My central thesis is that travel writing across Arabia, concerning British travellers, has been linked to the British imperial presence there and what we find is that your text is one of the first and most important to come out of the post-imperial period. So we find after Suez and then Aden in 1967 there's very little travel writing that comes out of there until your text arrives.

JR   Mine, of course, came after that notorious book by Linda Blandford which I actually didn't read myself but got a friend to read for me because I didn't want to know too much about what it said. It had come out before I went. It screwed up my own trip no end because Linda Blandford, who doesn't have a particularly Jewish name, was Jewish, probably is Jewish, and sort of smuggled herself into Saudi Arabia and then wrote what I gather was an intensely hostile account of Saudi Arabia. When I applied for a visa, I am actually not Jewish and come from about the longest line of Anglican clergymen in English history, but I do have a very odd second name which sounds about one vowel away from 'Rabin'. Plus I have an Old Testament first name. Obviously, I was a Jewish spy and they just would not grant me a visa. I mean I spent months trying to get a visa out of Saudi Arabia and after their experience with Linda Blandford whom they had let in unaware because she did not have a Jewish name, I never got my visa so I had to skirt around Saudi Arabia, rather to my embarrassment. To some extent writing about Arabia then without Saudi, was a little like writing Hamlet without the Prince.

JC   If you look at the 1980s, say, after your work there's very little writing, which is quite surprising if you think how much Arabia, and oil certainly, was in the news.

JR   Well, that's precisely why I don't like to be called a travel writer because the presupposition of the genre of travel writing is the places you must go to should be romantic and exotic and a place full of oil wells and cities and rich people rather defies the conventions of the genre. Arabia perhaps had been taken off the map by the very fact of its riches.

JC   Certainly, it was never depicted in those terms. It never was as rich when it was written about all through the earlier part of the century.

JR   Then it was 'the little brown boys'.

JC   I don't want to keep you for too long. It has been fascinating talking to you. I've just got a couple more questions. You've written a lot since 9/11; a lot more about Arabia. You've obviously gone back to that world as it's been more and more important. Do you see yourself going back to Arabia and writing in any sense 'from the ground'?

JR   I have thought about it and regret that I think it was possible when I went in the 1970s to travel with minimal, absolutely minimal, Arabic. In the world as it is at present constituted, it would be useless to go as a non-Arabic speaker. I just feel that I'd be a supernumerary there; just one more damn journalist. I thought recently about trying to go to Baghdad shortly after the invasion and then ditched that as being too old and frightened to go to Baghdad. I have thought more recently, perhaps if I set myself up in Jordan that would provide a point of perspective on what is happening now. Amman is a very international society, in which perhaps my Anglophone-ness would not be a great barrier. But no, I don't think I can be useful on the ground. Partly because that world is now flooded with journalists from one country or another and the moment a world does become flooded with journalists, it also becomes one in which people learn very fast how to put off and temporise and spin for journalists. I'm not up to all that spinning and temporising. The interesting thing about travelling then [in the 1970s] was that it was possible to have some interest in oneself. People were curious about what I was doing, people were on the whole glad to meet me, and were hospitable and eloquent when questioned. I was a kind of oddity, which is the best way, I think, of being a traveller. There was a curiosity about what I was doing. There wouldn't be any damn curiosity now. What I would be doing would be obvious and irritating.

JC   A lot of your material has been published in *New Yorker* or wherever. I've been reading it in *The Guardian*, as it tends to come to us, and obviously, through the internet. Two fascinating articles: 'Emasculating Arabia' which was linked with Abu Ghraib and came out over here in 2004; and 'The Greatest Gulf' which was about the role of imperial history in Iraq and sits perfectly with what I'm writing about.

JR   They're all collected in a small book called *My Holy War*. All the ones written up until about two years ago.

JC   It's fascinating that you have gone back to Arabia but it seems to be from a very different perspective: obviously it's going to be from a different perspective to the way you travelled in 1978.

JR   Yes, yes. It's the perspective of someone who was made sick to the heart at seeing Wolfowitz describing Iraq as a 'win, win situation' and how we would be welcomed as liberators. I watched him on C-SPAN. It's a free cable channel financed to provide 24 hour political coverage with no commercials. I'm a C-SPAN junky. At one in the morning one day, I switched on the television to find Paul Wolfowitz addressing some Californian think-tank of the right-wing kind and explaining what the immense benefits to America the invasion of Iraq would bring and I was just transfixed by the glibness of this man on the screen and pretty much everything I wrote touching on Arabia proceeded out of that moment. And rage at what this country and Britain did when they went in.

JC   You make valid use of British imperial history when you talk [in 'The Greatest Gulf'] about Bell in the setting up of Iraq trying to avoid the democracy situation. But it's interesting that

Edward Said gets referenced in both of those articles: you say you can't imagine Wolfowitz sitting down and reading *Orientalism* of an evening. You consider his work as still important?

JR   Well, I think so. I know the world is full of attacks on *Orientalism* and how Said got it wrong but it seems to me an immensely powerful and important book and in broad outline absolutely right. He caught perfectly the way in which the West has infantilised, trivialised, feminised the East for its own purpose. And although I'm sure you can pick detailed holes in the argument as he goes along, that essential conclusion seems to me to unequivocally stand.

JC   Just a final question. It's probably elevenses or something with you.

JR   It's O.K. I've got a cup of coffee. I'm happy. Take as much time as you need.

JC   Well, it's very interesting how you say you'd thought about going back to Arabia but that essentially you would just be one more Western body and that you wouldn't be able to get any angle and that you'd be treated badly in some ways. Where do you see the future of British travel writing on Arabia? I mean we've got someone like Rory Stewart, who I find quite fascinating. I don't know if you've read him.

JR   Oh yes. I read him with absolute avidity. I loved *The Places in Between*, but I loved particularly *Occupational Hazards* which I thought was quite brilliant as a book which absolutely conveyed the chaos. And very hard after he'd written the straight line form of his walk across Afghanistan, a narrative that had a sort of bullet-like trajectory from point A to point Z. He's then managed to write a book which conveyed chaos and found a form for chaos of an absolutely persuasive kind. I'm a terrific fan of Rory Stewart. I love the sort of 'education' which he describes in *Occupational Hazards*. In a way, he's a throwback to the age of Bell and Lawrence and those people. He seems to have stepped out of the pages of *Boy's Own Paper* in 1920 and yet at the same time is somebody who has been educated in a sort of very bruising way by actual experience of colonial occupation and is consequently able to give a more vivid picture of that precisely because of his sort of throwback quality than anybody else has done.

JC I think that's absolutely right. That's exactly how I see him. I see the comparisons, not exactly in the narrative style, but the comparison with someone like Bell does sit there. He writes a fantastic travelogue on Afghanistan. He suddenly then becomes Deputy Governor of Maysan Province and is writing a travelogue of his time there, but he is linked to the new British colonial presence in Arabia.

JR Yes. And of course is sitting right now, at least I presume right now, in Afghanistan running this non-profit organisation for Afghanistani crafts.

JC I should ask him, but it would be interesting to see how he sees himself within that canon. Well look, it's been brilliant and really, really useful for me to talk to you and on a personal level, it's just fantastic because I love your books. Anyway, I've read a lot of texts in the last four years or whatever it is, and *Arabia* stands there. I don't know if you've re-read it recently.

JR No, I haven't. I wouldn't dare.

JC Well, it stands up very well. It's still a great read. The way I'm placing it in my thesis is that it's the first great travelogue on Arabia of the post-modern age, the post-Thesiger age, let's say. It's fitted into two chapters so far and will get a third viewing in the final chapter which will draw everything together.

JR Well, I'm flattered.

Author's interview with Colin Thubron, 19 June 2007

JC   I want to start with *Mirror to Damascus*. You say that you chose Damascus because you were interested in the Syrian cities and because that city had been so little written about.

CT   Yes, unlike most of my contemporaries who I suppose have this fantasy about the Bedouin Arab and so on, the typical kind of Thesiger thing. I became interested because I did a sort of preliminary tour, I suppose I was about twenty, of the Middle East and I remember arriving in these Syrian cities like Aleppo, Hama, Homs, Damascus, the classic examples, and realising that I knew nothing about their history, what lay behind them, what kind of society was inhabiting these, classically these streets where you'd go down, say, the Bab al Charki area of Damascus which is within the walled city which seemed purposely to be occluding themselves, purposely saying we're not going to tell you anything. Mud walls, you know the sort of place. Somebody leaves a little door ajar and you look in and there's the marble courtyard with a fountain and a decorated stairway and that intrigued me intensely. A completely romantic instinct that I had initially. My head was full of *The Arabian Nights* and stuff and the kind of things that one had been served up since childhood on what the Arab world was like. And so I got fascinated with that and in the beauty of architecture …

JC   I presume you'd read Thesiger and Doughty and the desert romantic aspect to travel writing and yet weren't interested in following exactly.

CT   I was but not that. I was always intensely interested in history, the Ommayid particularly fascinated me and the early Arabian and Middle Eastern history. It sounds very naïve but the glamour of the history, the depth of it, the architecture it engendered, Islam itself, the richness that one found in Damascus everywhere, whether it was the Marmeluke, the Ommayid or whatever it was, that fascinated me more. I think it was an aesthetic fascination, in my head at least, with civilisation. So it was a very different thing. It was also an intense sense of ignorance, that this is a sort of mystery that one had to penetrate, and you could say the same of the Bedouin if you like, but when you're confronted by the complexity of the city, something so multilayered as Damascus, the so called oldest city in the world, to me the rich but confusing series of civilisations that had gone through that part of Syria that was riveting to me, together with the sense of being excluded from it which you get walking down those little streets. Damascus in those days, I'm talking about the early '60s now, the modern part was quite small; comparatively the walled city was a much greater element than it is now. It's all squashed in by suburbs. It was much more prominent. I didn't even know Islam or have any clue what that religion was about. So it was all to do with the civilisation rather than the nomadic. I had certainly read Thesiger. I don't know if I'd read Doughty by then. Probably. But I was familiar with the romance and books of Lawrence of Arabia if you like but it was the other that interested me.

JC   You say that you were inspired by the place. Were there writers that inspired you to Arabia as well?

CT   Not really. There were two writers that had an effect on me: Freya Stark and Patrick Leigh Fermor. I guess Patrick Leigh Fermor was the first, just, who did, but this was a stylistic matter. I loved the great richness and robustness of his style and the love of language and the love of all the byways of history. That was intoxicating to a young man. Just the sheer *joie de vivre* of it, if you like. Freya Stark came a year later probably and I think I was more influenced by her in the Lebanese book which is slightly more poetic. I think these influences aren't particularly fortunate in that when they're not absorbed properly, and probably at this stage neither influence was really absorbed completely into my own writing style. Freya Stark, of course, had written on Arabia … I loved her writing style. It was very seductive, that particular sort of tailored voice appealed. I could see that she was rather Victorian and sent out moral messages quite often but in the books that I've loved most I was very bewitched by her delicate sort of manner, I think. So it's more in style than in subject matter that it appealed to me. I think the main appeal of the Middle East at the time to me was that unknowingness, but as a writer I felt I could just about tackle it. If someone had said Japan, I'd have thought: 'That is a completely unknown civilisation; I can't deal with it.' But with the Middle East, as opposed to Arabia, I felt there are things here which historically I can hold on to, whether it's the recent imperial past, whether it's the crusades, whether it's the presence of the ancient worlds, ancient Greece and Rome which have always been a pet love of mine, ancient history. They were there in the Middle East so it wasn't hopelessly distant from us and yet it was sufficiently distant that it had this element of the exotic, I suppose a dirty word nowadays, but that element of drama and unknown-ness and romance. Additionally, there hadn't been a book on Damascus for a hundred years, so that was obviously, to a young man hoping desperately to be published, an opportunity to improve his chances.

JC　And you'd been in publishing so you were aware that was an important factor?

CT　Yes, that's right. I'd been four years in publishing. No, five years actually. I'd just come back from the States. I'd spent a year with a company in New York, or just less than a year. So I was acutely conscious of needing the money, needing to be published very urgently. I wasn't well off.

JC　Personally, I love the book. You start *Mirror to Damascus* with this view from Mount Kassioun When I was there in 1997, I went up there too, with your description, and had quite a different view.

CT　Probably smothered in high-rise buildings.

JC　Well, it's a decade ago for me, but there's a lot more concrete than you would have seen. But it's a fantastic opening, I think, to the book. So you have this lovely start and you work in your layers of history as we go along within the book which I think works so well. And you hire this bicycle. You must have cycled for miles.

CT　I didn't mind it.

JC　A young man.

CT　In the blazing sun. An idiot!

JC　You go to Ashrafiyeh and there's this lovely welcoming that you get in this village, and you stay up all night chatting away and then you're asked this question: 'What are the British doing in Aden?' and I think there's one other point in the book where this comes through as well, your concern or your slight fear that you're going to be asked this question again. Was that a question that kept being asked at the time?

CT　It must have been. You've reminded me of it. Yes, I think it was one of the things that were being highlighted by the ruler of

Egypt at the time, Gamel Abdul Nasser, whose broadcasts were being religiously listened to all over the Middle East particularly by Syrians, and anything that he was fussing about, they were fussing about, drinking in the propaganda. I was a very unpolitical animal. I was fascinated by history. I wanted these friendships with these people. I remember how naïve I was about Israel and the impact that Israel had had on them. With Aden, I'm sure I'd have thought, 'Oh dear, I'm going to get this' but it was sort of that feeling of it not being my fault and nothing to do with me. Typical of my sort of slightly apolitical British liberal: not wanting to be associated with my government in that way.

JC And you were young as well. I'm intrigued about these aspects. It seems like even though you were young, you deliberately create this text. It has these layers. You start from the high point [Mount Kassioun] and come down. Historically, you start from as far back. All these themes are running through. Did you deliberately work in dialogue there as you were writing it, just to kind of lighten the history of the book?

CT I don't quite know how it happened. Oddly enough after I wrote the book, I remember several people saying to me how much they'd liked the personal encounters. But I hadn't thought about them very much at the time. The important things to me were the history, the architecture, whatever and these bits which you mention, I remember thinking, 'It's nice when these things happen', and they give an idea, well some idea, of the people seen through rather naïve Anglo eyes. But they weren't as important to me as they later became – personal encounters. I wanted them but they tended to happen to me rather than my seeking them out. Later, I would tend to seek people out a bit more consciously.

JC That's quite interesting because it does seem as if you're working this in the text, perhaps not so deliberately in your early works on the Middle East. But I do think it works so well as this contrast to what's going on in the past. You have this present day, which can often be a lovely family scene, as we get to know the family in Damascus say, or it can be the political world, the wars that are occurring around you.

CT The Arabs being a very political people, as you know, it's bound to enter in somewhere. But yes, I think I was conscious that they produced another layer of reality in the book but I remember not being that self-conscious about it at the time. Whereas in later books, particularly on Russia and China, they almost pivot on the individual encounters. That's the sort of thing that I'm aware gives you an insight into a culture that is not normally easy, or wasn't when I first went to Russia which was then part of the Soviet Union, and was pretty difficult to access. So I realised the value of those kind of conversations in somewhere like China in the 1980s or any of these distant countries where meeting people is harder. Harder because in the case of the Soviet Union, or China, at that time, not only was the language difficult but because the people were wary of talking to you, were possibly being watched. All these things which make individual contact so precious; to the enemy, as it were. It wasn't like that in Syria. We weren't the obvious enemy. Nor were the conversations things which I sought as particularly valuable for the book. They were pleasantly innocent in a way, compared to my later encounters where I really did terribly miss meeting people. I'd imagine a very sterile part of the book in which I had made no interesting human contact in later books and that would worry me, but in this one, probably because my concern was with whopping great chapters on Damascus and history, I didn't feel that.

JC   When you go into these present day encounters, it's not necessarily driven by you but by the people you're meeting, the locals. I love the scene where you go to a Palestinian school. You're seeking the remaining Jewish population and you end up in a Palestinian school that's remembering Balfour Day. A wonderful scene. You're asked, 'Do you remember Balfour?' and you reply, 'I said I had heard of no other Englishman since entering Syria.' I presume you were asked that many times.

CT   I'd forgotten this.

JC   I'm sorry. It's not really fair.

CT   No, no it is fair. I don't much like reading my books after they've been published. Not being a political sort of animal, I mean I knew about Balfour ... yes, this kept coming up. Being somebody very naïve about Middle Eastern politics or any politics, I was surprised a little by the constancy with which the agreement came up like that. It sounds so naïve. And the way Israel was such an obsession. It seems amazing now, fifty year later practically, to think about how I was then, how little knowing I was about what was actually obsessing the Arab world and what England meant to them. Yes, the constant Balfour thing.

JC Well, I think it's completely acceptable to say 'I was innocent, I was naïve.' I've been reading the book again, so I have an unfair advantage on you. The way that this innocence comes across and you end the book, there's almost a kind of lamenting. I reread the ending today and it reminded me a little bit of Thesiger. I wonder if you've ever noticed that. You end with a kind of melancholic note of thinking you'll never see Damascus again in the same way, and it's kind of how Thesiger leaves the desert.

CT Sentimental, of course. I was leaving old Damascus, the water seller and the sherbet seller. I do remember the end of it. Unashamedly romantic, really. Again, a young man. I couldn't write such a thing now, and that's the benefit in a way of accepting that you were rather ignorant and a bit less cynical than now. I don't know about Thesiger. I must have had a feeling that this was on the way out and one was certainly very conscious even at the time of Salihiye and Kassioun, that the suburbs were backing up there and this was a doomed world probably. I didn't think that world would remain, the things that I loved. This is flagrant Orientalism by the standards of today but there we are. That's what one felt.

JC This is the thing. For someone like yourself, it's perhaps difficult to talk openly about those feelings then because of the pressures of being Saidian or something like that. It's very relativist because I don't think you can go back to the 1960s and say, 'You should have been writing in this way.' I don't go with that.

CT It always seems narrow in a way and rather self-righteous in as much as 'presentism' as they call it – I mean the idea that the present has all the knowledge, the judgement and the ethical clout that you're ever going to have – seems to be dreadfully narrow-minded in its way. It's much better to accept that you were a certain way at a certain time and that's the way things were and that's how the age was, that travel writing is one civilisation talking to another and both of them now are in flux and to pretend that you were other than you were is absurd. It always seems to me so wrong to condemn one society by the ethics of another without at least understanding what it was like. It seems so small. It also seems to be abrogating to yourself as a civilisation the total sum of good judgement and so on in the world at that time. In fifty years they're going to look back at us, and we won't see it because we can't see it now, to find us bitterly lacking in all sorts of ways, grossly insensitive, hideously prejudiced and all sorts of things we can't predict. I think this is a genuinely humbling thought for those that think they're in possession of the total sum of humanity.

JC When I read travel writing, I quite like the romance of the travelogue. That's partly why I read it and I'm sure that's why a lot of people read it.

CT And that's why people write it. If difference didn't exist, we wouldn't bother to travel. That's why people travel. To try to minimise it for PC reasons is absurd. One is fascinated by the other.

JC Had you read Thesiger at that time?

CT I think I'd read *Arabian Sands*. I'm pretty sure I had.

JC And *Marsh Arabs* came out in '64.

CT I'm not sure of *Marsh Arabs*. I think I'd read *Arabian Sands* and admired it.

JC It's a great desert book. And I do appreciate that I keep asking you questions about something that happened quite a while ago, which as I say is a little bit unfair.

CT You have to remind me.

JC Well, and then you go to *The Hills of Adonis* a year later, only just a year later, was it?

CT Yes. It took me quite a long time to write *Damascus*. I think it was published in 1967. I was in Damascus in '65 and I was writing it until '66 and it was a big effort because I overwrote it hideously and had to do a tremendous bashing down of my own text with some help. So it was the sort of struggle the way that a first book often is, especially a travel book, that you're finding your own style. At the end of it, I remember feeling a great dissatisfaction with it which I wanted to put right. It seemed to me too hefty in some way, too florid and I think here there was an influence of Freya Stark and *Lebanon* is more poetic and probably if one were to look at the sentences one would find each one to be a few words longer than the average one back in

Damascus, I'm not sure. Partly because I butchered *Damascus* because there were some hideously overwritten passages.

JC   I'd love to see the first draft.

CT   Patrick Leigh Fermor was an influence, of course, which wasn't a help with his verbosity, whereas Freya Stark is perhaps more lucid and streamlined. I mean I love Paddy but you emulate him at your peril. I conceived *Lebanon* as a corrective. A lot of my books have been correctives to the previous one. I think it was misplaced because I think it very likely that *Damascus* is probably the better book. But at the time, I thought I was putting right what had been too verbose, too florid in the previous book.

JC   And of course *Damascus* was a book about a city and then *Hills of Adonis* is a wandering travelogue.

CT   Yes, it's another task. That appealed to me too, doing something quite different.

JC   I've got my paperback edition and you say in '86 in the preface about 'a world irrevocably gone' and that the work 'belongs to a time of innocence, both Lebanon's and mine'. Again there's that sense of a lament coming in.

CT   That was a bit specific because the Six Day War had happened in the interval and I realised, it wasn't difficult to realise, that something was disappearing as indeed it has from the Lebanon. It wouldn't be possible probably to make a walk like that again. It seemed then to me, and I'm not normally particularly clear-sighted or politically driven as I say, but in this instant it seemed to be a tinkering with the make-up of something which was already very fragile in terms of government, the French legacy, so delicately poised and I felt that was all gone.

JC   I don't know if you intended to write it like this, but it works so well within that context because you start with this wonderful spring feeling: fecundity, you've got Adonis and you are free and you are wandering. And occasionally the present comes in with the policeman saying, 'What are you doing? Are you an Israeli spy?' and that reinforces what you are there doing – wandering.

CT   Innocent.

JC   It is. And then suddenly, page 148 or whatever it is, the reality of the situation kicks in. You're on the walk to Yammouneh and you're in a Christian hamlet and you discover that there are these guys walking round the fields with guns.

CT   I remember going into this crowded street and wondering what there was this crowd for. Had there been an accident? No, the Six Day War had just broken out. Maronite or Orthodox, I can't remember, Christian anyway, and they said avoid the Muslim villages and go over the mountains. In a way, there's a sort of excitement to the writer because in a crude way you're thinking, 'This is good copy' just like any journalist. There's this one part of you thinking you're in slight danger, and I didn't know if the whole country was going to break apart and they were going to start slaughtering foreigners. But there's the other one [part of you], the one who's writing about it as it were, sitting on your shoulder, the one who's travelling, saying, 'I can use this.' There was a certain something other than excitement. I was almost on a high for those few days. Partly because I escaped and partly because it was such good copy to use for the book.

JC   And you were youthful enough not to imagine that you were going to get into difficulty?

CT   Absolutely. It didn't really occur to me that I was going to be in serious trouble.

JC   I mean, even when you go to Tripolis and nearly get …

CT   Yes, that was no fun at all. There I was scared. The other time when I was walking over the mountains, I felt strangely disembodied, I just got a sense of unreality. But Tripolis was unpleasant.

JC   The only time I've been to Tripolis, I really didn't like the place. It's funny. But as a book, therefore, it seems to me that it works so well, because for a hundred and sixty pages or so you have this wonderful meandering through history etc., and suddenly the present comes in. Did you write it to work like that?

CT   No, I just wrote it as it happened. I was blithely confident that I was going to be OK. I knew that the Egyptians were building up a presence on the southern borders of Israel and that there might be an invasion. I remember my father warning me. But I couldn't believe it was going to affect me. My head was full of ancient history and the beauty of the landscape as well and it didn't occur to me. Of course, when it happened you just write it. It was luck if you like, or bad luck as it might have been.

JC   Well, I don't know. It works really well as a book. It's great. If I may move on. Then we go to *Jerusalem*. So you have a city, then a lovely wander. Why Jerusalem?

CT   Good question. The answer is the least romantic of all. It's the
      only book that I've written because my publisher wanted me to.
      I'd toyed with the idea of Jerusalem. I had a very paternalistic
      publisher who had taken me on, taken the book on Damascus
      after all by an unknown author and really plugged it and put his
      weight behind it. He was quite a well known publisher at the
      time, a man called Charles Pick. He was the managing director
      at Heinemann and a big noise in publishing and I was very
      flattered by his backing of me, very grateful. *Damascus* sold OK.
      It was very well reviewed but didn't do particularly well in the
      book stores and he put the same sort of spine into the Lebanese
      book, and so when he suggested I do the book on Jerusalem
      that had this particular format [indicating copy of the book]
      with colour illustrations ... It was a few years after Nancy
      Mitford had published an enormously successful book called
      The Sun King with a firm called Rainbird which was in that
      format and the format was beginning to be popularly copied by
      other publishers and this was meant to be an example of that
      sort of thing. He hoped it would take off. A misjudgement
      actually because it meant, because it was in that format with
      rather a lot of photographs, it wasn't reviewed much and so a
      lot of the clout that I had as a selling author (and it wasn't that
      great) was removed. It had come from reviews. I'd been well
      reviewed and people had bought the book from reviews. This
      one was barely reviewed because it was considered to be a
      coffee-table book. I wrote it in some hurry because it was
      written to schedule. I would write a very, very different book on
      Jerusalem now. It was done to a rather predictable format.
      History again, like *Damascus*. But rather dutifully I was covering
      practically every holy site in the place, too dutifully looking back
      on it. I should have been much bolder. I didn't have the
      confidence and wrote almost like a sort of glorified guide book
      that included everything and I would have been better advised I
      think to have been bolder. Anyway, there was an element of
      duty about it, I think, and not a feeling of being exactly out of
      my depth, I don't think I felt that literally, though I should have
      done. I think I was impressed by the vastness and importance of
      the subject, whereas in *Damascus* I could sort of crash into all
      these not really very much written about areas like the history of
      the Ommayids and so on, that all seemed glamorous and fun

and not really known. But here was Jerusalem, this great symbol of the city, and you had to make some sense of it. So it wasn't to my mind the most successful of my books.

JC   Well, that explains a lot to me. I wondered why you'd gone there. You start with, 'the history of Jerusalem is tragic'. In some ways that kind of comes through the book, though I still like it.

CT   I'm still very interested in the three great faiths, of course, and all that because I've always been interested in people's beliefs, what people's values are. But there was terribly little time. I remember having to write it in another year, after completing Lebanon in one, which is stupid.

JC   Big subject.

CT   Huge subject. I have to say it wasn't my publishers fault exactly but I think I should have resisted and said, 'I really can't do this.' But, of course, I was still really young and I took it on.

JC   What I'm looking at in my thesis is this idea of the relation between British travel writing and the British imperial presence in Arabia. In some ways it's quite simple to work out. In other ways, it's more complicated as is the case with Gertrude Bell. Gertrude Bell goes there as an independent traveller, then she starts working for the British Mandate and the setting up of Iraq. So it becomes more complex as British imperial policy becomes more complex. So that's where I'm coming from, to put a bit of background on it. You were writing at the end of British imperial concerns. How aware were you that you were writing at this particular historical time?

CT   I'm trying to think back. As I say, I was rather apolitical. I was always interested in a history where *these* people were great rather than *my* people. What interested me was their culture and not terribly much my culture. I've always been interested in the 'other'. Domestic policies here seem minimally interesting. I always go to the foreign pages of the newspaper. It always seems much more important. I wasn't very knowledgeable about empire. I certainly had no great developed or sophisticated thoughts about it. I was certainly aware that empire was over. It was over in 1960 as far as I could tell. It was the freeing of Cyprus, I suppose. I was shocked when I went back to Cyprus, which is the fourth book on the region, to find what the British had done. There was a schoolmaster there who'd been tortured by British Intelligence. Again there's the naïvety of my reaction which was, 'Surely not our boys?' At the time of these three books, how conscious was I of the end of empire? I think I was honestly a product of the end of empire in a way in so much as it just didn't feature much. I had a military father and I had seen the disintegration of Africa in the late '50s. I had been aware of the Mau Mau at school and this sort of stuff. I was aware of the disintegration of empire but it didn't feature as a part of what I wanted to write about or what was really in my mind. It came as an intrusion, as you have noticed, in the words of others saying, 'Look, Balfour! Look, Israel! Look what you're responsible for', in a way, and that took me by surprise.

JC   And it is a slightly unfair question, I think. I'm asking you to imagine what you were imagining at that time. But there were these previous writers on Arabia and I find it interesting this possible link with Thesiger. I see you as a different generation from Thesiger. He's the end of the last lot, if you see what I mean. I see you as the beginning of the modern generation. When you come in in the mid to late '60s, then really there's very little written on Arabia. You get Jonathan Raban writing in the late '70s.

CT   But on another Arabia, of course. A man who's certainly not a strenuous traveller in the sense that he's a sophisticated one.

JC   He flew from place to place and wanted to see the cities. He didn't want to see the desert. But he still says that he had romantic notions as to why he went there.

CT   He started on the Earl's Court Road as far as I can remember.

JC   That's right. But there's this big gap on writing about the whole Middle East in the 1980s as far as travel writing is concerned. Have you thought about that, why that might be?

CT   Interesting. I'd already left it by then so it didn't happen to impinge on me. My guess is that it became very familiar, too familiar for the sort of books that I was writing in the '60s. Syria sort of opened up, in spite of the Arab-Israel conflict continuing. Lebanon, not actually. I suppose Lebanon was out of bounds. Turkey had become a great venue, of course, for tourism which it hadn't been before. I was first in Turkey in the early '80s and nobody was there. City after ancient city all along the Aegean, lying in glamorous ruins without a soul there, no tourists. A wonderful time to be there.

JC   In the '80s in some ways the Arab countries became more and
       more well known to us in Britain and to the whole of the West
       as oil came in, and yet our travel writers weren't going out and
       telling us about their world.

CT   Interesting. The short answer is I don't know. These things have
       sort of fashions. I think travel writing by the early '80s had
       become terrifically fashionable as a literary genre here. Some
       people put it at the time of Paul Theroux's *The Great Railway
       Bazaar*, others later. Certainly by the late '70s, it was a literary
       genre which was to be considered. It had nothing to do with the
       travel writers. People always pointed and said, 'Look there's
       Theroux, there's Chatwin, there's Raban' and so on; these good
       writers appear. But actually if you look at the '60s and '70s, there
       are just as good writers then. Freya Stark was still writing,
       Patrick Leigh Fermor, and James Morris. So it was something in
       the air, but I don't understand it, that made almost a publishing
       sort of fashion. Suddenly, publishers seemed to realise there was
       this thing: travel literature. It became very much a cachet. All
       sorts of articles. I mean I was the recipient and very lucky in the
       '80s, and got all this attention which I never got in the '70s.
       Nobody sort of noticed travel writing before. Of course, more
       people were travelling; the gap year and God knows what things
       were starting up.

JC   Throughout this '80s period as travel writing boomed, the
       Middle East gets ignored.

CT   Funny. I can't quite understand it. It's interesting to know what
       the better known travel writers were writing about.

JC   And you'd moved on.

CT   Yes, I'd moved to these countries which were the traditional
       enemies like Russia and China, and it was a rather complicated
       decision. Paul Theroux was never going to just concentrate on
       one country or area. A peripatetic traveller.

JC   Chatwin the same.

CT   Chatwin the same. Very personal and eccentric choices. Raban
       went to the States.

JC   And maybe it was that Arabia had been 'done' by a whole load
       of British travellers up to Thesiger.

CT   Yes, Robin Fedden, I remember, was the only one just before
       me who had done anything substantial. I'm only guessing.

think it may have become a touch too familiar for some travel writers to feel they could really ...

JC   And we're just throwing ideas in the air. What I'm saying in my thesis is that perhaps we can put this down to the end of empire type period. That there's a breathing space if you like, and then a reflection because what you then get in the '90s is people writing and reflecting back quite differently on the way that the British Empire was operating before. People like Tim Mackintosh-Smith, for example, who is writing now.

CT   I know.

JC   Do you see that as being fair, me putting you in the modern gang, if you like, or do you see yourself more with Thesiger?

CT   No, I don't see myself with Thesiger. I feel very divorced from that, although I know you've suggested even a sort of romantic link. I don't think I was ever ennobling about the Arabs. I never felt that there was this glamorous race that Thesiger eulogised or supposed that they exist. That was all foreign to me. I think I'm probably modern in the sense that I'm entertaining of ordinary people in my books in a demotic kind of way, a way that is non-imperial. If you stage yourself in a particular way, in my case, it's pretty much unconscious. My feeling about the people I meet is that it's not as though I'm an inheritor of an imperial tradition or anything. One's just fascinated in making these friendships with these young guys on the whole. I mean, I was very young. In that sense, it is the modern tradition of attempted sympathy, empathy with the people you're travelling around, which you don't really get much with travel books before my time. To take a classic one, say Robert Byron, there's no sense there of any real empathy, let alone equality. There's an implied inequality and I don't think I did carry that with me in any sense. That's the way in which I feel most modern, in the attempted sympathy with the people who I come across.

JC   You talk about your desire to 'humanise the map' and that's why you set out to travel.

CT   Yes. That makes it sound very evangelical.

JC   I have got it slightly out of context.

CT   Well, you're right I have said it, that's true. If it's not why I have travelled, it's the effect I've hoped my books might have. I think one travels out of all sorts of selfish and complex reasons but you hope that the books will do that for you.

JC   To that extent, you've moved away from the Middle East, from
       Arabia. It's changed enormously, as we've said, since you were
       there. Do you have any plans to return and write a new book on
       the Middle East?

CT   I haven't immediately. I alternate between travel books and
       novels and I'm fiddling with a novel at the moment. It's usually
       what happens after a rather exacting travel book like the last
       one, *The Silk Road*. I find that I've left some area in myself
       fallow. That's where the novel comes from. It's, if you like, your
       personal life. A novel is usually extracted from some area other
       than the fascination of travel. With travel you're interested in a
       society that's miles away from your personal life. You disappear
       out of your personal life in your fascination with another
       culture. With a novel I find reverting inside my head to thinking,
       'What is now obsessing me?' which is usually something that's
       built up over the years in which you've been travelling and
       writing. So I swing between the two and at the moment it's a
       novel. If I were to return to the Middle East to travel, it would
       fascinate me to go back to Syria. I've always loved Syria.

JC   Have you been back during the Assad regime?

CT   No, I haven't been back for years. That, I think is partly why I
       want to go back. It's that feeling that mystery accumulates again
       when you've left the country. Immediately you've left the
       country, you can imagine that you've delved into it, had some
       understanding of it and transmitted that in some way to your
       reader. Actually, within a few years it's starting to accumulate
       mystique again in your head. You think, 'I've never really
       understood it.' And now that it's over forty years since I started
       in Syria, I feel I'd love to go back and try to explore it again.

JC   Obviously, Iraq is everywhere. In terms of that 'humanising the
       map' it would be amazing if you were to go to Iraq and write a
       book, talking to Iraqis. It would be humanising the world.

CT   Well, it's an idea. Iraq never appealed to me in the way that Syria
       did. For the crass reason that Syria had more ... sounds an
       awful word but 'cultural depth'. You could feel a sense of it in
       Damascus, I'm sure. You don't feel that in any Iraqi city. I mean
       Baghdad is nothing by comparison. It's a sort of mud shambles
       and I'm sure it's even more so now, poor place. Iraq always
       seemed of very secondary interest to me, in spite of the very
       ancient civilisations, of course, whether it be Assyria or Babylon.

That's another thing. It seems quite cut off from the Iraq that we know today and another cultural world altogether. I'd love to go back to the Middle East, but I'm not sure it would be Iraq. It might be. I tend to put these things on backburners while I'm on a novel, so I don't get too obsessive. I always get a bit too excited if I think I've found a subject for a travel book and that's the end of what you're doing at the moment, so I have to curb those sort of thoughts and feelings.

JC   I'm wondering where travel writing is going to go in Arabia, the Middle East, with Iraq obviously suddenly thrust in as this enormous aspect. Do we know? Do you know?

CT   No, one can't see it. It will be a long time before anybody dares to travel in Iraq in the way that I like to travel. You can imagine making specific destinations but that loose-footed way of travelling is going to be very hard to do.

JC   Have you read Rory Stewart? I'm not really going to be able to reference him fully as I'm going to be writing up to 2003. But he's an interesting figure. He travels in Afghanistan and then he writes *Occupational Hazards* about his time really within a new imperial force in Iraq. He's doing the Bell thing. He's replicating Gertrude Bell. I think it's fascinating if that's the way that travel writing is going to go ...

CT   His position was so unusual and anomalous in that second book, that nobody's going to emulate that. It's a peculiar thing to actually accept that post, a man with his sort of temperament, deeply suspicious and sceptical of the value of government. He says now about the only valuable thing he did was to create a secondary school or something in Maysan or wherever. Absolutely no sense of achievement at all. He's really hard-headed. I know him quite well. Well, I know him.

JC   He's in Afghanistan now, isn't he?

CT   He is. Yes, he's running a thing called 'Turquoise Mountain' – a charitable trust.

JC   Well, thank you very much for your time.

CT   Not at all.

BIBLIOGRAPHY

Primary Sources

Anderson, Jon Lee, 'Letter from Baghdad: "Invasions: Nervous Iraqis remember earlier conflicts"', *The New Yorker*, 24 March 2003, p. 1, www.newyorker.com/archive/2003/03/24/030324fa_fact (last accessed 7 Dec, 2007)

[Anon], 'British Explorer Arrested in Arabia: Ill-Treatment by Turkish Officials', *The Times*, 16 June 1911, p. 8

— 'Bad to Worse in Mesopotamia', *The Times*, 18 August 1920, p. 10

— 'Colonel Leachman's Murder', *The Times*, 20 August 1920, p. 9

— 'Across Arabian Deserts: Miss Bell's Journey to Hail, An Untold Story', *The Times*, 5 April 1927, p. 17

— 'Mrs Roland Wilkins: Work for Women on the Land', *The Times*, 25 January 1929, p. 21

— 'Across Arabia', *The Times*, 23 February 1931, p. 13

Asher, Michael, *The Last of the Bedu: In Search of the Myth* (London: Viking, 1996)

Barr, Robert, *The Unchanging East* (London: Chatto & Windus, 1900)

Bell, Gertrude, *The Desert and the Sown* [1907] (London: Virago, 1985)

— *Amurath to Amurath* [1911] (London: Macmillan, 1924)

— 'An Englishwoman's Desert Journey: Arab Intrigues', *The Times*, 13 June 1914, p. 7

— *The Arab of Mesopotamia* (Basrah: Government Press, 1918)

— *The Arab War: Confidential Information for General Headquarters from Gertrude Bell Being Despatches Reprinted from the Secret 'Arab Bulletin'* (London: Golden Cockerel Press, 1940)

Bell, Lady, ed., *The Letters of Gertrude Bell* [1927] (London: Penguin, 1987)

Bent, Mrs Theodore, 'Exploration in the Yafei and Fadhli Countries', *Geographical Journal*, 12 (1898), 41-63

Bent, Theodore, and Mrs Theodore Bent, *Southern Arabia* (London: Smith, Elder & Co., 1900)

Biggs, Rev. Charles, *Six Months in Jerusalem: Impressions of The Work of England in and for the Holy City* (Oxford: Mowbray, 1898)

Bigland, Eileen, *Journey to Egypt* (London: Jarrolds, 1948)

Blackmore, Charles, *In the Footsteps of Lawrence of Arabia* (London: Harrap, 1986)

Blandford, Linda, *Oil Sheikhs* (London: Weidenfeld & Nicolson, 1976)

Blunt, Wilfrid Scawen, *Secret History of the English Occupation of Egypt: Being a Personal Narrative of Events* (London: Fisher Unwin, 1907)

Brereton, Lt-Col. F. S., *On the Road to Bagdad* (London: Blackie, 1917)

— *With Allenby in Palestine: A Story of the Latest Crusade* (London: Blackie, 1919)

Budge, E. A. Wallis, *By Nile and Tigris: A Narrative of Journeys in Egypt and Mesopotamia on Behalf of The British Museum between the years 1886 and 1913* [1920] 2 vols (New York: AMS, 1975)

Bury, G. Wyman (Abdullah Mansûr), *The Land of Uz* (London: Macmillan, 1911)

Candler, Edmund, *On the Edge of the World* (London: Cassell, 1919)

Carruthers, Douglas, *Arabian Adventure: To the Great Nafud in Quest of the Oryx* (London: Witherby, 1935)

Cheeseman, Major R. E., *In Unknown Arabia* (London: Macmillan, 1926)

Clapp, Nicholas, *The Road to Ubar: Finding the Atlantis of the Sands* [1998] (London: Souvenir Press, 1999)

Cobbold, Lady Evelyn, *Pilgrimage to Mecca* (London: John Murray, 1934)

Dalrymple, William, *From the Holy Mountain: A Journey in the Shadow of Byzantium* [1997] (London: Flamingo, 1998)

De Gaury, Gerald, *Arabia Phoenix: An Account of a Visit to Ibn Saud, Chieftain of the Austere Wahabis and Powerful Arabian King* (London: Harrap, 1946)

Dickson, Harold, *The Arab of the Desert* [1949] (London: Allen & Unwin, 1983)

Dickson, Violet, *Forty Years in Kuwait* (London: Allen & Unwin, 1971)

Doughty, Charles M., *Travels in Arabia Deserta* [1888] (London: Jonathan Cape, 1926)

Douglas, Keith, *Alamein to Zem Zem* [1946] (London: Faber, 1966)

Edwards, Amelia B., *Pharaohs, Fellahs and Explorers* (London: Osgood, 1891)

Fiennes, Ranulph, *Atlantis of the Sands: The Search for the Lost City of Ubar* (London: Bloomsbury, 1992)

Fisk, Robert, 'The march of folly, that has led to a bloodbath', *Independent*, 20 March 2006, 1-2

Forbes, Rosita, *The Secret of the Sahara: Kufara* (London: Cassell, 1921)

— 'A Visit to the Idrisi Territory in 'Asir and Yemen', *Geographical Journal*, 62 (1923), 271-8

— *Women Called Wild* (London: Grayson, 1935)

Fountaine, Margaret, *Love Among the Butterflies: The Travels and Adventures of a Victorian Lady*, ed. by W. F. Cater [1980] (London: Penguin, 1982)

Fowle, Captain T. C., *Travels in the Middle East: Being Impressions by the Way in Turkish Arabia, Syria, and Persia* (London: Smith, Elder & Co., 1916)

Fraser, David, *The Short Cut to India: The Record of a Journey along the Route of the Baghdad Railway* (London: Blackwood, 1909)

Gairdner, Rev. W. H. T., *The Reproach of Islam* (London: Church Missionary Society, 1909)

Garnett, David, ed., *The Letters of T. E. Lawrence* (London: Jonathan Cape, 1938)

Glen, Douglas, *In the Steps of Lawrence of Arabia* (London: Rich & Cowan, 1941)

Glubb, Lt-Gen. Sir John Bagot (Glubb Pasha), *A Solider with the Arabs* (London: Hodder & Stoughton, 1957)

— *War in the Desert: An R.A.F. Frontier Campaign* (London: Hodder & Stoughton, 1960)

Haggard, H. Rider, *A Winter Pilgrimage: Being an Account of Travels through Palestine, Italy and the Island of Cyprus, accomplished in the Year 1900* (London: Longmans, 1901)

Hanauer, J. E., *Folk-lore of the Holy Land: Moslem, Christian and Jewish* (London: Duckworth, 1907)

Harris, Walter B., *A Journey Through the Yemen: And Some General Remarks Upon that Country* (London: Blackwood, 1893)

Hedgcock, S. E. ('Fulanain'), *Haji Rikkan: Marsh Arab* (London: Chatto & Windus, 1927)

Herbert, Aubrey, *Ben Kendim: A Record of Eastern Travel* (London: Hutchinson, 1924)

Hogarth, D. G., *The Wandering Scholar* (Oxford: Oxford University Press, 1925)

— 'Gertrude Bell's Journey to Hayil', *Geographical Journal*, 70 (1927), 1-16

Hubbard, G. E., *From the Gulf to Ararat: An Expedition through Mesopotamia and Kurdistan* (London: Blackwood, 1916)

Hutchison, Robert, *Juggernaut: Trucking to Saudi Arabia* (London: Heinemann, 1987)

Huxley, Julian, *From An Antique Land: Ancient and Modern in the Middle East* (London: Max Parrish, 1954)

Ingrams, Doreen, *A Time in Arabia* (London: John Murray, 1970)

Ingrams, Harold, *Arabia and the Isles* (London: John Murray, 1942)

Izzard, Ralph and Molly, *Smelling the Breezes: A Journey through the High Lebanon* (London: Hodder and Stoughton, 1959)

Jarvis, C. S., *Three Deserts* (London: John Murray, 1936)

— *Yesterday and To-day in Sinai* (London: Blackwood, 1931)

Jebb, Louisa, *By Desert Ways to Baghdad* [1908] (London: Nelson, 1912)

Johnston, Charles, *The View from Steamer Point: Being an Account of Three Years in Aden* (London: Collins, 1964)

Khan, Hadji, and Wilfrid Sparroy, *With the Pilgrims to Mecca* (London: John Lane, 1905)

Lane, Edward William, *An Account of the Manners and Customs of the Modern Egyptians* [1836] 2 vols (London: Charles Knight, 1837)

Lawrence, T. E., 'The Evolution of a Revolt', *The Army Quarterly*, 1 (Oct 1920 and Jan 1921), 55-69

— *Seven Pillars of Wisdom* [1926] Book Club edn (London: Jonathan Cape, 1976)

— *Secret Despatches from Arabia* (London: Golden Cockerel Press, 1939)

— *The Mint: A day-book of the R.A.F. Depot between August and December 1922 with later notes by 352087 A/c Ross* (London: Jonathan Cape, 1955)

— *Secret Despatches from Arabia and other writings*, ed. by Malcolm Brown (London: Bellew, 1991)

Leachman, Captain G. E., 'A Journey Through North-Eastern Arabia', *Geographical Journal*, 37 (1911), 265-74

— 'A Journey Through Central Arabia', *Geographical Journal*, 43 (1914), 500-520

Leeder, S. H., *Veiled Mysteries of Egypt and the Religion of Islam* (London: Eveleigh Nash, 1912)

Lewis, Norman, *Sand and Sea in Arabia* (London: Routledge, 1938)

Lyell, Thomas, *The Ins and Outs of Mesopotamia* (London: Philpot, 1923)

Mackintosh-Smith, Tim, *Yemen: Travels in Dictionary Land* [1997] (London: Picador, 1999)

— *Travels with a Tangerine* [2001] (London: Picador, 2002)

Mannin, Ethel, *A Lance for the Arabs: A Middle East Journey* (London: Hutchinson, 1963)

— *The Lovely Land: The Hashemite Kingdom of Jordan* (London: Hutchinson, 1965)

Maugham, Robin, *Nomad* (London: Chapman & Hall, 1947)

Maxwell, Donald, *A Dweller in Mesopotamia: Being the Adventures of an Official Artist in the Garden of Eden* (London: John Lane, 1921)

Maxwell, Gavin, *A Reed Shaken by the Wind* [1957] (London: Penguin, 1983)

McWilliams, H. H., *The Diabolical: An Account of the Adventures of Five People who set out in a Converted Ford Lorry to make a Journey from Palestine to England across Asia Minor and the Balkans* (London: Duckworth, 1934)

Moorehead, Caroline, ed., *Over the Rim of the World: Selected Letters of Freya Stark* (London: John Murray, 1988)

Morris, James (now Jan), *The Market of Seleukia* (London: Faber, 1957)

— *Sultan in Oman* [1957] (London: Sickle Moon, 2000)

— *Destinations: Essays from Rolling Stone* (Oxford: Oxford University Press, 1980)

— *A Writer's World: Travels 1950-2000* (London: Faber, 2003)

Morton, H. V., *In the Steps of the Master* [1934] (London: Methuen, 1984)

Neil, Rev. James, *Palestine Explored* [1881] (London: Nisbet, 1907)

O'Shea, Raymond, *The Sand Kings of Oman: Being the Experiences of an R.A.F. Officer in the little known regions of Trucial Oman Arabia* (London: Methuen, 1947)

Parfit, Joseph T., *Marvellous Mesopotamia: The World's Wonderland* (London: Partridge, 1920)

Pearn, Norman Stone, and Vincent Barlow, *Quest for Sheba* (London: Ivor Nicholson and Watson, 1937)

Pickthall, Marmaduke, *Oriental Encounters* (London: Collins, 1918)

Philby, Harry St John, *The Empty Quarter* [1933] (London: Century, 1986)

— *Sheba's Daughters: Being a Record of Travel in Southern Arabia* (London: Methuen, 1939)

Raban, Jonathan, *Arabia: Through the Looking Glass* [1979] (London: Picador, 1987)

Rawlinson, A., *Adventures in the Near-East 1918-1922* (London: Melrose, 1923)

Richmond, Lady, ed., *The Letters of Gertrude Bell* (London: Penguin, 1953)

Rodger, George, *Desert Journey* (London: Cresset Press, 1944)

Rolls, S. C., *Steel Chariots in the Desert: The Story of an Armoured-Car Driver with the Duke of Westminster in Libya and in Arabia with T. E. Lawrence* (London: Jonathan Cape, 1937)

Rushby, Kevin, *Eating the Flowers of Paradise: A Journey through the Drug Fields of Ethiopia and Yemen* [1998] (London: Robinson, 2003)

Rutter, Eldon, *The Holy Cities of Arabia*, 2 vols (London: Putnam, 1928)

Scott, Hugh, *In the High Yemen* (London: Murray, 1942)

—   *Western Arabia and the Red Sea* (London: Naval Intelligence, 1946)

Selby, Bettina, *Riding to Jerusalem* (London: Sidgwick & Jackson, 1985)

Shepherd, Anthony, *Arabian Adventure* (London: Collins, 1961)

Sladen, Douglas, *Oriental Cairo: The City of the 'Arabian Nights'* (London: Hurst & Blackett, 1911)

Soane, E. B., *To Mesopotamia and Kurdistan in Disguise: With Historical Notices of the Kurdish Tribes and the Chaldeans of Kurdistan* (London: John Murray, 1912)

Smiley, David, *Arabian Assignment* (London: Cooper, 1975)

Smith, Rev. Haskett, *Patrollers of Palestine* (London: Edward Arnold, 1906)

Stark, Freya ('Tharaya'), 'France in the Jebel Druse: A Fortnight's Travel Notes', *Cornhill Magazine*, 65 (1928), 534-56

—   *The Southern Gates of Arabia: A Journey in the Hadhramaut* [1936] (London: Century, 1982)

—   *Baghdad Sketches* [1937] (London: Guild Books, 1947)

—   Beyond Euphrates: Autobiography 1928-1933 [1951] (London: Century, 1983)

Stevens, E. S., *By Tigris and Euphrates* (London: Hurst & Blackett, 1923)

Stewart, Rory, *Occupational Hazards: My Time Governing in Iraq* (London: Picador, 2006)

Sykes, Mark, *Through Five Turkish Provinces* (London: Bickers, 1900)

—   *Dar-Ul-Islam: A Record of a Journey Through Ten of the Asiatic Provinces of Turkey* (London: Bickers, 1904)

Tennant, J. E. *In the Clouds Above Baghdad: Being the Records of an Air Commander* (London: Cecil Palmer, 1920)

Thesiger, Wilfred, 'The Marshmen of Southern Iraq', *Geographical Journal*, 120 (1954), 272-81

— *Arabian Sands* [1959] (London: Penguin, 1964)

— *Arabian Sands* [1959] (London: HarperCollins, 2000)

— *The Marsh Arabs* [1964] (London: Penguin Books, 1978)

— *Crossing the Sands* (London: Motivate, 1999)

Thomas, Bertram, *Alarms and Excursions in Arabia* (London: George Allen, 1931)

— '"The Empty Quarter" by H. J. B. Philby', *Royal Central Asian Society Journal*, 20 (1933), 438-44

— *Arabia Felix: Across the Empty Quarter of Arabia* [1932] (London: Jonathan Cape, 1938)

Thomas, Margaret, *Two Years in Palestine & Syria* (London: John C. Nimmo, 1900)

Thubron, Colin, *Mirror to Damascus* [1967] (London: Penguin, 1996)

— *The Hills of Adonis: A Journey in Lebanon* [1968] (London: Penguin, 1987)

— *Jerusalem* (London: Heinemann, 1969)

Tisdall, Rev. W. St Clair, *The Religion of the Crescent, Or Islam: Its Strength, Its Weakness, Its Origin, Its Influence* (London: Society for Promoting Christian Knowledge, 1895)

Toy, Barbara, *A Fool Strikes Oil: Across Saudi Arabia* (London: John Murray, 1957)

Vowles, Alfred, *Wanderings with a Camera in Mesopotamia (Babylonia)* (London: Simpkin, Marshall, Hamilton, Kent, 1920)

Wavell, A. J. B., *A Modern Pilgrim in Mecca: And a Siege in Sanaa* (London: Constable, 1912)

Woolley, C. Leonard, *Dead Towns and Living Men: Being Pages from an Antiquary's Notebook* (Oxford: Oxford University Press, 1920)

Wood, Michael, *In the Footsteps of Alexander the Great: A Journey from Greece to Asia* (London: BBC Books, 1997)

Young, Gavin, *Iraq: Land of Two Rivers* (London: Collins, 1980)

— *Return to the Marshes* [1977] (London: Penguin, 1989)

Secondary Sources

Adelson, Roger, *Mark Sykes: Portrait of an Amateur* (London: Jonathan Cape, 1975)

Al Yahya, Eid, ed., *Travellers in Arabia: British Explorers in Saudi Arabia* (London: Stacey, 2006)

[Anon], 'Books of the Week', *The Times*, 3 November 1893, p. 14

— 'Obituary: Mr. J. Theodore Bent', *The Times*, 7 May 1897, p. 11

Arberry, A. J., *British Orientalists* (London: Collins, 1943)

Asher, Michael, *Thesiger: A Biography* (London: Viking, 1994)

Assad, Thomas J., *Three Victorian Travellers: Burton, Blunt and Doughty* (London: Routledge & Kegan Paul, 1964)

Auerbach, Erich, *Mimesis: The Representation of Reality in Western Literature* [1946] (Princeton: Princeton University Press, 2003)

Balfour-Paul, Glen, *The End of Empire in the Middle East: Britain's Relinquishment of Power in Her Last Three Arab Dependencies* [1991] (Cambridge: Cambridge University Press, 1994)

Bartholomew, Michael, *In Search of H. V. Morton* (London: Methuen, 2004)

Bassnett, Susan, 'Travel writing and gender', in *The Cambridge Companion to Travel Writing*, ed. by Peter Hulme and Tim Youngs (Cambridge: Cambridge University Press, 2002), 225-41

Behdad, Ali, *Belated Travelers: Orientalism in the Age of Colonial Dissolution* (Cork: Cork University Press, 1994)

Bidwell, Robin, Introduction to *Southern Arabia* by Theodore and Mabel Bent (Reading: Garnet, 1994)

Bidwell, Robin, *Travellers in Arabia* (London: Hamlyn, 1976)

Birkett, Dea, ed., *Spinsters Abroad: Victorian Lady Explorers* (London: Gollancz, 1991)

Botting, Douglas, *Gavin Maxwell: A Life* (London: HarperCollins, 1993)

Bray, Major N. N. E., *Shifting Sands* (London: Unicorn Press, 1934)

— *A Paladin of Arabia* (London: Unicorn Press, 1936)

Brent, Peter, *Far Arabia: Explorers of the Myth* (London: Weidenfeld & Nicolson, 1977)

Butt, Gerald, *The Lion in the Sand: The British in the Middle East* (London: Bloomsbury, 1995)

Carr, Helen, 'Modernism and Travel (1880-1940)', in *The Cambridge Companion to Travel Writing*, ed. by Peter Hulme and Tim Youngs (Cambridge: Cambridge University Press, 2002), 70-101

Carruthers, Douglas, 'Captain Shakespear's Last Journey', *Geographical Journal*, 59 (1922), 321-34 and 401-18

Chalmers, Captain I., 'O. C. The Desert', *Blackwood's Magazine*, 23ʹ (1932), 259-67

Chaudhuri, Nupur, and Margaret Strobel, eds, *Western Women and Imperialism: Complicity and Resistance* (Indianapolis: Indiana University Press, 1992)

Childers, Erskine B., *The Road to Suez: A Study of Western-Arab Relations* (London: MacGibbon & Kee, 1962)

Clark, Peter, *Marmaduke Pickthall: British Muslim* (London: Quartet, 1986)

Clark, Steve, ed., *Travel Writing and Empire: Postcolonial Theory in Transit* (London: Zed Books, 1999)

Cleveland, William L., *A History of the Modern Middle East* (Boulder, Colorado: Westview, 2000)

Clifford, James, and George E. Marcus, eds, *Writing Culture: The Poetics and Politics of Ethnography* (Berkeley and Los Angeles: University of California Press, 1986)

Cocker, Mark, *Loneliness and Time: The Story of British Travel Writing* (New York: Pantheon Books, 1992)

Damiani, Anita, *Enlightened Observers: British Travellers to the Near East 1715-1850* (Beirut: American University of Beirut, 1979)

Dresch, Paul, *A History of Modern Yemen* (Cambridge: Cambridge University Press, 2000)

Driver, Felix, *Geography Militant* (Oxford: Blackwell, 2001)

Duncan, James, and Derek Gregory, *Writes of Passage: Reading Travel Writing* (London: Routledge, 1999)

Fairley, Barker, *Charles M. Doughty* (London: Jonathan Cape, 1927)

Fedden, Robin, *English Travellers in the Near East* (London: Longmans, Green & Co., 1958)

Ffinch, Michael, *Donald Maxwell* (Kendal, Cumbria: The Maxwell Estate, 1995)

Ffrench, Yvonne, *Six Great Englishwomen* (London: Hamish Hamilton, 1953)

Fieldhouse, D. K., ed., *Kurds, Arabs and Britons: The Memoir of Wallace Lyon in Iraq 1918-1944* (London: I.B.Tauris, 2002)

Fisher, John, *Gentleman Spies: Intelligence Agents in the British Empire and Beyond* (Stroud: Sutton, 2002)

Foss, Michael, 'Dangerous Guides: English Writers and the Desert', *New Middle East*, 9 (June 1969), 38-42

Foster, Shirley, and Sara Mills, eds, *An Anthology of Women's Travel Writing* (Manchester: Manchester University Press, 2002)

Fremantle, Anne, *Loyal Enemy* (London: Hutchinson, 1938)

Freeth, Zahra, and H. V. F. Winstone, *Explorers of Arabia: From the Renaissance to the End of the Victorian Era* (London: George Allen & Unwin, 1978)

Frere, Richard, *Maxwell's Ghost: An Epilogue to Gavin Maxwell's Camusfearna* (London: Gollancz, 1976)

Fromkin, David, *A Peace to End All Peace: Creating the Modern Middle East 1914-1922* [1989] (London: Penguin, 1991)

Fyfe, H. Hamilton, *The New Spirit in Egypt* (London: Blackwood, 1911)

Garcia-Ramon, Maria-Dolors, 'Gender and the colonial encounter in the Arab world: examining women's experiences and narratives', *Environment and Planning D: Society and Space*, 21 (2003), 653-72

Geniesse, Jane Fletcher, *Freya Stark: Passionate Nomad* (London: Chatto & Windus, 1999)

Graham, Desmond, *Keith Douglas 1920 – 1944: A Biography* (London: Oxford University Press, 1974)

— Introduction to *Alamein to Zem Zem* by Keith Douglas (Oxford: Oxford University Press, 1979)

Green, Martin, *Dreams of Adventure, Deeds of Empire* (London: Routledge & Kegan Paul, 1980)

Green, Timothy, *The Adventurers: Four Profiles of Contemporary Travellers* (London: Michael Joseph, 1970)

Halliday, Fred, *Arabia Without Sultans* [1974] 2nd edn (London: Saqi, 2002)

Hindle, E., 'Obituary: Dr. Hugh Scott', *Geographical Journal*, 127 (1961), p. 142

Hodgson, Barbara, *Dreaming of East: Western Women and the Exotic Allure of the Orient* (Vancouver: Greystone, 2005)

Hogarth, D. G., *The Nearer East* (London: Heinemann, 1902)

— *The Penetration of Arabia: A Record of the Development of Western Knowledge Concerning the Arabian Peninsula* (London: Lawrence and Bull, 1904)

— *The Life of Charles M. Doughty* (London: Humphrey Milford, 1928)

Holden, David, *Farewell to Arabia* (London: Faber, 1966)

— and Richard Johns, *The House of Saud* [1981] 2nd edn (London: Pan, 1982)

Holland, Patrick, and Graham Huggan, *Tourists with Typewriters: Critical Reflections of Contemporary Travel Writing* (Ann Arbor, Michigan: University of Michigan Press, 1998)

Hooper, Glen, and Tim Youngs, eds, *Perspectives on Travel Writing* (Aldershot, Hants: Ashgate, 2004)

Hopwood, Derek, *Sexual Encounters in the Middle East: The British, the French and the Arabs* (Reading, UK: Ithaca Press, 1999)

Hout, Syrine C., 'Critical Encounters: Feminism, Exoticism, and Orientalism in Freya Stark's *The Southern Gates of Arabia*', *Studies in Travel Writing*, 6 (2002), 54-77

Hudson, Kenneth, and Julian Pettifer, *Diamonds in the Sky: A Social History of Air Travel* (London: Bodley Head, 1979)

Hughes, Hugh, *Middle Eastern Railways* (Harrow, Middlesex: The Continental Railways Circle, 1981)

Hulme, Peter, and Tim Youngs, eds, *The Cambridge Companion to Travel Writing* (Cambridge: Cambridge University Press, 2002)

— and Russell McDougall, eds, *Writing, Travel and Empire: In the Margins of Anthropology* (London: I.B.Tauris, 2007)

Ireland, Philip Willard, *Iraq: A Study in Political Development* (London: Jonathan Cape, 1937)

Izzard, Molly, *Freya Stark: A Biography* (London: Hodder & Stoughton, 1993)

Joyce, Miriam, *The Sultanate of Oman: A Twentieth Century History* (Westport, Connecticut: Praeger, 1995)

Kabbani, Rana, *Imperial Fictions* [1986] (London: Pandora, 1994)

Kedourie, Elie, *England and the Middle East: The Destruction of the Ottoman Empire 1914-1921* [1956] (London: Mansell, 1987)

— *The Chatham House Version and Other Middle-Eastern Studies* (London: Weidenfeld & Nicolson, 1970)

Kelly, J. B., *Arabia, the Gulf and the West* (London: Weidenfeld & Nicolson, 1980)

— 'Jeux sans frontières: Philby's Travels in Southern Arabia', in *The Islamic World from Classical to Modern Times: Essays in Honor of Bernard Lewis*, ed. by C. E. Bosworth and others (Princeton, New Jersey: Darwin, 1989), 701-32

Kent, Marian, *Oil and Empire: British policy and Mesopotamian Oil 1900-1920* (London: Macmillan, 1976)

Kiernan, R. H., *The Unveiling of Arabia* (London: Harrap, 1937)

Korte, Barbara, *English Travel Writing from Pilgrimages to Postcolonial Explorations* (London: Macmillan, 2000)

Kyle, Keith, *Suez* (London: Weidenfeld & Nicolson, 1991)

Lawrence, T. E., *An Essay on Flecker* (London: Corvinus Press, 1937)

Leslie, Shane, *Mark Sykes: His Life and Letters* (London: Cassell, 1923)

Lewis, Andrea, 'Englishness in Rosita Forbes', *Ariel*, 27 (1996), 47-67

Lane-Poole, Stanley, '"The Desert and the Sown" by Gertrude Bell', *The Times Literary Supplement*, 25 January 1907, p. 28

Longrigg, Stephen Hemsley, *Oil in the Middle East: Its Discovery and Development* [1954] (Oxford: Oxford University Press, 1968)

Lowe, Lisa, *Critical Terrains: French and British Orientalisms* (Ithaca, NY: Cornell University Press, 1991)

Lucas, W. Scott, *Divided We Stand: Britain, the US and the Suez Crisis* (London: Hodder and Stoughton, 1996)

Lynch, H. F. B., 'Railways in the Middle East', *Proceedings of the Central Asian Society* (1910-11), 1-25

Malone, J. J., 'Involvement and Change: the Coming of the Oil Age to Saudi Arabia', in *Social and Economic Development in the Arab Gulf*, ed. by Tim Niblock (London: Croom Helm, 1980), 22-48

Mansfield, Peter, *The Arabs* [1976] 3rd edn (London: Penguin, 1992)

—   *A History of the Middle East* [1991] 2nd edn (London: Penguin, 2003)

Marshall, Brian, 'Bertram Thomas and the Crossing of Al Rub' Al-Khālī', *Arabian Studies*, VII (1985), 139-50

Marvin, Charles, *Our Unappreciated Petroleum Empire: Oil Discoveries in the Colonies* (London: Anderson, 1889)

Maunsell, Captain F. R., 'The Mesopotamian Petroleum Field', *Geographical Journal*, 9 (1897), 528-32

McEwan, Cheryl, *Gender, Geography and Empire: Victorian Women Travellers in West Africa* (Aldershot, Hampshire: Ashgate, 2000)

McLoughlin, Leslie, 'Abdullah Philby's Crossing of the Empty Quarter', *Asian Affairs*, 22 (1991), 142-51

—   *In a Sea of Knowledge: British Arabists in the Twentieth Century* (Reading, UK: Ithaca Press, 2002)

McMurray, Jonathan S., *Distant Ties: Germany, the Ottoman Empire, and the Construction of the Baghdad Railway* (Westport, Connecticut: Praeger, 2001)

Melman, Billie, *Women and the Popular Imagination in the Twenties: Flapper and Nymphs* (London: Macmillan, 1986)

—   *Women's Orients: English Women and the Middle East, 1718-1918. Sexuality, Religion and Work* [1992] 2nd edn (London: Macmillan, 1995)

Meyers, Jeremy, *The Wounded Spirit: A Study of Seven Pillars of Wisdom* [1973] (London: Macmillan, 1989)

Mills, Sara, *Discourses of Difference: An Analysis of Women's Travel Writing and Colonialism* (London: Routledge, 1991)

— 'Knowledge, Gender and Empire', in *Writing Women and Space: Colonial and Postcolonial Geographies*, ed. by Alison Blunt and Gillian Rose (New York: Guilford, 1994), 29-50

Monroe, Elizabeth, *Britain's Moment in the Middle East 1914-1956* (London: Chatto & Windus, 1963)

— *Britain's Moment in the Middle East: 1914-1971* [1963] rev. edn (London: Chatto & Windus, 1981)

— *Philby of Arabia* [1973] 2nd edn (Reading: Garnet, 1998)

Morris, James (now Jan), *The Hashemite Kings* (London: Faber, 1959)

— 'Marshmen of Iraq', *Geographical Journal*, 130 (1964), 540-1

— *Farewell the Trumpets: An Imperial Retreat* (London: Faber, 1978)

Morris, Mary, ed., *Maiden Voyages: Writings of Women Travellers* (New York: Vintage, 1993)

Nash, Geoffrey, *From Empire to Orient: Travellers to the Middle East 1830-1926* (London: I.B.Tauris, 2005)

Neill, Stephen, *A History of Christian Missions* (London: Penguin, 1964)

Onley, James, *The Arabian Frontier of the British Raj: Merchants, Rulers, and the British in the Nineteenth-Century Gulf* (Oxford: Oxford University Press, 2007)

Owen, Tim, *Beyond the Empty Quarter* (London: Serendipity, 2003)

Padwick, Constance E., *Temple Gairdner of Cairo* (London: Society for Promoting Christian Knowledge, 1929)

Peters, F. E., *The Hajj: The Muslim Pilgrimage to Mecca and the Holy Places* (Princeton: Princeton University Press, 1994)

Porter, Dennis, *Haunted Journeys: Desire and Transgression in European Travel Writing* (Princeton, New Jersey: Princeton University Press, 1991)

Porter, Andrew, *Religion versus Empire? British Protestant Missionaries and Overseas Expansion, 1700-1914* (Manchester: Manchester University Press, 2004)

Potter, Jennifer, *The Long Lost Journey* (London: Bloomsbury, 1989)

Pratt, Mary Louise, *Imperial Eyes: Travel Writing and Transculturation* (New York: Routledge, 1992)

Raby, Peter, *Bright Paradise* (London: Pimlico, 1997)

Ralli, Augustus, *Christians at Mecca* (London: Heinemann, 1909)

Redouane, Joëlle, *L'Orient arabe vu par les voyageurs anglais* (Alger: Enterprise nationale du livre, 1988)

Rich, Paul, *Iraq and Imperialism: Thomas Lyell's The Ins and Outs of Mesopotamia* (Cambridge, England: Alborough Publishing, 1991)

Rosaldo, Renato, 'Imperial Nostalgia', *Representations*, 26 (1989), 107-22

Rubiés, Joan Pau, 'Travel Writing and Ethnography', in *The Cambridge Companion to Travel Writing*, ed. by Peter Hulme and Tim Youngs (Cambridge: Cambridge University Press, 2002), 242-60

Russell, Alison, *Crossing Boundaries: Postmodern Travel Literature* (New York: Palgrave, 2000)

Said, Edward W., *Orientalism* [1978] (New York: Vintage, 1979)

— *Culture and Imperialism* [1993] (London: Vintage, 1994)

Saleh, Zaki, *Britain and Iraq: A Study in British Foreign Affairs* [1966] (London: Books & Books, 1995)

Sattin, Anthony, *Lifting the Veil: British Society in Egypt 1768-1956* (London: Dent, 1988)

Searight, Sarah, *The British in the Middle East* (London: Weidenfeld & Nicholson, 1969)

— and Malcolm Wagstaff, eds, *Travellers in the Levant: Voyagers and Visionaries* (Durham: Astene Publications, 2001)

Sheffy, Yigal, *British Military Intelligence in the Palestine Campaign 1914-1918* (London: Frank Cass, 1998)

Siegel, Kristi, ed., *Gender, Genre and Identity in Women's Travel Writing* (New York: Peter Lang, 2004)

Simmons, James C., *Passionate Pilgrims: English Travelers to the World of the Desert Arabs* (New York: William Morrow, 1987)

Sluggett, Peter, *Britain in Iraq 1914-1932* (London: Ithaca Press, 1976)

Smith, Clive, *Introduction to The Land of Uz by G. Wyman Bury* [1911] (Reading: Garnet, 1998)

Smith, I., *To Islam I Go (Temple Gairdner of Cairo)* (London: Edinburgh House Press, 1939)

Spurr, David, *The Rhetoric of Empire: Colonial Discourse in Journalism, Travel Writing and Imperial Administration* (Durham and London: Duke University Press, 1993)

Starkey, Janet, and Okasha El Daly, eds, *Desert Travellers: from Herodotus to T. E. Lawrence* (Durham: ASTENE Publications, 2000)

Starkey, Paul, and Janet Starkey, eds, *Interpreting the Orient: Travellers in Egypt and the Near East* (Reading: Ithaca Press, 2001)

— *Unfolding the Orient: Travellers in the Near East* (Reading, UK Ithaca Press, 2001)

Stewart, Desmond, and John Haylock, *New Babylon: A Portrait of Iraq* (London: Collins, 1956)

Storrs, Ronald, *Orientations* (London: Ivor Nicholson & Watson, 1937)

Sugnet, Charles, 'Vile Bodies, Vile Places: Traveling with Granta', *Transition*, 51 (1991), 70-85

Tabachnick, Stephen E., ed., *Explorations in Doughty's Arabia Deserta* (Athens, Georgia: University of Georgia Press, 1987)

— and Christopher Matheson, *Images of Lawrence* (London: Jonathan Cape, 1988)

Taylor, Andrew, *God's Fugitive* (London: HarperCollins, 1999)

Thomas, Nicholas, *Colonialism's Culture: Anthropology, Travel and Government* (Cambridge: Polity Press, 1994)

Tidrick, Kathryn, *Heart-beguiling Araby* (Cambridge: Cambridge University Press, 1981)

Trench, Richard, *Arabian Travellers* (London: Macmillan, 1986)

Treneer, Anne, *Charles M. Doughty: A Study of his Prose and Verse* (London: Jonathan Cape, 1935)

Tripp, Charles, *A History of Iraq* [2000] 2nd edn (Cambridge: Cambridge University Press, 2002)

Tuson, Penelope, *Playing the Game: The Story of Western Women in Arabia* (London: I.B.Tauris, 2003)

Ure, John, *In Search of Nomads: An English Obsession from Hester Stanhope to Bruce Chatwin* (London: Constable, 2003)

Vassiliev, Alexei, *The History of Saudi Arabia* [1998] (London: Saqi, 2000)

Venn, Fiona, *Oil Diplomacy in the Twentieth Century* (London: Macmillan, 1986)

— "A Futile Paper Chase': Anglo-American Relations and Middle East Oil, 1918-34', *Diplomacy and Statecraft*, 1 (1990), 165-84

Wallach, Janet, *Desert Queen: The Extraordinary Life of Gertrude Bell Adventurer, Advisor to Kings, Ally of Lawrence of Arabia* (London: Weidenfeld & Nicolson, 1996)

Westrate, Bruce, *The Arab Bureau: British Policy in the Middle East, 1916-1920* (Pennsylvania: Pennsylvania State University Press, 1992)

Wilson, Arnold, 'E. B. Soane – A Memoir', in *To Mesopotamia and Kurdistan in Disguise: With Historical Notices of the Kurdish Tribes and the Chaldeans of Kurdistan* by E. B. Soane [1912] (London: John Murray, 1926)

Winstone, H. V. F., *Captain Shakespear: A Portrait* (London: Jonathan Cape, 1976)

— *Gertrude Bell* (London: Jonathan Cape, 1978)

—   *Leachman: 'OC Desert': The Life of Lieutenant-Colonel Gerard Leachman D.S.O.* (London: Quartet Books, 1982)

—   *The Illicit Adventure: The Story of Political and Military Intelligence in the Middle East from 1898 to 1926* (London: Jonathan Cape, 1982)

Wroe, Nicholas, 'The Great Escapist' in *The Guardian*, 11 November 2000. http://books.guardian.co.uk/departments/artsandenter tainment/story/0,6000,395859,00.html (last accessed 27 March 2007)

Yapp, M. E., *The Near East since the First World War: A History to 1995* [1991] 2nd edn (London: Longman, 1996)

Youngs, Tim, *Travellers in Africa: British Travelogues, 1850-1900* (Manchester: Manchester University Press, 1994)

—   'Buttons and Souls: Some Thoughts on Commodities and Identity in Women's Travel Writing', *Studies in Travel Writing*, 1 (1997), 117-40

—   'Interview with William Dalrymple', *Studies in Travel Writing*, 9 (2005), 37-63

Government Archives

National Archives, Foreign Office
NA, FO 78/4414
NA, FO 78/4416
NA, FO 371/1245
NA, FO 371/1249

Oriental, India and Commonwealth Office (O.I.C.O.), Political and Secret Records
L/P&S/10/135 'Arabia: Travellers; Mr G W Bury 1904-1911'
L/P&S/10/259 'Arabian travellers 1909-1920'
L/P&S/10/617 'Mesopotamia'
L/P&S/11/175 Political and Secret files 1920

O.I.C.O. Records of the British Administration in Aden, 1839-1967
R/20/A/1456 'Travels and Exploration'
R/20/E/184 'Mukalla: Mr Theodore Bent'
R/20/E/187 'Bent's visit to Mukalla'
R/20/E/1363 'Personal Files: Mr. G. W. Bury'

Other Archive Materials

Douglas, Keith, Manuscript of *Alamein to Zem Zem* (British Library Add. Ms. 53774)

Lawrence, T. E., Reader's report (1929) for the publisher George Allen & Unwin on the manuscript *The Legend of Lijman* by Harry St John Philby (George Allen & Unwin archive, Reading University library MS3282) www.library.rdg.ac.uk/colls/special/featureditem/lawrence/index.html (last accessed July 2006)

Personal Correspondence and Interviews

Author's interview with William Dalrymple, 22 May 2007

Author's interview with Tim Mackintosh-Smith, 2 July 2007

Author's interview with Jonathan Raban, 12 June 2007

Author's interview with Colin Thubron, 19 June 2007

Email from Tim Mackintosh-Smith, 17 June 2007

Email from Jonathan Raban, 30 May 2007

Email from Jonathan Raban, 5 June 2007

Personal correspondence with G. M. C. Bott, archivist for Jonathan Cape, 6 Feb 2004 re: *Seven Pillars of Wisdom* publication figures

INDEX

Abu Dhabi
  Al Ain, 103
Aden, 5, 9
  and British authorities, 182, 187-9,
    192-3
  Bury in, 170-6
  Harris in, 155-8
  Mackintosh-Smith in, 187-8
  occupation of, 39
  tribes of, 174
Aden Protectorate, 11, 179-80, 182
Adonis, 199-200
air travel, 93-5
  Imperial Airways, 94
  Iraqi Airways, 129-30
Al-Murshidi, 210
Amara
  and Thesiger, 146, 153
  and Young, 153
Anglo-Persian Oil Company, 96
anthropology, 41-2
  and smuggling of antiquities, 138
Arab Bulletin, 63-4
Arab Bureau in Cairo, 62
Arabia
  Arab inferiority, 16
  British withdrawal from, 6-7, 9-10,
    214
  changing nature of, 9-10
  colonial activity in, 5-6
  imperial knowledge of, 60-1
  post-imperial, 11

southern, 8-9, 11
Turkish, 131
use of the term, 3
Arabian Nights
  see *One Thousand and One Nights*
archaeology
  Bell and, 115, 118
Astarte, 199-200
Auda Abu Tayih, 90

Baghdad, 9, 10-1, 215
  and *Arabian Nights*, 130-1
  British community in, 139-40
  under British occupation, 131
  Budge in, 137-8
  Fraser in, 136
  modernisation of, 132-3
  and *One Thousand and One Nights*,
    129-32
  railway, 135
  romanticism of, 132-3
  Soane in, 135
  Starke in, 119-20
  Thomas in, 139
  Young on, 132-3
Balfour, Arthur, 196-7
Balfour Declaration, 196-7
Barr, Robert (Luke Sharp), 93
Bartholomew, Michael, 27
Bassnett, Susan, 125-6
Bedouin, the
  Carruthers and, 70

encampment of, 102
exhibition on, 101
Lawrence and, 55, 66
modernised, 103-4
Raban and, 101-4
romanticised, 103
Shakespear and, 61
Thesiger and, 48-56
Bell, Gertrude, 9, 10, 92, 109, 122-3,
138
  Amurath to Amurath, 8, 62, 115-6
  The Arab of Mesopotamia, 63, 116
  and archaeology, 115, 118
  and colonial administration, 116-8,
  126
  The Desert and the Sown, 114-5
  and the First World War, 62-3
  on Forbes, 114
  in Hayil, 117-8
  imprisoned, 117
  journey to Jebel Druze, 120
  and Lawrence, 118
  Leachman's editor, 63
  on Mesopotamia, 132
  'Pleasant Sunday Afternoon'
    gatherings, 139
  and Stark, 118-20
  Sykes on, 115
  'A Tribe of the Tigris', 62-3
Bent, Mabel, 109, 180
  Southern Arabia, 124, 165-70
Bent, Theodore, and Mabel Bent, 123-
4, 188, 212
  and British authorities, 165, 169-70
  death of Theodore Bent, 166-7
  in Hadhramaut, 165-70
  harrassed and shot at, 168-9
Biggs, Reverend Charles
  Six Months in Jerusalem, 24
Bigland, Eileen, 121
bin Ghabaisha
  and Thesiger, 55
bin Kabina, Salim, 55, 56
  and Thesiger, 52
  Thesiger's description of, 50-1
bin Taimur, Said (Sultan of Oman), 97-
100

Blunt, Wilfred Scawen
  and Lady Anne Blunt, 4, 123
  *Secret History of the English Occupation
    of Egypt*, 4
British authorities, 7-8, 169, 178-9
  and Aden, 182, 187-9, 192-3
  and Arabia, 5-7, 9-11, 60-1, 214
  and Bell, 116-8, 126
  and the Bents, 165-70
  and Bury, 170-6
  and Forbes, 112, 114
  and Harris, 160-1
  and Herbert, 176-7
  and Lewis, 179
  and the Ottoman Empire, 159-61
  and Philby, 181-2
  and Scott, 178-9
  and Soane, 133-5
  and Stark, 121
  and Wavell, 161-5, 175
  and women travellers, 108-9, 121
  and Yemen, 158-9, 177, 187-8
  see also women travellers, colonial
    wives
British Museum, 138, 172
Britton, Everard
  in Yemen, 177-9
Buddicom, Venetia, 118-9
Budge, E. A. Wallis, 137-8
Burton, Sir Richard, 123
  conversion to Islam, 18
  and Isabel Burton, 123
  *Personal Narrative of a Pilgrimage to El-
    Medinah and Meccah*, 4
  A Pilgrimage to Mecca, 18
Bury, Wyman, 189
  as 'Abdullah Mansûr', 170, *171*, 175
  in Aden, 170-6
  Arabia Infelix, 175
  bribery charges against, 170-2, 175-
  6
  and the British authorities, 170-6
  and the British Museum, 172
  and the Empty Quarter, 174-6
  The Land Of Uz, 170, 174-6
  and the Royal Geographical Societ*
  173

in Turkish Yemen, 175
Buxton, Leland
and Herbert, 176-7
Buxton, Victoria
see Jebb, Louisa, and Victoria
Buxton

camels, 88, 90, 91, 92
Candler, Edmund
On the Edge of the World, 132
Carr, Helen, 48
Carruthers, Douglas
Arabian Adventure, 69-70
and the Bedouin, 70
and Lawrence, 69-70
'Shakespear's Last Journey', 61-2
cars, 85-93, 97-8
armoured, 87-90
in the First World War, 87-90
and imperial administrators, 91
in museums, 101-2
Christianity, 23, 194-5, 204-9
see also missionaries
Church Missionary Society, 23
Clare-Ford, Sir Francis, 160-1
Cobbold, Lady Evelyn Zainab, 124
Coptic Christians, 208
Cromer, Evelyn Baring, 1st Earl of,
114, 115
Currie, Sir Philip, 166

Dalrymple, William, 193
in Beirut, 72
From the Holy Mountain, 204-9, 213
and Moschos, 204-5, 208-9
Damascus, 109, 193-201
fall of, 78-9
history of, 195-7
Jews in, 195-6
Mackintosh-Smith in, 211-2
Thesiger and, 197-8
Darwin, Major Leonard, 163
De Brath, Major-General, 172-3
de la Mare, Walter
Arabia, 38, 40, 50
Dickson, Violet, 109, 122-3
Doughty, Charles Montagu (Khalil)

attacked and threatened, 20-2
and Mohammed Aly, 19-20
and religion, 17-23
Travels in Arabia Deserta, 4, 17-22, 45
use of third person, 18-9
Douglas, Keith
Alamein to Zem Zem, 10, 74-7
and Lawrence, 75, 77
narrative style, 75-6
and the Second World War, 74-7
travel reading, 77
wounded and killed, 77

Egypt, 2, 3, 114-6, 121, 208, 210
Alexandria, 209-10
Asyut, 208
British rule in, 17
Cairo, 23, 62, 126
El Alamein, 74, 77
missionaries in, 23
and the Suez War, 79-81
Ein Fara monastery, Palestine, 208
Empty Quarter, the, 8-9, 10, 39
Bury and, 174-6
inhabitants of, 38-9
Leachman and, 65
oil in, 46, 51
Philby and, 39-40, 43-7
romanticisation and feminisation
of, 38
Thesiger and, 48-56
Thomas and, 37-43

Feisal, King, 90, 94, 131
First World War, 5-6, 10, 60-71, 179
and aircraft, 94
and Bell, 62-3
and cars, 87-90
and Lawrence, 63-71
and Leachman, 57-65
and Mesopotamia, 131-3
writers and reporters of, 77-81
Fisk, Robert, 207
'Three Years of War in Iraq', 1
Flecker, James Elroy, 133
Forbes, Rosita, 113
and the British establishment, 112,

and cars, 90
and the harem, 125
and Philby, 112
The Secret of the Sahara, 111-4
Fountaine, Margaret, 109-11
Fraser, David
in Baghdad, 136
and the Marsh Arabs, 141
in Mesopotamia, 135-6
French, Thomas Valpy, 23

Gairdner, Reverend (Temple Gairdner of Cairo)
The Reproach of Islam, 23-4
gender, 107, 125-7
see also women travellers
geology
Philby and, 45-6
Glen, Douglas
in Lawrence's footsteps, 70-1
Glubb, Sir John (Glubb Pasha), 59
and Maugham, 73
Greater Syria, 114

Hadhramaut, 91-3, 120, 124, 179-82
the Bents and, 165-70
Haggard, H. Rider, 93
hajj, the
Doughty on, 18
Khan on, 28-9
Hanauer, James E.
Folk-lore of the Holy Land, 16
Walks About Jerusalem, 24
Hardinge, Lord Charles (Viceroy of India), 60
harem, the, 120-1, 124-5
Harris, Walter, 188, 189
and Aden, 155-8
and British authorities, 160-1
imprisonment in San'a, 160
A Journey Through the Yemen, 155-61
Hassanein, Ahmed, 111
Hauran, plains of, 114
Hedgcock, Stuart (Fulanain)
Haji Rikkan, 142-3
on the Marsh Arabs, 142-3
and Monica Hedgcock, 142

Hejaz railway, 85
Helfritz, Hans, 181
Herbert, Aubrey, 188-9
and British authorities, 176-7
and Buxton, 176-7
Hogarth, D. G.
and the *Arab Bulletin*, 64
on Bell, 118
on Doughty, 18
homosexuality, 52
Hubbard, Gilbert E.
on the Marsh Arabs, 141-2
in Mesopotamia, 137

Ibadhiya (Islamic sect), 98
Ibn Battutah, 209-13
Travels, 209-10
Ibn Saud (King Abdul-Aziz of Saudi Arabia), 45, 47, 60-1, 62, 117-8
and Philby, 43-4
and transport, 92
Imperial Airways, 94
imperial wars, 9-10, 59-60
see also First World War; Second World War; Suez War
India Office, 173
Ingrams, Doreen, 109, 123
and the harem, 124
Ingrams, Harold, and Doreen Ingrams, 180
in the Hadhramaut, 91-2
'Ingrams' Peace', 91, 94, 123, 157, 180, 182
Iraq, 8-9
Basra, 131
British military in, 1-2
marshes of, 9, 131, 141
post-invasion, 214-6
see also Baghdad
Iraqi Airways, 129-30
Islam
anti-Muslim sentiments, 18, 23-4
conversion to (Burton), 18
conversion to (Philby), 43, 46-7
conversion to (Pickthall), 17
the hajj, 18, 28-9
sympathy towards, 24

Israel
  attacked, 200
  settlements of, 208
  and the Suez War, 79-81
Izzard, Ralph, and Molly Izzard
  Smelling the Breeze, 198-9

Jebb, Louisa, and Victoria Buxton
  By Desert Ways to Baghdad, 105-9
Jerusalem, 207-8

Kabbani, Rana
  on Thesiger, 55
Khalil
  see Doughty, Charles Montagu
  (Khalil)
Khan, Hadji
  and the hajj, 28-9
Khan, Hadji, and Wilfrid Sparroy
  With the Pilgrims to Mecca, 28-9
Khawar tribe, 212-3

Lawrence, T. E. ('Lawrence of
  Arabia'), 8, 57, 59, *89*, 94
  and the Bedouin, 55, 66
  and Bell, 118
  and camels, 88, 90
  and Carruthers, 69-70
  and cars, 88-90
  and Douglas, 75, 77
  and the First World War, 63-4, 65-
  71
  on Flecker, 133
  on Leachman, 67-9
  'Military Notes', 63-4
  The Mint, 76
  Seven Pillars of Wisdom, 1-2, 49, 63-7,
  69-74, 87-8
  travel reading, 77
Leachman, Gerard, 57
  accounts of travels, 59, 64-5
  and the Arab tribes, 59, 64-5, 68-9
  'Below Kut' ('Brief Note on Tribes
  of the Tigris Below Baghdad'), 63
  biography of, 68-9
  death of, 58-9
  and the Empty Quarter, 65

and the First World War, 57-65
  on Lawrence, 67-9
Lebanon
  Beirut, 72, 207
  Izzards in, 198-9
  Rayak railway station, 83-4
  Sidon, 199
  Thubron in, 198-201
Leeder, S. H.
  *Veiled Mysteries of Egypt and the
  Religion of Islam*, 24
Lewis, Norman, 93
  and British authorities, 179
  Sand and Sea in Arabia, 179
  on tribal warfare, 94-5
Lowther, Sir G. (Foreign Office), 163-
  4

McEwan, Cheryl, 108
Mackintosh-Smith, Tim, 11, 159, 193,
  204, 215
  in Aden, 187-8
  in Alexandria, 209-10
  and Battutah, 209-13
  in Damascus, 211-2
  narrative, 185-6
  in Oman, 212-3
  style, 187-8, 211, 213
  Travels with a Tangerine, 209-13
  Yemen, 183-8, 210
McLoughlin, Leslie, 45
McWilliams, H. H.
  The Diabolical, 90
Madan
  see Marsh Arabs (Madan)
Maitland, Major-General Pelham, 170
Mannin, Ethel
  A Lance for the Arabs, 121-2
Marsh Arabs (Madan), 11, 215-6
  Fraser on, 141
  Hedgcock on, 142-3
  Hubbard on, 141-2
  Maxwell on, 148-51
  and modernity, 154
  Stevens on, 140-1
  Thesiger on, 143-8
  Vowels on, 142

Young on, 152-4
marshes of southern Iraq, 9, 131, 141
Marvin, Charles, 95
Masaudi
  with Wavell, 31
Maugham, Robin
  and Glubb, 73
  and Lawrence, 72-4
  and the Second World War, 72-4
Maxwell, Donald, 132
  A Dweller in Mesopotamia, 85-7
  on oil, 95-6
Maxwell, Gavin, 131, 143-4
  and animals in the marshes, 150-1
  on the Marsh Arabs, 148-51
  A Reed Shaken by the Wind, 149-51
  Ring of Bright Water, 148, 154
  and Young, 143-4, 151-2
Mecca
  Burton and, 18
  Khan and, 28-9
  Ralli and, 29
  Rutter and, 31-5
  seized, 31
  Wavell and, 29-31
Mesopotamia, 57-9, 131, 135-6
  Bell on, 132
  and the First World War, 131-3
  Fraser in, 135-6
  Hubbard in, 137
  tribes of, 116-8
military travellers, 62
  war reporters, 77-81
  see also First World War; Second
    World War; Suez War
Mills, Sara, 108
missionaries, 110
  in Egypt, 23
  Pickthall and, 15-7
  Stark and, 119
modernisation, 6-7, 51
  of Baghdad, 132-3
  of the Bedouin, 103-4
  Morris on, 97-9
  Raban on, 100-4
  Thesiger on, 96-7, 197-8
  Thubron on, 197

Monroe, Elizabeth, 84
Montez, Maria, 129-30
Morris, James (Jan Morris), 79-81, 109,
  125
  on cars, 97-8
  and gender, 125-7
  The Market of Seleukia, 60, 79-81
  on modernisation, 97-9
  on oil, 98-100
  in Oman, 97-100
  and the Suez War, 79-81
  Sultan in Oman, 204
Morton, H. V.
  In the Steps of St Paul, 27
  In the Steps of the Master, 27
Moschos, John, 208-9
  The Spiritual Meadow, 204-5
Munroe, Elizabeth, 5

native dress
  Bury and, 171
  Forbes and, 113
  Ralli and, 29
  Rutter and, 32-6
  Smith and, 24-7, 26
  Soane and, 133-4
  Wavell and, 29-31, 30
Neil, Reverend James
  Palestine Explored, 24
Neimy, Khalil, 109-11
nostalgia, 6, 51-2, 54

oil, 6, 94-100, 131
  and Basra, 131
  in the Empty Quarter, 46, 51
  and the military, 96
  in Qatar, 100-4
  in Saudi Arabia, 96
Oman, 97-100, 212-3
One Thousand and One Nights, 129-30
  and Baghdad, 130-2
Orientalism, 7, 193, 203
Ottoman Empire, 158
  and the British, 159-61

Padwick, Constance, 23
Palestine, 121-2, 182, 196-7, 208

Anglicanism in, 23
Morton and, 27
Smith and, 24-5
Palestinians
in Jerusalem, 207-8
Pearn, Norman, 214
in Hadhramaut, 180-1
Quest for Sheba, 181
Philby, Harry St John, 8, 10, 52, 56,
180, 189
and British authorities, 181-2
and cars, 92-3
conversion to Islam, 43, 46-7
diaries of, 45
and the Empty Quarter, 39-40
The Empty Quarter, 43-7, 48
and Forbes, 112
and geology, 45-6
and Ibn Saud (King Abdul-Aziz of
Saudi Arabia), 43-4, 47
and Leachman's biography, 68-9
and oil, 96
and religious metaphors, 46-7
Sheba's Daughters, 181-2
writing style, 45
Pickthall, Marmaduke, 8
Oriental Encounters, 13-7
and religion, 15-7, 22-3

qat chewing
and *kayf*, 184-6
Qatar
Doha, 101-2
oil in, 100-4

Raban, Jonathan, 193, 196-7, 215
Arabia: Through the Looking Glass, 3,
6-7, 100-4, 201-4
on the Bedouin, 101-4
on modernisation, 100-4
on Morris, 126
post-modern style of, 203
on Stewart, 215-6
on Thesiger, 102-3, 201-3
Rahman, Abdel
Umm Ziin, 102
rail travel, 83-5, 87, 93, 210-1

Baghdad railway, 135
Hejaz railway, 85
Rayak railway station, 83-4
Ralli, Augustus
Christians in Mecca, 29
Rashid tribes, 117-8
religion, 9-10, 98
Doughty and, 17-23
Morton and, 27
Pickthall and, 15-7, 22-3
Rutter and, 32-5
Smith and, 24-7
see also Christianity; Islam;
missionaries
Rodger, George
Desert Journey, 78-9
and the Second World War, 77-9
Rolls, S. C.
Steel Chariots in the Desert, 87-9
war memoirs of, 70
Royal Geographical Society, 162, 164,
173
Rub' al Khali
see Empty Quarter, the
Rushby, Kevin, 159
Eating the Flowers of Paradise, 184-5
Rutter, Eldon
dual identity adopted, 34-5
The Holy Cities of Arabia, 32-6
Mecca and, 31-5
native dress and, 32-6
religion and, 32-5

Sahara desert, 111
Said, Edward
Orientalism, 7, 193, 203
St Clair-Tisdall, Reverend William
The Religion of the Crescent, 24
Saint Sarkiss monastery, Maloula, Syria,
194-5
St Symeon Stylites, 204-6
Saleh, Zaki, 131
San'a, 158, 160-5, 176-8, 183-5
Saudi Arabia, 121
Ayn el Zeyma, 21
Hayil, 116-8
Medain Saleh monuments, 18-21

oil in, 96
Saud tribes, 117-8
scientific research, 138, 177-9
Bell and, 115
the Bents and, 167, 169-70
Philby and, 45-6
Thomas and, 41-2
Wavell and, 161-4
Scott, Hugh, 188
and British authorities, 178-9
In the High Yemen, 178
in San'a, 178
and the Second World War, 178
Western Arabia and the Red Sea, 178-9
in Yemen, 177-9
Second World War, 6, 10, 60, 71-9
and Douglas, 74-7
and Maugham, 72-4
and mechanisation, 71, 74-7, 81
and Rodger, 77-9
and Scott, 178
Seidnaya convent, Syria, 194, 206
Shakespear, Captain William, 60-2
Sharabishiyyah (Hatter's college), 211
Sharp, Luke
see Barr, Robert (Luke Sharp)
shipping, 131
steamers, 93-4
slavery, 28
Smith, Reverend Hasket, *26*
Patrollers of Palestine, 24-6
Soane, Ely, 138
to Baghdad, 133-4
in Baghdad, 135
and the British government, 133-5
in disguise, 133-4
Sparroy, Wilfrid
see Khan, Hadji, and Wilfrid Sparroy
spying, 158, 161-2
Wavell and, 162
Standard Oil Company of California
(Socal), 96
Stark, Freya, 2, 8, 109, 118-21, 180
in Baghdad, 119-20
Baghdad Sketches, 139-40
and Bell, 118-9, 120
Beyond Euphrates, 119

and colonial policy, 121
on the harem and women's
quarters, 120-1
and missionaries, 119
rescued by air, 95
The Southern Gates of Arabia, 95, 120,
181
The Valleys of the Assassins, 120
Stevens, Ethel
on the Marsh Arabs, 140-1, 154
Stewart, Dugald, 144
Stewart, Rory
Occupational Hazards, 215-6
Thubron on, 216
Suez War, 6, 10, 60, 79-81
Sykes, Mark, 83-5, 87
on Bell, 115
Sykes-Picot agreement (1916), 84, 196-
7
Syria, 194-5, 206
Dalrymple in, 206
Greater Syria, 114
Jebel Druze, 118-20
Maloula, 194

Tel Ada monastery, 206
Tel es Salihiye, 194
Temple Gairdner of Cairo, 23-4
Tennant, Lieutenant-Colonel J. E.
In the Clouds Above Baghdad, 57-8
Thesiger, Wilfred, 2, 50, 102-3
and al Auf, 53-4
and Amara, 146, 153
Arabian Sands, 6, 48-56, 96-7, 100,
197-8, 212-3
and the Bedouin, 48-56
on Bell, 115
and bin Ghabaisha, 55
companions of, 50-1
and Damascus, 197-8
dangers of the journey, 53-4
and the Empty Quarter, 48-56
on homosexuality, 52
on Kabbani, 55
on Lawrence's *Seven Pillars of
Wisdom*, 49
The Marsh Arabs, 6, 131, 143-8, 153

and Maxwell, 151
as a medic, 145
on modernisation, 96-7, 197-8
and nostalgia, 51-2, 54
on Philby's writing, 45
Raban on, 102-3, 202-3
and Salim bin Kabina, 50-1, 52
style of, 48-9, 145
Thubron on, 198
and Young, 152
Thief of Baghdad, The, 129-30
Thomas, Bertram, 9, 10, 52, 56
   Alarms and Excursions in Arabia, 142
   and anthropology, 41-2
   Arabia Felix, 37-43, 48
   in Baghdad, 139
   on *The Empty Quarter* (Philby), 46-7
Thomas, Lowell
   on T. E. Lawrence, 59, 69-71
Thubron, Colin, 6, 203, 205, 215
   The Hills of Adonis, 198-201
   in Lebanon, 198-201
   Mirror to Damascus, 191-2, 193-8
   on Stewart, 216
   on Thesiger, 198
Toy, Barbara, 121
transport, 6, 83-93, 88
   see also air travel; camels; cars; rail
      travel; shipping

Umayyid Mosque, 211-2

Veidt, Conrad, 129-30
Virago Press, 108
Vowles, Alfred
   on the Marsh Arabs, 142
   *Wanderings with a Camera in
      Mesopotamia*, 131-2

war reporters
   Morris, 79-81
   Rodger, 77-9
Wavell, Arthur, *30*, 188
   arrested, 163
   and British authorities, 161-5, 175
   *A Modern Pilgrim in Mecca: And a
      Siege in Sanaa*, 161-5

native dress and, 29-31
return to England, 164-5
in San'a, 162-5
scientific work, 161-4
and spying, 161-4
Wilson, Sir Arnold, 58-9
   *Memorandum on Self-Determination in
      Mesopotamia*, 138
women travellers, 9-10
   appearance and dress concerns,
      108, 111
   and Arab lovers, 109-11
   colonial wives, 109, 122-4, 126-7
   feminine, 114, 121
   and the harem, 120-1, 124
   and imperialism, 108-9, 121
   independent, 107, 109-22
   masculine, 115
   as 'proto-feminist', 108
   role of, 126-7
   and social norms, 107-8

Yahya, Imam, 158
   in San'a, 162
Yemen, 11, 120, 182
   and the Bents, 165-8
   and British authorities, 158-9, 177,
      187-8
   and Britton, 177-9
   and Harris, 155-8
   and Mackintosh-Smith, 183-8, 210
   and Rushby, 184-5
   and Scott, 177-9
   Shabwa, 180-1
   Shibam, 168, 181
   Sief, 167-8
   Turkish, 158-61, 175
   and Wavell, 161-5
   see also Aden; San'a
Young, Gavin, 129-31, 143-4
   and Amara, 153
   in Baghdad, 132-3, 136
   and Maxwell, 143-4, 151-2
   as a medic, 153
   Return to the Marshes, 152-4
   and Thesiger, 152